LEARNING CENTRE

CLASS NO: 651.75 BLY

ACC NO: 067423

KT-557-403

Revised Edition

The Encyclopedia of Business Letters, Faxes, and E-Mail

Harrow College
Harrow Weald Campus, Learning Centre
Brookshill, Harrow Weald, Middx.
HA3 6RR   0208 909 6248

**Features Hundreds of
Model Letters, Faxes, and E-Mail
to Give Your Business Writing
the Attention It Deserves**

Robert W. Bly
and
Regina Anne Kelly

CAREER PRESS

Pompton Plains, NJ

HARROW COLLEGE

067423

Copyright © 2009 by Robert W. Bly and Regina Anne Kelly

All rights reserved under the Pan-American and International Copyright Conventions. This book may not be reproduced, in whole or in part, in any form or by any means electronic or mechanical, including photocopying, recording, or by any information storage and retrieval system now known or hereafter invented, without written permission from the publisher, The Career Press.

THE ENCYCLOPEDIA OF BUSINESS LETTERS, FAXES, AND E-MAIL
EDITED BY KATE HENCHES
TYPESET BY MICHAEL FITZGIBBON
Cover design by Rob Johnson/Johnson Design
Printed in the U.S.A.

To order this title, please call toll-free 1-800-CAREER-1 (NJ and Canada: 201-848-0310) to order using VISA or MasterCard, or for further information on books from Career Press.

The Career Press, Inc.
220 West Parkway, Unit 12
Pompton Plains, NJ 07444
www.careerpress.com

Library of Congress Cataloging-in-Publication Data
Bly, Robert W.
  The encyclopedia of business letters, faxes, and e-mail : features hundreds of model letters, faxes, and e-mail to give your business writing the attention is deserves. — Rev. ed. / by Robert W. Bly and Regina Anne Kelly.
      p. cm.
  Includes index.
  ISBN 978-1-60163-029-2
  1. Commercial correspondence—Handbooks, manuals, etc. 2. Memorandums—Handbooks, manuals, etc. 3. Electronic mail messages—Handbooks, manuals, etc. 4. Facsimile transmission—Handbooks, manuals, etc. I. Kelly, Regina Anne. II. Title. III. Title: Businessletters, faxes, and email.

HF5721.B59 2009
651.7'4--dc22

                                                              2008041695

To the memory of Burton Pincus, one of the greatest letter-writers of all time; and to Bob Jurick, who has mailed more letters than anyone I know.
—Robert W. Bly

To my daughter, Maren. Too bad you're still too little to type.
—Regina Anne Kelly

Acknowledgments

Thanks to the many organizations and individuals who allowed us to reprint their letters in this book.

Thanks also to our editors at Career Press for making this book much better than it was when it first crossed their desks.

Contents

Introduction

Business Writing Basics in the Age of Electronic Communications

Mastering the skills of clear, concise writing can certainly give you an edge in today's business world, where communications are too often dominated by jargon, double-talk, and weak, watered-down prose. Most business communications today descend into what E.B. White, the essayist and coauthor of *The Elements of Style*, called "the language of mutilation."

Some examples: A commercial describes a new television series as "the most unique show of the season"—an impossible claim, considering that *unique* means "one of a kind." A Detroit automobile manufacturer bases a series of print ads on the theme "new innovations." Is there such a thing as an *old* innovation? An advertiser describes a dental splint created to hold loose teeth in place as a product designed "to stabilize mobile dentition." Dentition is what you brush every day. When's the last time you heard of someone being punched in the mouth and getting mobile dentition—or the dentition fairy leaving money under your pillow? A brochure for a storage silo informs us that material is "gravimetrically conveyed," not dumped. And, of course, every system, product, and service now sold to businesses is said to be "cost-effective." How refreshing it would be to read about a product that was inexpensive, low-priced, or just plain cheap.

English-speaking people have not always embraced such obfuscation. Approximately 70 percent of the words in Lincoln's Gettysburg Address contain less than six letters. Winston Churchill, faced with Hitler's armed forces, said to Americans, "Give us the tools and we will do the job." He did not say: "Aid our organization in the procurement of the necessary equipments and we will, in turn, implement the program to accomplish its planned objectives."

Many businesspeople of the 21st century struggle to write clear, lucid prose. They may know the basics (sentence structure, grammar, punctuation, exposition), but a few poor stylistic habits continually mar their writing, making it dull and difficult to read. Part of the problem may lie in their approach to writing—

they may view it as a time-consuming, unimportant, and unpleasant task. Or perhaps the underlying problem is a lack of confidence in their ability to communicate, uncertainty about how to get started, or insufficient training. Whatever the obstacle, they also face an additional challenge: the need to be well versed in the nuances of electronic communications, which have all but overhauled the way people communicate in business and industry.

The era of long, leisurely letters is gone; we have entered the age of frantic thumb-typing on laptops and handheld devices that can transmit e-mail messages whether we are in the train station, the airport, or the board room. Concise letters, fast faxes, and, especially, instant e-mail have replaced the chatty correspondence of yesteryear. In this environment, your reader doesn't have time to waste, and neither do you. You need to get your message across clearly, easily, and quickly so that you can cut down on writing time and focus on more important tasks.

Observing the rules of good business writing is the first step toward achieving this goal, whether you're typing an e-mail or composing a letter. The following tips identify common pitfalls in business writing and offer ways to overcome them.

12 general tips for better business writing

1. Get organized.

Poor organization is a leading problem in business writing. A computer programmer might never think of writing a complex program without first drawing a flowchart, but he'd probably knock out a draft of a user's manual without making notes or an outline. Writer Jerry Bacchetti points out, "If the reader believes the content has some importance to him, he can plow through a report even if it is dull or has lengthy sentences and big words. But if it's poorly organized—forget it. There's no way to make sense of what is written."

Poor organization stems from poor planning. Before you write, plan. Create a rough outline that spells out the contents and organization of your document. The outline need not be formal. A simple list, doodles, or rough notes will do; use whatever form suits you. By the time you finish writing, some things in the final draft might be different from the outline. That's okay. The outline is a tool to aid in organization, not a commandment cast in stone. If you want to change it as you go along—fine.

An outline helps you divide the writing project into many smaller, easy-to-handle pieces and parts. The organization of these parts depends on the type of document you're writing. In general, it's best to stick with standard formats. For example, a speech begins with an introduction, presents three to four key points in the body, then closes with a summary of the main points made in the body. An operating manual includes a summary; an introduction; a description of the equipment; instructions for routine operation, troubleshooting, maintenance, and emergency operation; and an appendix containing a parts list, spare-parts list, drawings, figures, and manufacturer's literature. Standard formats such as these allow for an easier time writing and for better understanding.

If the type of document you are writing doesn't strictly define the format, select the organizational scheme that best fits the material. Some common formats include:

- **Order of location.** An article on the planets of the solar system might begin with Mercury (the planet nearest the sun) and end with Pluto (the planet farthest out).

- **Order of increasing difficulty.** Computer manuals often start with the easiest material and, as the user masters basic principles, move on to more complex operations.

- **Alphabetical order.** This is a logical way to arrange a booklet on vitamins (A, B-3, B-12, C, D, E, and so on) or a directory of company employees.

- **Chronological order.** Here you present the facts in the order in which they happened. History books are written this way. So are many case histories, feature stories, corporate biographies, and trip reports.

- **Problem/solution.** Another format appropriate to case histories and many types of reports, the problem/solution organizational scheme begins with "Here's what the problem was" and ends with "Here's how we solved it."

- **Inverted pyramid.** News reporting follows this format. The lead paragraph summarizes the story, and the paragraphs that follow it present the facts in order of decreasing importance. You can use this format in journal articles, letters, memos, and reports.

- **Deductive order.** You can start with a generalization, then support it with particulars. Scientists use this format in research papers; they begin with the findings and then state the supporting evidence.

- **Inductive order.** Another approach is to begin with specifics and then lead the reader to the idea or general principles the specifics suggest. This is an excellent way to approach trade journal feature stories.

- **List.** Articles, memos, instructions, procedures, and reports can be organized in list form. A list procedure might be titled "Six Tips for Designing a Website" or "Seven Steps to a Greener Household."

2. Know the reader

Written communication is most effective when it is targeted and personal. Your writing should be built around the needs, interests, and desires of the reader. Know your reader, especially in relation to the following categories:

- **Job title.** A person's job influences his or her perspective of your product, service, or idea. For example, techies are interested in your processor's reliability and performance, whereas a purchasing agent is concerned about the cost. Are you writing for plant engineers? Office managers? CEOs? Machinists? Make the tone and content of your writing compatible with the professional interests of your readers.

- **Education.** Consider the education of your audience. Is your reader a PhD or a high-school dropout? Does he or she understand computer programming, thermodynamics, physical chemistry, statistics, and the calculus of variations? Target the knowledge level of your readership appropriately. On the other hand, be sure to write simply enough so that even the least technical of your readers can understand what you are saying.

- **Industry.** When plant managers buy a reverse-osmosis water purification system for the town water supply, they want to know every technical detail down to the last pipe, pump, fan, and filter. Fishermen buying portable units for fishing boats, however, have only two basic questions: "What does it cost?" and "How reliable is it?" Especially in promotional writing, know what features of your product appeal to various markets.

- **Level of interest.** A prospect who responded to an advertisement is more likely to be receptive to a salesperson's call than one who is called on "cold turkey." Is your reader interested or disinterested? Friendly or hostile? Receptive or resistant? Understanding the reader's state of mind helps you tailor your message to meet his or her needs.

If you don't know enough about your reader, there are ways of finding out. If you are writing to a potential business client, for example, visit its Website to get background on the company and study it before you write. If you are presenting a paper at a conference, look at the conference brochure to get a feel for the audience who will be attending your session. If you are contributing text to product descriptions, ask the marketing or publications department the format in which the material will be distributed and who will be reading it.

3. Avoid "corporatese"

Corporatese is language more complex than the concepts it serves to communicate. Often you will find it in the writings of technicians and bureaucrats, who hide behind a jumble of incomprehensible memos and reports loaded with jargon, clichés, antiquated phrases, passive sentences, and excess adjectives. This pompous, overblown style can make a business document sound as if a computer or a corporation, instead of a human being, wrote it.

Here are a few samples of corporatese from diverse sources. All of these excerpts are real. Note how the authors seem to be writing to impress rather than to express:

"Will you please advise me at your earliest convenience of the correct status of this product?"

—Memo from an advertising manager

"All of the bonds in the above-described account having been heretofore disposed of, we are this day terminating same. We accordingly enclose herein check in the amount of $30,050, same being your share realized therein, as per statement attached."

—Letter from a stockbroker

"This procedure enables users to document data fields described in master files that were parsed and analyzed by the program dictionary."

—Software user's manual

This type of verbal gobbledygook has also turned the concept of firing into the following pieces of gibberish:

- "Downsizing."
- "Eliminating redundancies in the human resources area."
- "Indefinite idling."
- "Involuntary separation."
- "Managing our human resources down."
- "Restructuring."
- "Realignment."
- "Reductions in overhead, process improvements, facility rationalization, and purchasing and logistics savings."
- "Reengineering."
- "Right-sizing."
- "Volume-related production schedule adjustment."

How do you eliminate corporatese from your writing? Start by avoiding jargon. Legal scholar Tamar Frankel notes that when you avoid jargon, your writing can be read easily by novices and experienced professionals alike. Many industries have their own special jargon. Although this language may sometimes be helpful shorthand when you're communicating within your profession, it confuses readers who do not have your specialized background. Take the word *yield*, for example. To a chemical manufacturer, *yield* is a measure of how much product a reaction produces. But, to car drivers, *yield* means "to slow down" (and stop, if necessary) at an intersection. This is where knowing your reader, as explained previously, becomes important.

To eliminate corporatese in your writing, you should also avoid clichés and antiquated phrases. Write simply. Don't use a technical term unless it communicates your meaning precisely. Never write *mobile dentition* when *loose teeth* will do just as well. Some executives prefer to use big, important-sounding words instead of short, simple words. This is a mistake; fancy language just frustrates the reader. Write in plain, ordinary English and your readers will love you for it.

Here are a few big words that occur frequently in business and technical literature; the column on the right presents a shorter and preferable substitution:

Big word	Substitution
terminate	end
utilize	use
incombustible	fireproof
substantiate	prove
eliminate	get rid of

4. Favor the active voice

In the active voice, action is expressed directly: "John performed the experiment." In the passive voice, the action is indirect: "The experiment was performed by John." When you use the active voice, your writing will be more direct and vigorous; your sentences, more concise. As you can see in the samples below, the passive voice seems puny and stiff in comparison to the active voice:

Passive voice	Active voice
Control of the bearing-oil supply is provided by the end shutoff valves.	Shutoff valves control the bearing-oil supply.
Leaking of the seals is prevented by the use of O-rings.	0-rings keep the seals from leaking.
Fuel-cost savings were realized through the installation of thermal insulation.	The installation of thermal insulation cut fuel costs.

5. Avoid lengthy sentences

Lengthy sentences tire the reader and make your writing hard to read. A survey by Harvard professor D.H. Menzel indicates that in technical papers, the sentences become difficult to understand when they exceed 34 words. One measure of writing complexity, the Fog Index, takes into account sentence length and word length in a short (100- to 200-word) writing sample. Here's how it works: First, determine the average sentence length in the writing sample. To do this, divide the number of words in the sample by the number of sentences. If parts of a sentence are separated by a semicolon (;), count each part as a separate sentence. Next, calculate the number of big words (words with three or more syllables) per 100 words of the sample. Do not include capitalized words, combinations of short words (*everywhere*, *moreover*), or verbs made three syllables by adding *ed* or *es* (*accepted*, *responses*). Finally, add the average sentence length to the number of big words per 100 words, then multiply it by 0.4. This gives you the Fog Index for the sample.

The Fog Index corresponds to the years of schooling needed to read and understand the sample. A score of eight or nine indicates high school level; 13, a college freshman; 17, a college graduate. Popular magazines have Fog Indexes ranging from eight to 13. Technical journals should rate no higher than 17. Obviously, the higher the Fog Index, the more difficult the writing is to read.

In his book *Gene Control in the Living Cell* (Basic Books, 1968), J.A.V. Butler leads off with a single 79-word sentence: *In this book I have attempted an accurate but at the same time readable account of recent work on the subject of how gene controls operate, a large subject which is rapidly acquiring a central position in the biology of today and which will inevitably become even more prominent in the future, in the efforts of scientists of numerous different specialists to explain how a single organism can contain cells of many different kinds developed from a common origin.* This sample has a Fog Index of 40, which is equivalent to a reading level of 28 years of college education! Obviously, this sentence is way too long. Here's a rewrite with a Fog Index of only 14: *This book is about how gene controls operate—a subject of growing importance in modern biology.*

Give your writing the Fog Index test. If you score in the upper teens or higher, it's time to trim sentence length. Read over your text, breaking long sentences into two or more separate sentences. To further reduce average sentence length and add variety to your writing, you can occasionally use an extremely short sentence or sentence fragments of only three to four words or so. Short sentences are easier to grasp than long ones. A good guide for keeping sentence length under control is to write sentences that can be spoken aloud without losing your breath (do not take a deep breath before doing this test).

6. Be specific

Businesspeople are interested in specifics—facts, figures, conclusions, and recommendations. Do not be content to say something is good, bad, fast, or slow when you can say how good, how bad, how fast, or how slow. Be specific whenever possible.

General	Specific
a tall spray dryer	a 40-foot-tall spray dryer
plant	oil refinery
unit	evaporator
unfavorable weather	rain
structural degradation	a leaky roof
high performance	95 percent efficiency

7. Be simple

The key to success in business writing is to keep it simple. Write to express, not to impress. A relaxed, conversational style can add vigor and clarity to your work.

Formal style	Informal conversational style
The data provided by direct examination of samples under the lens of the microscope are insufficient for the purpose of making a proper identification of the components of the substance.	We can't tell what it is made of by looking at it under the microscope.
We have found during conversations with customers that even the most experienced of extruder specialists have a tendency to avoid the extrusion of silicone profiles or hoses.	Our customers tell us that experienced extruder specialists avoid extruding silicone profiles or hoses.
The corporation terminated the employment of Mr. Joseph Smith.	Joe was fired.

8. Define your topic

Effective writing relies on clear definition of the specific topic about which you want to write. A big mistake that many of us make is to tackle a topic that's too broad. For example, the title *Project Management* is too all-encompassing for a business paper. You could write a whole book on the subject. By narrowing the scope with a title such as *Managing Chemical Plant Construction Projects With Budgets Under $500,000*, you get a clearer definition and a more manageable topic.

It's also important to know the purpose of the document. You may say, "That's easy; the purpose is to give business information." But think again. Do you want the reader to buy a product? Change methods of working? Look for the hidden agenda beyond the mere transmission of facts.

9. Develop adequate content

Once you've identified your reader and defined your topic and purpose, do some homework and gather information on the topic at hand. Even though you're an expert, your knowledge may be limited and your viewpoint lopsided. Gathering adequate information from other sources helps round out your knowledge or, at the very least, verify your own thinking. Backing up your claims with facts is also a real credibility builder.

10. Be consistent in usage

Inconsistencies in business writing will confuse your readers and convince them that your work and reasoning are as sloppy and unorganized as your prose.

Good business writers strive for consistency in the use of numbers, hyphens, units of measure, punctuation, equations, grammar, symbols, capitalization, business terms, and abbreviations.

For example, many writers are inconsistent in the use of hyphens. The rule is: Two words that form an adjective are hyphenated. Thus, write: first-order reaction, fluidized-bed combustion, high-sulfur coal, space-time continuum, and so forth.

The U.S. Government Printing Office *Style Manual*, Strunk and White's *The Elements of Style*, and your organization's writing manual can guide you in the basics of grammar, punctuation, abbreviation, and capitalization.

11. Shun dull, wordy prose

Business professionals, especially those in the industry, are busy people. Make your writing less time-consuming for them to read by telling the whole story in the fewest possible words.

How can you make your writing more concise? One way is to avoid redundancies, a needless form of wordiness in which a modifier repeats an idea already contained within the word being modified. Some redundancies that arise in business literature are listed below, along with the correct way to rewrite them:

Redundancy	Rewrite
advance plan	plan
actual experience	experience
two cubic feet in volume	two cubic feet
cylindrical in shape	cylindrical
uniformly homogeneous	homogeneous

Another good strategy is to avoid wordy phrases that often appear in business literature. The following list identifies some of these and offers suggested substitute words:

Wordy phrase	Suggested substitute
during the course of	during
in the form of	as
in many cases	often
in the event of	if
exhibits the ability to	can

Also avoid overblown expressions such as *the fact that, it is well known that,* and *it is the purpose of this writer to show that.* These take up space but add little to no meaning or clarity.

12. Use short blocks of text

To enhance readability, break your writing up into short sections. Long, unbroken blocks of text are stumbling blocks that intimidate and bore readers. Breaking your writing up into short sections and short paragraphs makes it easier to read.

These tips cover the basics of effective business writing. Following them should help eliminate some of the fear and anxiety you may have about writing, making the task easier and more productive. Of course, though, to keep pace with our electronically oriented business world, you don't just need the basics—you need to know which form of communication (e-mail? fax? standard letter?) is best suited to your message. In addition, you need to be adept at the ever-evolving rules of e-mail etiquette and avoid the kinds of business e-mail blunders that can potentially damage your reputation—or even put your job on the line.

So, how does one master the precarious art of electronic business communications? The first, most fundamental step is knowing when an e-mail, a fax, or a letter is the most appropriate medium for your message.

How to determine the best medium for your message

Knowing when and how to use e-mails, faxes, and letters can help you shine as a business professional. Obviously, you don't send a fax to congratulate someone on his or her retirement, and you don't send a formal letter to tell employees there's a new snack machine in the lobby. But, of course, the biggest challenge today is not really sorting faxes from letters; it's knowing when to use e-mail. One hundred eighty-three billion e-mails were sent each day in 2006, reported the technology market research firm The Radicati Group, which also estimated that the number of e-mail users was 1.2 billion in 2007 and would increase to 1.6 billion by 2011. E-mail has become the chosen form of communication for so many kinds of messages that probably the most valuable skill today is knowing when *not* to use it.

Although there is no single "right" way to determine when to shun e-mail in favor of a more formal missive, there are definitely some business communications that simply ought to be sent the traditional way—that is, mailed through the post office (or, at the very least, communicated via a phone conversation, meeting, memo, or even fax instead). The acronym **POST** is an easy way to remember which business communications these are. A **POST** message has the following qualities:

Personal and/or **P**rivate

Official

Sensitive

Telling

A brief explanation of each of these qualities follows.

Personal and/or private

Rule #1: Don't use business e-mail for personal communications. Most corporations' electronic communications usage policies prohibit the use of workplace e-mail accounts to transmit or receive personal messages. Chances are, you've had to sign one of these policies in agreement. Although you might be aware of people who violate the rules all the time—sending messages to make dinner plans with friends, vent about relationship woes, share the most popular YouTube video, or, worse yet, gripe to family and friends about the boss—taking these policies seriously is the mark of a true professional. When an e-mail is *about* your personal life, or its intended recipients belong to what you would consider your personal life, don't send it using your corporate e-mail account. And don't assume that management doesn't have the technology in place to routinely archive and review every e-mail you send. Remember that once your message is out there, you can't get it back. It will not only serve as proof that you have violated your corporate e-mail policy, but it may embarrass you or, worse yet, result in your firing. Refer to "Tips for avoiding common e-mail blunders" in Chapter 1 for advice on keeping your business communications out of the personal fray. Even if you are the business owner yourself, keeping your personal life separate from your daily business communications is a good practice that encourages better management of your time and resources.

Now, to address "private." All e-mail can be forwarded, searched, and stored, so there is really no such thing as a private or confidential e-mail, no matter what high-end encryption functions your e-mail program might feature. If you have a private or confidential business matter to discuss, such as contract negotiations, personnel issues, or company proprietary information, or if you need to send a message that includes a Social Security number, personal identification code, credit card number, or a client's financial account or similarly confidential information, don't send an e-mail, either internally or externally. With e-mail, you can never be certain that your message won't end up in the hands of an unintended recipient.

Confidential details and issues are best expressed in a printed memo or letter, or in a face-to-face meeting that is followed up by a printed memo or letter—preferably in an envelope labeled *confidential*. At the very least, before sending an e-mail that addresses potentially sensitive information, ask someone knowledgeable in your organization. Remember that you represent your organization, not just yourself, in every business message you send. You don't want to leave yourself, or the company you represent, open to legal action for releasing information that someone expected to remain under wraps. By the same token, revealing information your own organization intended to keep close to the vest can damage your employment record or even be enough to get you fired if you previously signed a confidentiality agreement. Examples include details about a proprietary strategy for launching a product or contracts with external vendors for work that a client believed was being completed in-house.

A good rule of thumb: If you don't want a message made public, don't use e-mail.

Official

By "official," we mean the types of correspondence for which you require either delivery confirmation or detailed documentation and recordkeeping. Some examples: messages pertaining to contracts, agreements, and other legal obligations; notifications of firing, salary, or job classification changes; communications about employee benefits and other personnel issues; tax-related information; employment offers; official notices about important information; formal announcements about changes in company structure; and notarized or signed documents.

There are many reasons why e-mail is not suitable for communications like these. Although e-mail can be a written record, it's electronic, which means there's a potential to lose messages to software or hardware glitches. In addition, many corporate e-mail servers have memory storage limits and automatically delete e-mails when users go over these limits. It's also possible to have the content of your e-mail changed, falsified, or manipulated by another user (who can simply type over parts of your message). And, although "read receipts" are available with e-mail, most e-mail programs allow users to opt out of sending these receipts.

Furthermore, even if you print a copy of an e-mail for your records, your recipient may not necessarily do the same—or even save your e-mail. You can, of course, scan important documents and attach them to an e-mail, provided they do not need added security (for example, if they don't include personal identification codes or account numbers). In most cases, however, proper documentation of the kinds of messages we're discussing here requires the genuine article—the original hard copy.

Sensitive

By *sensitive*, we are referring to the kinds of messages in which emotion is (or ought to be) involved. Occasionally in business you will need to congratulate, give thanks, express condolence or personal concern, reprimand, state disapproval, or lavish praise—and do it in writing. If you want the thought or feeling behind your message to come across as you intended and to correspond with the medium in which it was sent, e-mail is *not* the way to go. It can't convey emotion in the same way that the stationery or writing style of a letter can (much less the facial expressions, vocal inflections, and gestures of a face-to-face meeting).

For example, in a letter, the use of exclamation points, all capital letters, and ellipses (three or four periods in a row) can be effective, but in an e-mail, the use of these often backfires. Why? The inherent brevity of e-mail, along with its stark, utilitarian setting within a computer screen, leaves little room for expression. In e-mail, liberally used exclamation points suggest overexcitement, while all capital letters look like shouting and ellipses appear to underlie an indecisiveness about what to say next.

Even if you add special formatting to enhance your e-mail, such as background "stationery" with expressive colors or scenes, you can't be certain that what you see on your screen will be what your recipient sees. That's because he or she may have different software or hardware, or settings that filter out graphics and/or HyperText Markup Language (HTML).

Of course, there are always "smileys" or "emoticons"—face-like symbols composed of different characters on a computer keypad, commonly used to express emotion in e-mail. Here are some popular emoticons, along with their meanings:

Emoticon	Meaning
:)	Smile
;)	Wink
:(	Frown
:-D	Laugh
:-X	No comment
:'(	Crying
:-I	Tongue in cheek
:->	Sarcastic
=:O	Surprise

Although many people use emoticons freely, they are not recommended for business communications. Some readers may not understand their meaning, and emoticons can also leave the impression that you're being irreverent or cutesy.

When it comes to sensitive messages, the other drawback of e-mail is that it can be risky when you have an emotionally charged or touchy situation to address. E-mail is like the "convenience store" of written communications; typically, it's brief, to the point, composed quickly, and lacking any backstory. Because of this, short statements made in the context of a sensitive subject matter can be misinterpreted, and one's intended tone easily gets lost in translation. Often, the direct language that characterizes an e-mail is misread as curt, cold, or accusatory. Recently, a study published in the *Journal of Personality and Social Psychology* reported that e-mails are misinterpreted 50 percent of the time, and a Canadian study revealed that 32 percent of people considered e-mail to be ineffective at conveying tone, intent, and emotional context. In addition, when you're faced with a business situation that irks you, e-mail's convenience makes you more likely to fire off a response before carefully choosing your words as you would when composing a letter. Add that to the inherently abrupt tone of e-mail, and you can end up making a bad situation even worse.

So, in sum: If you're actively trying to convey emotion or you need to address a sensitive situation, avoid e-mail. It's probably best to go with a printed letter or memo. In this age of fast, impersonal e-mails and text messages, your reader will appreciate it.

Telling

A dictionary definition of the word *telling* is "producing a strong effect" or "powerfully persuasive." For a message to be "telling"—that is, to make a distinct impression—the best medium is a printed letter, not an e-mail. In today's e-mail–oriented business world, letters have symbolic importance. Letters are tangible; you can hold them and read them. Their visual and tactile features have impact. For example, crisp, textured stationery; clean, professional company letterhead; and an elegantly penned signature suggest class and formality. A handwritten note suggests warmth and personal attention. E-mail, on the other hand, lacks personality. It is functional, not symbolic.

So, for correspondence that is meant to make a strong impression, the post office is usually the best way to go. Examples include promotional mailings, brochures, and letters introducing your company to potential clients. You can, of course, transmit such documents by e-mail, attaching them as portable document format (PDF) files, but these files sometimes look different on different computers because of variations in operating platforms and selected printer fonts. The bottom line is: If you want your message to make a real impression, avoid e-mail.

That covers the basics of knowing when not to use e-mail in business situations. To make it even easier to identify the specific kinds of correspondence discussed in this book for which e-mail is inappropriate, we use the following icon: 🚫. Look for this icon above sample messages in each chapter.

In addition, here are a few more guidelines on when to use a business letter or a fax.

- The business letter is used to communicate formal matters in business, jurisprudence, or otherwise. You can use this form of correspondence when you want to send a cover letter to accompany your resume, write a letter announcing business news to colleagues outside your company, or notify vendors of a change in your ordering procedures. You can file an official complaint or compliment with such a letter, or use it for any number of other business occasions.

- The facsimile machine dramatically changed the pace of business communication about two decades ago, but its use has somewhat declined with the advent of e-mail. Still, knowing how to correctly and appropriately use this form of quick correspondence will help you boost your business image.

  Here are some basics: Use faxes only when the message needs immediate attention. Do not use the fax machine to send documents or information in which the appearance is important. Despite advances in image quality and plain paper fax machines, faxed messages still do not arrive with the same professional look that personal letters or reports offer.

Of course, communicating effectively in business today not only involves knowing whether you should send your correspondence by e-mail, fax, or letter. It also means being able to use e-mail wisely, navigating the ever-evolving rules of e-mail etiquette. The next chapter offers valuable rules, tips, and guidelines related to e-mail etiquette and more.

1

Special Rules, Tips, and Guidelines for Writing Business E-Mails

E-mail has revolutionized daily communications. Ninety-one percent of U.S. Internet users have gone online and used e-mail, with 56 percent doing so as part of their daily routine, according to the Pew Internet & American Life Project in 2007. According to some estimates, working Americans typically spend about two hours per day managing their business e-mail. The number of business e-mail users totaled 780 million in 2007, according to Ferris Research, and 3.4 billion business e-mails are sent in North America on an average day, reported IDC, a technology research firm. With e-mail entrenched in daily life and dominating the way businesspeople communicate, we thought a chapter devoted to its do's and don'ts could help guide you in using this technology more effectively on a daily basis.

Three basic rules of business e-mail etiquette

Because e-mail is continually evolving as a communication tool, it can be difficult to navigate its ambiguous rules of conduct. To help you with this task, we've distilled the fundamentals of business e-mail etiquette down to three simple rules: *Keep it simple. Keep it clean. Keep it professional.*

1. Keep it simple

Simplicity is the key to composing effective e-mails, because e-mail is meant to be quick and direct. A properly written business e-mail has the following characteristics:

Simplicity of language. Following the "Be simple" rule of business writing that we discussed in "12 general tips for better business writing" in the Introduction of this book is *critical* when it comes to e-mail. That's because e-mail style exudes speed and brevity. You can dispense with the formality and hackneyed phrases that have plagued so much business correspondence in the past ("enclosed please find," "as per your request," and "please be informed," for example). Instead of "as per your request," just send the document as an attached file with a cover e-mail that says, "Here is the PowerPoint presentation you asked me to send." People have so many other e-mails to read that succinctness and clarity are essential. Don't waste your readers' time by sending an e-mail that requires them to follow up to clarify what you meant.

Don't write a book. Keep your e-mails brief. Limit them to one to three short paragraphs; if you need to write more, don't go beyond the equivalent of one printed page. Anything longer will need some other forum, such as a printed letter or a meeting, to resolve your issue. Similarly, if there is lengthy explanatory or supporting material, consider sending it along with your e-mail as an attached file. This makes it easier for the recipient to download and file the information onto his or her own hard drive.

Simplicity of subject. E-mail was designed for the speedy transfer of files and messages from computer to computer over a network—regardless of where these computers are located or whether they're all online at the same time. Because recipients may retrieve their messages at different times, problems arise when groups of people, particularly in the workplace, attempt to use e-mail to reach a consensus on an issue or to engage in a lengthy "conversation." Such e-mail exchanges easily get out of synch, with some individuals replying to older e-mails in the e-mail string. This leads to confusion, which further lengthens the discussion and clogs up participants' inboxes with additional e-mails. Inevitably, a phone call or a meeting is needed to settle things.

So, restrict your e-mail messages to one topic per message, and don't use them for conversations or for consensus-seeking (save these for meetings, phone calls, or instant messages). An easy-to-remember guideline: Use e-mail to send simple messages that are "actionable"—messages that solicit a specific, uncomplicated response or action.

Unfortunately, it is easy to get entangled in interoffice e-mail exchanges that are *not* actionable. Here's a brief list of the most common kinds of *non*actionable business e-mails that you should avoid:

- E-mails whose purpose is to prove that you're right about something (for example, e-mailing a history of previous e-mails to prove you already sent your recipient his or her copy of your quarterly report).

- E-mails that serve as a delaying tactic (for example, e-mailing questions whose answers affect your ability to complete a project just before that project is due).

- Gratuitous replies to e-mails that have already ended the discussion (for example, someone has written, "Thank you" or "Perfect," and you respond "Oh, it's no problem" or "You can count on me!").

- Unsolicited advertisements and promotions; these are considered spam and will likely be blocked and reported to an e-mail administrator, with possible legal implications for you.
- E-mails composed "under the influence"—of anger, disappointment, boredom, confusion, guilt, gossip, insomnia, insecurity, and so on.

If you are angry or upset about a costly mistake that someone in your department made, wait until your feelings cool before sending an e-mail about the matter. Although it may be tempting to fire off an e-mail to avoid the discomfort of an actual confrontation, resist the urge. If you don't, you may regret what you say, and the object of your disdain will likely respond just as vehemently. A heated e-mail conversation you never intended to have may ensue (and could go on indefinitely, taking you away from important tasks that you need to complete).

Similarly, e-mailing when you're confused about an e-mail you were sent will inevitably cause your inbox to fill up with replies you *still* don't understand. If you need clarification on a confusing e-mail, call the sender.

E-mailing to apologize or admit guilt can be risky. For example, there could be serious repercussions if you use e-mail to admit a company error to a client without consulting with your superiors first.

Avoid e-mail for dishing the latest office gossip. What you say becomes a permanent record that may come back to haunt you.

E-mailing in the dead of night about a work issue that is keeping you awake is also a bad idea. Give yourself a chance to "sleep on it" and see if you still feel the same way about the issue the next day.

Finally, e-mail is not the forum for seeking reassurance on a work-related action you feel insecure about; your recipient will likely consider your e-mail a waste of his or her valuable time, as well as your own.

Finally, there is one last tip for "keeping it simple": Set aside a half-hour or an hour each day when you do not log into your e-mail account but simply focus on getting your work completed. This will help make you more productive and protect you from e-mail "information overload."

2. Keep it clean

Keeping your business e-mails "clean" doesn't just mean avoiding profanities or offensive statements—that goes without saying. It refers to the way your e-mail messages are presented. "E-mail especially, with its convenience and lightning-fast speed, has introduced new sloppiness into business communication," says Dr. Lester Hoff, a communications consultant based in New York City. He notes that the majority of interoffice e-mail, for example, is not proofread in hard copy (because the messages are never printed out by the writer) or even with a spell-checker on the screen. The result: ineffective, error-plagued communication.

Certainly, e-mail has a reputation for informal language, lax grammar, cryptic acronyms, emoticons, chain letters, trifling forwards, offensive jokes, spam, and spreading computer viruses. But that doesn't mean you should allow the quality of your own business e-mails to suffer. Grammatical errors, unintelligible content, misspellings, and typos in your e-mails will turn off your associates, managers, and clients alike. Carefully proofread your e-mails before you send them. Errors are no more acceptable in e-mails than in printed documents.

Take your time composing your e-mails. You might try having another person in your company read and give you feedback on your most important e-mails (for example, e-mails intended for clients or potential clients) before you send them.

Check your spelling carefully, with special attention to the spelling of recipients' names. Don't leave everything up to your spell-checker, though. Be careful about automatically accepting its suggestions for proper nouns and personal names. We once knew a colleague who, because of overdependence on his spell-checker, sent a message addressed to a Dr. Fishbone (whose name was really Dr. Fishbane).

Closely examine your punctuation, formatting, and capitalization as well. Stay clear of the kinds of overpunctuation, excessive type-styling, and formatting that are misguidedly used to express emotion in e-mail. Examples:

- **Emoticons:** These should be avoided for the reasons explained in "How to determine the best medium for your message" in the Introduction.

- **Ellipses:** These are intended to signify that words have been omitted from a direct quotation—not that one's thoughts have trailed off or that a pause has occurred. (There really is no place for a pause in an e-mail. Pauses are for conversations.)

- **All capital letters:** Words and phrases typed in all capital letters are not only difficult to read, they are perceived as YELLING. To stress a word, boldface or italicize it.

- **Overuse of exclamation points and question marks:** Avoid concluding too many sentences with exclamation points or using a series of exclamation points and/or question marks in a row. These impart a sense of desperation, instability, or bossiness.

- **E-mail/text message acronyms and lingo:** These will make your e-mail message seem too casual or unprofessional, plus confuse readers who are unfamiliar with them. In fact, the time you save by typing in an acronym will be more than compensated by the time it takes your recipient to figure out what you meant.

  Although the acronyms are not recommended for business e-mail messages, you will encounter them frequently, warranting that you know what they mean. Here are a few of the more popular acronyms and their meanings:

Acronyms	Meaning
b/c	Because
BRB	Be right back
BTW	By the way
COB	Close of business
CUL8R	See you later
ETA	Estimated time of arrival
<g>	Grin
GTG	Got to go
IMO	In my opinion
JIC	Just in case
LOL	Laugh out loud
NC	No comment
OIC	Oh, I see
OTOH	On the other hand
TTFN	Ta ta for now
TTUL	Talk to you later
w/	With
w/o	Without
WTG	Way to go

▪ **Fanciful formatting, graphics, backgrounds, icons, logos, clip art, and so forth:** As mentioned previously, because of differences in hardware, software, and filter settings, what you see on your screen may not be the same as what your recipient sees. So, jazzing up your e-mail with such features may be a waste of time. Your e-mail might even get dumped into your recipient's junk or spam folder because of its unrecognizable attachments.

Composing e-mail messages in HTML can also be problematic if your reader's e-mail program isn't set up to view HTML messages. Many computer users don't have the capability to read anything but plain text in ASCII format. Trying to add drawings, even ones made by ASCII characters that "should" be readable by everyone, isn't worth the risk of sending illegible material.

You can also keep your business e-mails "clean" by being meticulous about the way you handle attachments. Before attaching files, confirm that the person you are corresponding with has the software to open them and that his or her e-mail server can handle their size. Instead of attaching large files to an e-mail, you could post the files on an FTP (file transfer protocol) site where they can be downloaded, or include a link to a Website where the information contained in the attachment can be displayed.

3. Keep it professional

This may sound like a vague piece of advice. But there are very specific ways you can ensure that your e-mail is professional and courteous:

- Be careful about sending jokes or using humor. If the content of your e-mail or its attachments offend your reader (sexist comments and jokes, for example), you could be reprimanded, accused of workplace harassment, even sued. Your e-mail could also be forwarded to people with whom you would rather not have shared it. This can embarrass you or damage your reputation. Also, remember that employers routinely archive e-mail and monitor their e-mail systems.

- Follow your company's e-mail usage policy. Even if your organization has not issued a formal, written policy, observe any statements the management have made about properly using the company's communications systems. Use your common sense.

- As we stressed in the previous chapter, avoid sending personal e-mail using your business e-mail account. This includes forwarding jokes, reflections, chain letters, and the like.

- Be complete. If you're responding to an e-mail that posed questions or requested information, make sure you have provided all the details asked of you. If you're using an e-mail to introduce your company's products or services to a potential client, give him or her all the information needed to make a decision about what you're offering.

- Don't be too informal. Although the tendency is to write less formally in e-mail than in an official letter or memo, if you are sending a message to a client, an associate, or your boss, be just as professional as you would in a typical memo or letter.

- Be sure all the recipients who are relevant to your e-mail are included in the "To" and "CC" fields. Accidentally leaving someone out can become a politically sensitive sore spot. For example, if you are using e-mail to thank your team for their fine work on the last project, be sure to include all the team members, and carbon-copy the appropriate managers.

- Verify the accuracy of any facts, claims, statistics, or information that you put into your message. This is particularly important if your e-mail introduces your product or services to a potential customer.

- Finally, be genuine, and don't make your messages to clients sound like advertisements. No one likes a cheesy sales pitch.

Tips for avoiding common e-mail blunders

We've all heard stories about the regrettable consequences of workplace e-mail transgressions, such as sending a colleague disparaging remarks about a manager. Here are some ways to keep yourself out of e-mail trouble:

1. Use instant messaging, instead of e-mail, for brief online conversations with coworkers. That way, if you slip up and say something you shouldn't have, there's no permanent record. This will also keep your e-mail inbox from overflowing with insignificant little messages.

2. To avoid receiving personal e-mails in the workplace, make it a policy to not disclose your business e-mail address to friends and family. If it's too late for that, at least let them know that if they want you to respond to personal e-mails, they should use your personal e-mail address. Ask them to delete your business e-mail address from their online address books.

3. Get into the habit of completing the "To" and "CC" fields of e-mail messages as the *last* step before sending a message. This prevents you from prematurely hitting the "Send" button before you've carefully proofed your message. You should complete your e-mail, proofread it, double-check any attachments, and only fill in the "To" and "CC" fields when you're absolutely ready to hit "Send."

   If you're responding to a message, clear the "To" and "CC" fields by hitting "Forward" instead of "Reply." Then type your reply, carefully proof it, remove any unnecessary attachments automatically picked up by selecting "Forward," and enter the e-mail addresses of your recipients last. If others are anxiously awaiting your reply, let them wait the few extra seconds or minutes it takes to ensure that you don't send a message that is missing an attachment or key details, filled with errors, incomplete, or addressed to the wrong person.

4. If you find yourself typing an angry or emotionally charged e-mail, leave off the recipient's address and save the message as a draft. Return to the message later and evaluate whether sending it still seems like a good idea.

5. Double-check files after attaching them. Open them up to make sure you have attached the correct version (or even the correct file). There's nothing more embarrassing than having to resend an e-mail because you realized you attached the wrong file, omitted something, or forgot a correction.

Guidelines for crafting the most effective business e-mails

Now you know the basic do's and don'ts of writing business e-mails. But how can you be sure your e-mail messages do more than just adhere to the rules of etiquette, but also make a real impact? Here are some guidelines for using e-mail more effectively:

- Carefully choose the day and time you send your messages to customers or potential customers. For example, Monday morning is generally a time when people sift through all the e-mails that have piled up since the last Friday. Try to send your message when it isn't competing with dozens of other messages for your recipient's attention.

- Don't be slow in replying to e-mail. Check your mailbox at least daily (some people check hourly) to get your messages and ensure you can respond quickly. "The biggest appeal of e-mail is its immediacy," says Marcia Layton, author of *The Complete Idiot's Guide to Terrific Business Writing* (Alpha Books). "People don't like to wait days to hear back from you."

- Don't use e-mail to avoid phone conversations. E-mail is convenient because it allows you to send people a message at your convenience and they can pick it up at their convenience. But if you never pick up the phone to speak directly to someone, you might give the message that you're avoiding him or her. Personal contact from time to time is necessary to solidify business and personal relationships.

- When reaching out to clients or potential clients via e-mail, don't allow your messages to look like everyone else's. Subscribe to your competitors' e-mails to customers in order to analyze these messages and find ways to make yours stand out.

- Don't forget that e-mail is not always the appropriate communication tool. Before automatically sending an e-mail, ask yourself if what you're sending would have more impact as a letter, a memo, or a mailing.

- Look for the **E-mail Empowerment Tips** throughout the book. This special feature points out easy ways to use business e-mail more effectively.

Keep in mind that success in writing, no matter what form of communication you use, is largely a matter of attitude. If you don't think writing is important enough to take the time to do it right and you don't really care about improving, you probably won't get better at it. But if you believe that writing is important and you want to improve, you will.

2

How to Format Your Business Letter, Fax, Memo, or E-Mail

The mechanics of writing a letter, fax, or e-mail are just as important as the content. The way these messages look immediately tells the reader how seriously he or she should take the contents. You can throw a few words on a piece of paper and look like an amateur to your readers, or you can learn the rules for writing business correspondence and look like you know what you're doing. It's all in perception. The following rules and tips will set your stylistic eye straight.

Letters

You will want to use the formal format to emphasize the importance of the contents to your reader. The rules are simple; however, be sure not to break them.

Letter formatting basics

Business letters should be written in the following manner:

- Print your letter on high-quality white or light-colored paper with black ink.
- Set your margins to 1 to 1 1/2 inches all around.
- Use a colon after the salutation.
- Leave four returns between the complimentary close and your name.
- Place your signature in between the complimentary close and your name.

Sample business letter on letterhead paper

There are many formats you can use, but to keep things simple we recommend the full-blocked style in which everything is placed flush with the left margin. (This includes the dateline, inside address, salutation, paragraph openings, complimentary close, and writer's name.) See the sample below:

Fictional Firm Letterhead
0000 Make-Believe Street
Noplace Real, NJ 10000

Date: [put the date here]

Inside Address: [This is the company or person you are writing your letter to.]

Street Name
Town, State, ZIP Code

Salutation: [This is your "hello" greeting. If you do not know the person's name, use: *Dear Sir or Madam:* and when you are writing to an organization rather than an individual, you can write: *Dear Ladies and Gentlemen:*]

Body: [The body, as its name suggests, is the primary part of the letter. It follows the salutation. Most often business letters are single-spaced, unless they are very short and double-spacing will better fill up the page.]

When you start a new paragraph, drop down two line spaces and begin. In this full-blocked style you do not indent the first line.

Closing: [This is where you say, *Sincerely yours,* or *Best wishes,* or *Very truly yours.* Note the first word of the complimentary close is capitalized; the second word is not.]

[Your signature goes here.]
Type your name below it

Sample business letter on plain paper without letterhead

If you are writing a business letter on paper without letterhead, put your company's name and address directly above the dateline and then proceed with the same format as above:

```
Fictional Firm
0000 Make Believe Street
Noplace Real, NJ 10000


Dateline


Dear Salutation:
```

Faxes

Not every businessperson has his or her own personal fax machine. Often fax transmissions arrive in a common area and then are routed to the proper recipient. The facsimile transmission cover form has been developed to route your communication to the correct person and to provide details you'd find on a business letter, such as the sender's name, address, and date. It also includes subject matter, as well as the number of pages being transmitted. It's smart to keep your fax cover sheet as brief as possible. The fax machine will read all print on the sheet including borders, margins, and lines. Something as simple as a heavy border around the cover sheet can double your fax transmission time.

Fax transmission cover form

Be sure this type of cover form precedes your fax communications. Here is a simple format you can use or adapt any way you like:

Date _____   **Time** _____
To: _____
From: _____

Phone: _____
Fax: _____
Subject: _____

We are transmitting _____ pages including this cover sheet. If you do not receive all the pages or they are not legible, please call back as soon as possible. Thank you.

Fax formatting basics

If you want your fax messages to receive a positive reception, follow these basic guidelines:

- Avoid heavy, dark graphics on a fax. In addition to doubling transmission time, recipients who have an inkjet fax may get a page that is moist from the heavy application of ink.
- In addition to the cover form, format your fax message in either the standard business letter or memo form.
- Use a simple, legible type for your fax messages. Helvetica, Times New Roman, and Courier all transmit very clearly.
- Avoid handwritten notes. Text written with a pen or pencil often does not fax well.
- Make the type at least 11 or 12 points in size.
- To double-check the appearance of your fax correspondence, run the original through your fax machine using copy mode. The document the recipient gets will look like this copy.
- Before we move on, here is one caveat about faxing: In-trays by fax machines are rapidly becoming as cluttered as in-baskets or regular mailboxes. Communicating via fax does not assure the reader's undivided attention.

Memos

The word *memo* is short for *memorandum*. A memo is a short "note" passed in an office. Memos are brief reminders, quick announcements, or concise pieces of information. Memos were once the communication lifeline for interoffice correspondence, but they have been supplanted by e-mail for most of their original purposes—except where a printed document is preferable because of confidentiality issues or the need to create a paper trail. (But when you do use the memo format, be sure you're not trying to communicate something of vital importance.)

Memos tend to be given less attention and importance than correspondence written on company letterhead. Memos should also be used sparingly for communications outside the office. When writing to colleagues, customers, clients, vendors, or others, you should use the more formal business letter format, or use e-mail, if appropriate.

You will notice that we use the memo format only occasionally in this book, as e-mail is now preferable for many of the situations that used to call for a memo.

Memo formatting basics

There is no rule carved in stone about how to set up the format of a memo. But you should pick one format and stick with it. The top of the paper should contain four pieces of information: the date, the recipient, the sender, and the subject matter (*Re:* means "regarding").

The memo format you'll see used throughout this book looks like this:

```
Date

To: _____

From: _____

Re: _____
```

E-mails

The business letter has its full-blocked style; the fax has its cover sheet, the memo has its "to/from/re" heading. E-mail has its format built right in. The computer supplies the recipient with a record of the sender, the sender's e-mail address, the date and time, and the subject. You don't have to add these things to your message. You simply begin, "Dear So-and-So."

One of the best things about e-mail is the ease of a reply. With a click of the "Reply" button, you can respond to your e-mail and send along the original correspondence as well. With paper communication, you have to remind the person of the original correspondence ("In response to your memo of 5/8/09, let me point out that..."). With e-mail, the automatic inclusion of the original message in your reply eliminates the need to establish that link.

Much of the correspondence in this book can be sent via e-mail. In some cases, the e-mail message itself serves as a cover message, with a more formal letter attached.

E-mail formatting basics

- Keep your margins wide. "You can use narrow margins on regular letters, but online your wide sentences may not get seen, or they may get reproduced in an irregular format. It'll be very tough to read," says Joe Vitale, author of *Cyberwriting* (Amacom, 1996). He advises that e-mail letters should have margins set at 20 and 80, so every sentence is very short and will get displayed on any screen, even if it's a laptop, without odd text breaks.

- Widthwise, adjust your e-mail program's setting for wrapping lines to accommodate a line length of no more than 65 characters across. And, as we stressed in the previous chapter, never write more than what would amount to one page lengthwise. E-mail that requires excessive scrolling either horizontally or vertically will eventually lose its recipient's attention and be shuttled away. "My own rule of thumb is to keep text down to 60 characters wide," Vitale explains. "As I'm typing, I'm looking at the screen. When the lines look as if they are beyond four inches, I hit my return key to force a carriage return. This way all my posts are narrow enough to be read by virtually everyone online without difficulty."

- Demonstrate courtesy. Don't launch right into your message without a formal salutation, such as "Hi, Gloria" or "Dear Brian." Also, include at least the basic introductory headers and addresses you would normally include in a letter (refer to the sample business letters in this chapter), unless you are corresponding with a coworker or are on familiar terms with your correspondent, in which case you can simply begin with the salutation.

- Be sure to include your contact information in the body of your message, either in a closing statement or, preferably, in an automatic e-mail signature.

Automatic e-mail signatures are really a form of letterhead. Usually appearing at the end of your message, separated by a rule, they should include your full name, title, company, address, phone number, fax number, e-mail address, and Website link (if applicable). To automatically append a signature to all of your outgoing messages, access the "Signature" feature in your e-mail program and enter the information you'd like displayed.

Limit your signature to 10 lines. More than that is too much to read and makes you look self-important. Here is a sample signature for a business professional:

Ian Smith
President
Fictional Firm
0000 Make-Believe Street
Noplace Real, NJ 10000
Phone: (000) 000-0000
Fax: (000) 000-0000
Mobile: (000) 000-0000
E-mail: myname@fictionalfirm.com
Website: *www.fictionalfirm.com*

Here is a sample nonbusiness signature (for example, one that a consumer would use to write to a company):

Ian Smith
0000 Home Address Street
Noplace Real, NJ 10000
Phone: (000) 000-0000
Fax: (000) 000-0000
Mobile: (000) 000-0000
E-mail: myname@personale-maildomain.com

- Prepare a direct, self-explanatory subject line. The subject line is the first thing your recipient sees.

- Use the special tools and functions that come with your e-mail program wisely. For example, don't overdo it with "high priority" messages. We know some people who mark just about every message as high priority, putting the fear of that red-exclamation-point-in-the-inbox into the hearts of many a colleague! Reserve this e-mail feature for messages that pertain to immediate deadlines, egregious errors, or last-minute premeeting notes or attachments.

  Similarly, don't digitally encrypt your messages (encryption is another feature available with many e-mail programs). They may not translate correctly on your recipient's end.

  Avoid the blind carbon-copy (bcc) feature unless your bcc buddy has requested it. Otherwise, this person may wonder why you feel the need to "BCC" him or her.

  On the other hand, it is a good idea to request "read receipts," even though whether you will actually receive them will be hit-or-miss (it all depends on how your correspondents have set up their read-receipt–sending preferences).

  Some options or preferences in your e-mail program that you should *always* choose include: automatic names and e-mail address suggestions; a display of recently used addresses when you're typing e-mail addresses; inclusion of previous messages in replies (this helps to minimize confusion about what you're replying to); and placement of your replies at the beginning of outgoing messages, not at the end.

- If you're replying to only a couple of points in a message, you can briefly reference the items to which you are responding from the original text without including the entire original message. But if you have been sent a list of specific questions to answer, ensure that you answer in full by typing your responses next to the sender's questions, using brackets, asterisks, or another character to set your answers apart from the sender's text. Preface your reply by noting this method you've used for answering the questions.

- If sending a link to a Website address, be sure that the link is active and accurate. Also make sure the length of the Web link does not surpass the margin of your e-mail. If it does, it will break onto a new line on your recipient's end, and the link will not work correctly for him or her. If you have the option of e-mailing content from the site as an attachment instead, it may be preferable to do that. On the other hand, if your e-mail message refers to an online document that your reader can access without any problems, include the Web address in the text of your e-mail message so he or she can visit it directly.

3

Job-Hunting and Employment-Related Correspondence

The employment correspondence in this chapter includes messages to land a job and messages to reject a job (with samples to help you secure the kind of job that will put you in a position to write lots of business letters!). You will also find the letters you need if you're the one doing the hiring and firing, with samples you can adapt to your personal needs whether you are entry-level, middle management, or an experienced executive.

In years past, much of the correspondence addressed in this chapter, particularly related to hiring and job hunting, would have been typed on crisp, formal letterhead, faithfully reflecting the business letter formatting shown in Chapter 2. Today, however, employers routinely solicit job applications electronically and provide an e-mail address to which job seekers can send cover e-mails about their credentials, along with their resumes as attachments. Those looking for employment, too, commonly attach their resumes to cover e-mails, or they may post their relevant experience and background on career-related Websites.

Indeed, in today's business climate, job candidates who are not afraid to sell themselves by using e-mail or posting a resume online—and employers who can interact effortlessly with job candidates via e-mail or employment-related Websites—are more appealing than those who shy away from such technology. This ability to keep current with technology not only makes a good impression; it can save lots of time, allowing for quick electronic access to career-related information and offering the ability to schedule interviews through an electronic meetings calendar tied to one's e-mail program. Many employers do, in fact, arrange interviews via e-mail, with their first exposure to a job candidate's voice actually being the face-to-face interview.

That being said, be aware that, if you use e-mail for the kinds of correspondence in this chapter, you still need to include several elements of a standard business letter. For example:

- Always insert a header for your addressee at the top of your cover e-mail (that is, one that includes the recipient's name, title, and address).
- Include a salutation and a cordial closing.
- Provide your contact information in an e-mail signature appended to the end of your message, and draw your addressee's attention to this signature in the last paragraph of your message.

Taking these steps will show that you have spent time crafting your message and tailoring it to its recipient instead of simply jettisoning off a prefabricated "form" e-mail from your "drafts" folder. In fact, you might want to attach a formal cover letter and resume as separate documents, rather than using the e-mail message itself as your cover letter. If you choose this route, your e-mail message can be a brief statement such as "Attached are my cover letter and resume for your consideration for the position of such-and-such." (See pages 41 and 42 for two e-mail samples you can adapt to your own needs.)

If you are a job seeker who wants to stand out by mailing a formal cover letter along with a professionally designed resume on matching high-quality stock paper, be aware that your correspondence may reach your prospective employer much later than the e-mail messages of the other candidates who are vying for the same position (assuming the employer has included an e-mail address to which to send these items). A better strategy would be to send electronic files of your cover letter and resume by e-mail first, then follow up with the more formal hard copies by regular mail. Also, if the employer has specifically requested you apply by e-mail only, comply with this request.

Furthermore, remember that e-mail is still inappropriate for some of the letters described in this chapter—for example, letters about firing or specific personnel decisions. Be on the lookout for the ⊘ icon.

Correspondence to gain employment

The following letters will help bring your job-search process from application to interview to acceptance. Almost all of these letters may be sent via e-mail, whether as attachments or typed directly into the body of an e-mail message; just follow the guidance in the e-mail samples provided.

Recent college grad cover letter (traditional)

Background: Recent college graduates are often (but not always) light on experience. Most often, they have degrees and extracurricular activities, as do most other candidates, but summer job experience that doesn't relate to the position they're seeking. Therefore, their letters should be short and sweet. If you're a recent college grad, don't try to cover up your beginner status in the work world with hype.

On the other hand, if you have some experience that differentiates you from the crowd—say, you started a successful business or climbed Mt. Everest—the cover letter is the best place to stress it.

Essential elements: This simple and short letter doesn't waste the recipient's time. It gets right to the point with three main details:

1. Enclosed resume and spotlight on important experience.
2. Request for a job interview.
3. Promise of a follow-up call.

Samples:

Letter

Dear Ms. Rushiski:

As my enclosed resume shows, I am a recent graduate of HigherEd University with a major in English. My experience includes an internship with a large publishing company and word processing a novel for a best-selling author. I would like to meet with you to discuss the possibility of gaining an entry-level editorial position with your company. I look forward to hearing from you to discuss the possibility of an interview. [*If mailing a standard letter, state your contact information here. If using e-mail, include a statement that directs attention to your e-mail signature.*] I will follow up with you on Tuesday, October 2. Thanks for your time and consideration.

Sincerely,

E-mail

1. E-mail sample without a separate cover letter as an attachment

---

From: Your Name <yourname@e-maildomain.com>
Date: Thursday, September 15, 20XX
To: Maria Rushiski <president@fictionalfirm.com>
Subject: Entry-level editorial position
Attachments: Resume.doc

Maria Rushiski
President
Fictional Firm
0000 Make-Believe Street
Noplace Real, NJ 10000

Dear Mrs. Rushiski,

As my attached resume shows, I am a recent graduate of HigherEd University with a major in English. My experience includes an internship with a large publishing company and word processing a novel for a best-selling author. I would like to meet with you to discuss the possibility of gaining an entry-level editorial position with your company. My contact information is provided below. I look forward to hearing from you and will follow up with you on Tuesday, October 2, to discuss the possibility of an interview. Thanks for your time and consideration.

Cordially,
[*Automatic e-mail signature should appear here; see the sample signatures in Chapter 2.*]

2. E-mail sample with a separate cover letter as an attachment

From: Your Name <yourname@e-maildomain.com>
Date: Thursday, September 15, 20XX
To: Maria Rushiski <president@fictionalfirm.com>
Subject: Entry-level editorial position
Attachments: Coverletter.doc, Resume.doc

Maria Rushiski
President
Fictional Firm
0000 Make-Believe Street
Noplace Real, NJ 10000

Dear Mrs. Rushiski,

Attached are my resume and cover letter, outlining my credentials for an entry-level editorial position with your company. Thank you for your time and consideration.

Cordially,
[*Automatic e-mail signature should appear here; see the sample signatures in Chapter 2.*]

E-Mail Empowerment Tip

Apply this sample e-mail structure, while adapting the content, to the "Correspondence to hire employees" letters described in this chapter, except where e-mail is specifically not recommended.

Recent college grad cover letter (nontraditional)

Background: This kind of letter is risky—it may turn some people off, but if it works, it can make you stand out clearly from the crowd. (The real writer of this letter actually got the interview.)

Essential element: This letter is a little different, a bit bolder than the conventional cover letter above.

Sample:

Dear Mr. Petrelli,

The only problem with working at the cutting edge of communications is staying ahead of the blade. To stay ahead, you need aggressive people willing to take chances. People who are confident, flexible, dedicated. People who want to learn—who are not afraid to ask questions. I am one of those people—one of the people you should have on your staff. Let me prove it. Start by reading my resume. It shows I can take on any challenge and succeed. I want to succeed for you. But if you're looking for someone comfortable with covering the same old ground, count me out. If you want to work at the cutting edge, call me. I won't get cut. [*If mailing a standard letter, state your contact information here. If using e-mail, include a statement that directs attention to your e-mail signature.*]

Sincerely,

Recent college grad cover letter emphasizing experience

Background: A *Forbes* magazine article once predicted that a college degree would become superfluous in today's technology-oriented business world. Whether that's true remains to be seen. However, a college degree is usually a basic qualification, not a differentiator.

Potential employers have always been impressed with college grads who combine their degrees with real-world experience. If you have such experience, add it to your resume and highlight it prominently in your cover letter.

Essential elements: This letter contains just the right touch of salesmanship. It presents the main details of a recent graduate's real-world experience (in the case of the sample letter, internship experience) and then explains why that experience will be good for the recipient's company. The goal isn't to convince a potential employer that your experience has been good for you, but rather to explain how that experience will benefit his or her company.

Sample:

Dear Mr. Hendricks:

Your ad in *Chemical Engineering Progress* says Chemco is looking for chemical engineering seniors to work as junior process engineers. I'd like to interview for one of these positions.

Like most seniors in engineering, I've been educated in the chemical engineering fundamentals. But, unlike most, I also know what it takes to apply those skills in the real business world. During two summer internships at Kodansha Chemicals, I worked on project teams involved in major projects: a scale-up of a dry scrubbing system from pilot plant to semi-works one summer, and then commercialization of the dry scrubber design in the next. This experience enabled me to see chemical engineering from a business as well as a technical perspective. I'm guessing it takes time to orient college students to the work world. But I've already been there, which means I can be productive right from my first day on the job.

I will travel to your offices or meet with your college recruiter on campus, whichever you prefer. I am available to start immediately after my May 27 graduation. I look forward to presenting myself as a candidate for the process engineer position. [*If mailing a standard letter, state your contact information here. If using e-mail, include a statement that directs attention to your e-mail signature.*]

Sincerely,

Experienced manager cover letter

Background: If you have been in the job market awhile and have previous work experience, your cover letter will stress your background and goals.

Essential elements: This letter by an experienced manager stresses two strong points:

1. Specific results achieved in previous positions.
2. How the writer fits in with the potential employer's organization, corporate culture, goals, and requirements.

Sample:

> Dear Mr. Halloway:
>
> As vice president of an audiovisual production company, I expanded the Acme, Incorporated, account from $5,000 to $65,000 per year. I also brought in Procter and Gamble, New York Telephone, Prime Computers, and Dean Witter.
>
> If you are looking for someone with strong communications sales experience, you just found him. Let me mention some specific accomplishments:
>
> - Developed 17 new accounts that generated $425,000 in total income.
> - Increased my total billing 40 percent each year for three years.
> - Initiated an aggressive marketing campaign to three trade shows per year, generating at least one new client for each show.
>
> With eight years of experience in all aspects of sales and production, I believe I can generate sales and profits for your company. If the timing is right, I would be happy to meet with you at your convenience. [*If mailing a standard letter, state your contact information here. If using e-mail, include a statement that directs attention to your e-mail signature.*]
>
> Sincerely,

Response to a classified ad

Background: If you send your resume to a company in response to a classified ad, be sure to include a meticulously crafted cover letter. One tool available to the letter writer in this circumstance is the "Re:" line. This is typed below the recipient's name and address and above the salutation. "Re" is short for *Regarding*, and the "Re:" line allows quick identification of the subject matter. Because there may be hundreds of responses to one ad, try to personalize your letter. If the ad gives the name of the person to whom you should send your correspondence, be sure to use the name in the salutation of your letter. If the ad supplies only the person's title, use that, as in "Dear Creative Director." If you are not given any information about the person to whom the letter is directed, you can call and ask for a name (if a phone number is given), or you can resort to using "To whom it may concern."

Be careful about responding to blind ads (ads that do not give a company name). Your very own employer might have placed these!

Essential elements: When you respond to a classified ad, be sure to directly state three things:

1. Where you read about the job opening.
2. Your special qualifications that match the needs mentioned in the ad.
3. Your availability for an interview.

Sample:

Re: Your ad for "copywriter wanted" in *Adweek* magazine

Dear Personnel Director:

Your help-wanted ad caught my attention. You're looking for a copywriter with heavy software background—and that's my specialty. As my enclosed resume indicates, I've worked on a number of computer-related accountings, including Dell and IBM. An ad campaign I wrote for Parsons Software was the company's most profitable ever. I can send a portfolio or visit your offices for an interview—whichever you prefer. Please let me know what you want to happen next. [*If mailing a standard letter, state your contact information here. If using e-mail, include a statement that directs attention to your e-mail signature.*]

Sincerely,

Unsolicited request for an interview

Background: Many firms have occasional or even frequent job openings that they do not advertise. Therefore, there is often less competition for these positions. To be considered, write a letter requesting an interview. The key to this unsolicited request is to establish that you are familiar with the company and have a strong interest in working for its personnel based on who they are and what they do.

Gaining such inside corporate knowledge is easy when you use the Internet. Before writing a letter requesting an interview, log onto the company's Website and browse it carefully. The home page should give you a good overview of what the company does. Check the most recent press releases for news items you can work into your letter. The recipient will be impressed that you know what's going on with the company.

Essential elements: Be sure this letter clearly states four things:

1. A piece of company information that shows you are familiar with its operations.
2. A highlight of your business experience.
3. Your interest in an interview.
4. How your skills will benefit the company.

Dear Ms. Parks:

Congratulations on Acme's recent acquisition of Ace Company. This will certainly strengthen Acme's product offerings for digital prepress. That's the reason I'm writing you.

As an area sales rep for Grayco, I have been the number-one producer for my company for the past three years. This year, I exceeded last year's prepress equipment revenues by more than 65 percent. Now I am looking for my next challenge.

I'd love to interview for any area or regional sales rep positions you have open now or might have in the near future. As my resume indicates, I have broad experience in sales of many different products to the printing and photographic markets. With your newly acquired line of Ace systems, Acme will clearly provide the single-source solution prepress operations are demanding. I think my solution-selling experience is a good fit for your current direction and would welcome the chance to discuss how I can help increase Acme's market share. Just let me know when and where! [*If mailing a standard letter, state your contact information here. If using e-mail, include a statement that directs attention to your e-mail signature.*]

Sincerely,

Request for an informational interview

Background: Informational interviews, which are interviews with potential employers or sources of referral who have no immediate opportunity for you, serve two purposes: They give you an inside view of an industry and its hot career opportunities, and they allow you to present yourself to people who would not otherwise see you for a "job interview" because no immediate position exists. Do the informational interview well, and you may suddenly find yourself called in or recommended by that person for a "real" interview for the next position that opens up—often more quickly than you'd think.

Essential elements: In a letter that requests an informational interview, be sure to note:

1. How you know about the potential interviewer.
2. Who you are.
3. Why you would like to talk.
4. A promise to call to set up the interview.
5. A subtle piece of flattery.

Dear Ms. Tonnely:

Elizabeth Abrams suggested that I write to you. Would you consider meeting with me to discuss instructional design and your experiences in the profession? Liz suggested you might have some helpful advice for me. I am a computer programmer who became interested in computer-based training six months ago after taking several courses offered through my company.

I have always loved learning and am now thinking of making a career move to instructional design, emphasizing computer-based courseware in technical skills. I am also currently taking a night course at Generic University.

I'd greatly appreciate it if you could call or e-mail me. [*If mailing a standard letter, state your contact information here. If using e-mail, include a statement that directs attention to your e-mail signature.*] If I don't hear from you in the next week or so, I'll call to see if you have time to meet at your convenience.

Your experiences in training and development would be invaluable to me. Thank you for your time and consideration.

Sincerely,

Acceptance of an offer to interview

Background: If you are offered an interview, confirm it in writing. E-mail is especially appropriate for this written confirmation if your interview is just days away.

Essential elements: After you confirm your interview, send one or two more communications to the interviewer, such as a testimonial letter from a satisfied customer or an article about the interviewer's industry. This keeps your name in mind and shows that you're thinking of the potential employer.

Sample:

Dear Ms. Parks:

Thanks for your prompt response to my message. As we previously discussed, I will meet you in your corporate offices on Thursday, March 22, at 2 p.m. If you have to change the appointment, let me know. [*If mailing a standard letter, state your contact information here. If using e-mail, include a statement that directs attention to your e-mail signature.]* I look forward to meeting you and continuing our discussion in person!

Sincerely,

Thank-you note for an interview

Background: Sending thank-you notes has become a lost art, yet in today's busy world people appreciate them more than ever. This situation can work to your advantage. Because most people don't send thank-you notes any more, yours will stand out and make a lasting impression. Although a mailed thank-you letter may impress your potential employer more than a thank-you message conveniently launched from cyberspace, either way your thoughtfulness will be appreciated. Plus, an e-mail stands a better chance of reaching the employer before thank-yous sent by competing job candidates.

Essential elements: Thank-you notes are short and sweet. Remind the recipient of when you met and what position you interviewed for. Add an interesting note about something you talked about at the interview, and you're done.

Sample:

Dear Ms. Parks:

Thanks for taking the time to meet with me last Thursday to discuss sales opportunities with Acme Co. I'm excited about the possibility of your creating a new position for an additional rep in the Northeast. And I look forward to being considered for the assignment.

Enclosed is the information on the sales training program we discussed. Grayco's training department sends most of the sales force through this program. I found the techniques well worth learning. Overall, we saw a lift in our closing rates. Please contact me if you would like to discuss my candidacy for this position further. *[If mailing a standard letter, state your contact information here. If using e-mail, include a statement that directs attention to your e-mail signature.]*

Sincerely,

Request for a letter of recommendation ⊗

Background: When you want a former employer, supervisor, colleague, customer, vendor, or professor to write you a letter of recommendation for employment, make your request in writing. Be realistic about to whom you send such a letter. Someone who thought highly of you is more likely to comply with your request than a boss you disliked or a professor who flunked you.

Essential elements: Letters asking for a recommendation should include:

1. A request, not a demand, for a favor. Too many people make the mistake of thinking their request can't be refused and pose their request as an order ("I need a letter of recommendation. Send it to the address below.").

2. Statement of the skills and attributes you'd like mentioned in the letter. This isn't being pompous; it's being helpful. Give specifics, such as: "The company to which I am applying is looking for information about attributes such as my ability to work on a team, to meet deadlines, to work hard, and to meet goals." Factors such as perseverance, loyalty, and job commitment might also be suggested. You will get the letter you want if you supply the writer with information that does not merely repeat what is on your application. This will make it much easier for the recipient to dash off a good letter.

3. The complete name and address you would like the letter of recommendation written to (or whether you would like a specific address left off so that you can make photocopies of the letter for future use).

4. A stamped envelope addressed to the person to receive the recommendation, whether this be the prospective employer or yourself. This is why you would not e-mail your request for a recommendation letter. A recommendation letter is best supplied in hard copy, which gives it more official and credible feel for the prospective employer and also supplies you with a base hard copy to use for future photocopies.

Sample:

Dear Norman:

Would you do me a favor? I need a letter of recommendation from you to aid in my current job search. Could you write and send such a brief note?

The company to which I am applying is looking for someone who is able to work on tight deadlines and stay organized. The employee must have superior communication skills and the ability to work on team projects. Could you please mention in your letter how these attributes were evident in my work with you?

Please send your letter to:
Ms. Jane Smith
XYZ Company
54 Broad Street
New York, NY 10012

I appreciate the opportunities I had while working for you, and I thank you for considering me for this additional favor.

Sincerely,

P.S. An addressed and stamped envelope is enclosed for your convenience.

Negotiating a job offer

Background: If two firms offer you a job, and one position is more desirable than the other but offers considerably lower pay, you can respond to your first-choice offer by straightforwardly explaining the facts of the competing offer. This may spur the preferred prospective employer to increase its original offer, getting you the job you really wanted.

Essential elements: If you want to negotiate your terms of employment, consider the following, and use what's appropriate in your letter:

1. Your performance. Have you done something to warrant better terms?

2. The going rate in the marketplace. Check the employment classifieds, consult an online salary-tracking resource, and talk with colleagues in other firms to find the salary range for someone with your education and background experience.

3. Other benefits you might consider, such as a company car or more vacation, in place of increased salary.

Sample:

Dear Mr. Smith:

Thanks for your letter and the job offer. I enjoyed our time together and know that I would like to work for you. However, Koch Engineering in New York City has offered me $43,000 a year. Given that my fellow chemical engineering classmates average $40,000 a year, I just can't accept your offer of $36,000.

If it's possible to increase your offer or add additional benefits, let me know. I'd be interested in pursuing the position with you. If not, I still learned a lot from the time we spent together.

Sincerely,

Acceptance of a job offer

Background: Years ago, employment contracts were common. Today, they are becoming much less so. Therefore, the confirmation letter you send accepting a job offer is a good place to spell out the basic terms and conditions of employment. This gives everyone a clear sense of what has been agreed upon and also documents the offer in writing.

This is an important letter that can save you many headaches down the line. It often happens that when you arrive at your new job, no one quite remembers offering you your own office or promising a two-week vacation. Protect yourself by asking for a signature of agreement on your confirmation letter (if you choose to mail it) or a confirming reply (if you choose to e-mail it). This will show you're an astute businessperson who leaves nothing to chance.

Essential elements: Letters accepting job offer must include:

1. All terms of employment; include starting date, salary, benefits, hours, perks, and so forth.
2. A request for a signature of agreement and an enclosed self-addressed, stamped envelope, or a request for a confirming reply by e-mail.
3. A positive note of enthusiasm about the new job.

Sample:

Dear Mr. Mutsakis:

Thanks for your call today.

I accept your offer of a position as advertising manager at a salary of $47,000 a year. Based on our phone conversation, I understand that in addition to Oak Engineering's standard benefits plan, I will receive two weeks of vacation the first year. As discussed, I will also be given a private office (not a cubicle) with a PC, fax, and printer. I will share an administrative assistant with Joe Bulges, your trade show manager. My starting date will be Monday, June 12. Oak will reimburse me for mover's fees for relocating from Baltimore to Secaucus.

If I have understood the terms of my employment correctly, please sign in the space provided below and return this letter to me in the enclosed self-addressed, stamped envelope. [*If using e-mail, request a reply expressing agreement to the terms stated.*]

I'm thrilled about starting with Oak and look forward to a long and productive relationship. On a personal note, I'm also delighted that you're going to be my boss!

Sincerely,

Agreed: Date:

Rejection of a job offer

Background: On a lucky day, you might be able to reject a job offer. This rejection letter should be very professional with no personal information added. For example, if you have a superior offer that you've already accepted, don't boast about it. You might meet that person again someday or find yourself in the situation of wanting to accept the position you turned down.

Essential elements: Note that rejecting a job offer requires some sensitive communication skills:

1. State immediately that you cannot take position.
2. Explain why the company you chose was a better match for your needs. (Or you can skip this part completely if you'd rather not compare companies or explain your reasons.) End the letter on a positive note that leaves the door open for the future.

Sample:

Dear Terry:

Thanks for your call. However, after much thought, I have decided to take a position with General Motors in Flint and must turn down your generous offer. I'm sure I would have enjoyed working with you and the Process Design Group. But the opportunity with General Motors is a management position—one of my goals as I had mentioned in our interview. This position is more in line with my career objectives than the staff position you had available.

I'm sure we will meet again, perhaps at the upcoming Process Design Society Conference. Perhaps we can meet at your booth for a cup of coffee—on me, of course.

Sincerely,

Resignation on good terms ⊘

Background: Company loyalty isn't as crucial as it once was. Employees routinely hop from job to job looking to advance in position and salary. When you find it necessary to move on, notify your employer in writing immediately. It is best to avoid e-mail for this kind of letter because you need to maintain a signed printed copy for yourself and be certain that you have the terms of your resignation properly documented, both for yourself and your employer's files.

Essential elements: To resign from a company on good terms, it's best to include:

1. Statement of your resignation.
2. Exact date of your leave.
3. An offer to stick around for a specific period while the company looks for a replacement. Never make this offer open-ended by saying something such as "I'll stay until you find a replacement." Give an exact period of time.
4. Indication that you're willing to be on call for a while after you leave.
5. A positive statement about your experience with the company.
6. A reason for leaving, if you choose. Most bosses understand when you explain that you received an offer you simply couldn't refuse.

Sample:

Dear Mr. Jones:

This letter is to notify you that I'm resigning from my position at Global Affiliates to take a new position at Associated Systems.

My last day will be October 11. By giving you six weeks' notice I'm hoping to provide you with some extra time to find a replacement. After October 11, I'll still be available if you need help locating resources or getting answers to any questions the new employee may have about procedures or records. You will be able to reach me at my new number, 123-456-7890, or through e-mail at yourname@e-maildomain.com.

For the record, I enjoyed my job and our association here at Global. But the position at Associated has significantly higher compensation, and in our annual reviews, you indicated the salary for someone in my classification could not come near this level. So, the decision is mainly a financial one. However, I'll miss you and the whole group in our department.

Sincerely,

Resignation on bad terms ⊘

Background: Make this letter simple and straightforward. No embellishments, no explanation. The boss already knows why you are resigning. It's a sore spot, so why bring it out into the open? No one benefits, and it just makes one or both of you look bad. It is especially important to maintain a signed printed copy of this kind of resignation letter for yourself, so don't use e-mail. If relations between you and your employer are particularly bad, the worst thing you could do is to send an e-mail that the employer might later claim was never received— or, worse, falsify your resignation terms by typing over your message.

Essential elements: This is as simple as business letters get. State your resignation and the date you are leaving.

Sample:

Dear Mr. Smith:

This letter is to notify you that I'm resigning from my position at Global Affiliates to take a new position at Associated Systems.

My last day will be October 11. By giving you six weeks' notice I'm hoping to provide you with some extra time to find a replacement.

Sincerely,

Correspondence to hire employees

Response to a job-seeker when no positions are open

Background: This letter answers an unsolicited employment inquiry when the candidate appears qualified but there are no openings available.

Essential elements: This kind of letter answering a job-seeker should always include:

1. A cordial opening that thanks the applicant for thinking of your company.
2. A clear statement, without any ambiguity, that there are no positions open.
3. A promise to keep the application on file and an invitation to follow up at a later date.

Samples:

Letter

> Dear Ms. Brigetto:
>
> Your letter of inquiry about employment opportunities in our company was forwarded to me from our human resources department because of your interest in obtaining a position in quality assurance. I am pleased you thought of Remco Widgets.
>
> At this time, all our supervisory slots in manufacturing and production are filled, and the job responsibilities in those positions include quality assurance. I do not think there will be an opening for a manager dedicated to quality assurance this year.
>
> I will ask our human resources department to keep your letter on file, because you certainly seem qualified in the quality assurance field. If you don't hear from them by April, call Ronny Bruce, our personnel manager, at 123-456-7890 to see if anything has opened up for you.
>
> Sincerely,

E-mail

> **From:** Brian Kelly <president@fictionalfirm.com>
> **Date:** Monday, January 15, 20XX
> **To:** Maren Brigetto <yourname@e-maildomain.com>
> **Subject:** Quality assurance position
>
> Maren Brigetto
> 0000 Make-Believe Street
> Noplace Real, NJ 10000
>
> Dear Ms. Brigetto:
>
> Your e-mail inquiring about employment opportunities in our company was forwarded to me from our human resources department because of your interest in obtaining a position in quality assurance. I am pleased you thought of Remco Widgets.

At this time, all our supervisory slots in manufacturing and production are filled, and the job responsibilities in those positions include quality assurance. I do not think there will be an opening for a manager dedicated to quality assurance this year.

I will ask the human resources department to keep your e-mail on file, because you certainly seem qualified in the quality assurance field. If you don't hear from them by April, e-mail Ronny Bruce, our personnel manager, at rbruce@e-maildomain.com to see if anything has opened up for you.

Sincerely,

[*Automatic e-mail signature should appear here; see the sample signatures in Chapter 2.*]

E-Mail Empowerment Tip

Apply this sample e-mail structure, while adapting the content, to the "Correspondence to hire employees" letters described in this chapter (page 55), except where e-mail is specifically not recommended.

Reference check 🚫

Background: This letter is used to request information from an applicant's former employer.

Essential elements: A letter asking for an employment reference check should include:

1. The applicant's name and the position for which he or she is applying.
2. An understanding that this person was previously employed by the recipient of the letter.
3. A request for information that zeros in on specific work skills and characteristics you are most interested in knowing about.
4. A deadline for reply.
5. An offer of confidentiality that will make the recipient more comfortable about telling the truth. With this need to ensure confidentiality, out of consideration for the recipient it is best not to e-mail this letter because the person may not be comfortable with sending a reply by e-mail.
6. A thank-you.

Sample:

> Dear Mr. Carlson:
>
> We recently received an application from George Olmstede for the position of master electrician with our firm. We understand you previously employed him. We would appreciate any information you could give us concerning Mr. Olmstead's work habits, expertise as a master electrician, and attitude. We would also appreciate your sharing with us the reason he no longer works for your firm.
>
> We look forward to hearing from you. If you could reply by early March, it would be very helpful. [*State your contact information here.*] Please advise us if the information you provide is confidential. Thank you for your time in considering this request.
>
> Sincerely,

Rejection of an employee's application for an in-house position

Background: Inside people don't always have the inside track on new positions, especially if these opportunities are in areas outside of their core skill set. Because the applicant is also an employee, your letter must motivate and encourage even as it rejects. Out of consideration for the employee's privacy, it is best to use a traditional letter that can be hand-delivered to the employee, rather than send an e-mail.

Essential elements: A letter rejecting a current employee applying to an open in-house position needs to be carefully crafted. It should include:

1. An opening that acknowledges the employee's application and presents a form of active listening that shows you've read his or her application letter carefully—you understand why the employee is applying for the open position.

2. A clear statement of the skills or training required for this job that the employee does not possess.

3. An acknowledgment that you have a number of qualified applicants and will choose from that pool.

4. A paragraph that praises the work of this employee and opens the door to future advancement in a more appropriate direction.

Sample:

Dear Dan:

Thanks for your interest in becoming part of SunStar's marketing communications department as a communications coordinator. Yes, I agree that as a sales rep, you know what motivates customers to buy our products. I also appreciate your desire to reduce your travel and make the change from personal selling to mass communications.

Unfortunately, your field sales background has not given you many of the skills this position requires, including copywriting, editing, desktop publishing, database marketing, and mailing list selection and analysis. You also don't have the necessary proficiency with Website development software.

We've received applications from several candidates who, in addition to having these requisite skills, have a background in lines of equipment and markets similar to ours. We will probably fill the current opening from these applicants.

Although you are not being selected for this position, I am aware that you wish to change your department and upgrade your level within the company. I encourage you to do so. Your sales record is good and your appraisal reports are positive. I am sure that we can find a position that best matches your experiences, background, and career goals.

Again, I appreciate your interest and hard work at SunStar, and good luck in all your future promotions.

Sincerely,

Invitation to a job interview

Background: If you are in human resources or a hiring manager, you will need to communicate with candidates for open positions at your firm, including inviting them to job interviews.

Essential elements: A letter that offers an invitation to a job interview should include:

1. A cordial thank-you for the interest shown in working for your company.
2. An invitation to an interview. You can either state a time or ask the applicant to e-mail or call you to set up an appointment at a mutually convenient time.
3. A closing that says, "I look forward to meeting with you."

Sample:

Dear Mr. Plowman:

Thank you for taking the time to explore employment opportunities with our company. I am very impressed with your application, background, and experience. I would like to schedule an interview to talk further about your career interests and our employment needs. Can you meet with me and our department supervisor on Monday the 21st at 9 a.m. for about one hour?

Please contact my office to confirm this appointment. [*If mailing a standard letter, state your contact information here. If using e-mail, include a statement that directs attention to your e-mail signature.*] I look forward to meeting with you.

Sincerely,

Rejection following a job interview

Background: A less pleasant communications task is to notify an applicant after the interview that he or she did not get the job.

Essential elements: A letter of rejection following a job interview should include:

1. A positive opening that compliments the applicant.
2. A straightforward rejection that does not get into detailed reasons. (If you explain exactly why a candidate is not right for a position, you open the door to arguments and pleading.)
3. A sincere thank-you and a wish for luck in the job search.

Sample:

Dear Mr. Mayers:

It was a pleasure to meet with you last week in our offices at Integrated Network Solutions, Inc. Your programming background and corporate experience give you skills that will be useful in many IS positions.

We have reviewed your credentials but unfortunately do not find a suitable match between your background and experience and the opening in our company.

Thank you for your interest in our company. Good luck in your job search.

Sincerely,

Job offer

Background: The letter of a job offer should outline the essential information the employee needs to make a decision. The tone of the letter should be upbeat and enthusiastic to help the employee decide in favor of accepting the offer. Any terms stated in the letter will become part of your employment agreement with the applicant if he or she takes the job. Although you could send this letter as an attachment to an e-mail, it would be better, for documentation purposes, to send it through snail mail or at least to follow up on the e-mail by sending the original letter through snail mail.

Essential elements: A letter making a job offer should include:

1. A statement of the job offer.
2. Details of employment.
3. Information about starting date, time, and place.
4. A request for a confirmation of acceptance.

Sample:

Dear Ms. Myers:

With great pleasure, I am able to offer you a position at Artech Semiconductor as a quality engineer.

The position pays $38,000 annually, in equal increments, every other Friday. Additionally, you will receive two weeks paid vacation every 12 months, a bonus equaling two weeks' salary the payday before Christmas, health benefits, and $25,000 in life insurance. The position is a one-year agreement, after which it may be renegotiated. Either party can terminate with a two-week notice.

We are very pleased to offer you this position. Your starting date will be April 3rd at 9 a.m. You will report to Ms. Johnson, the senior supervisor. Please signify your acceptance of this offer by calling my office or e-mailing me before Friday the 15th.

On a personal note, I think you'll enjoy working at Artech and will fit in well with our department. If you have any questions, please call me anytime.

Sincerely,

New employee introduction

Background: This is an easy note to write, and an e-mail sent to a company or departmental distribution list is the recommended format (see sample). An easy way to get this letter written is to ask the new hire to draft a summary of his or her background. Then you simply add the essential elements, edit, and distribute. If you want a more in-depth profile of the new hire, perhaps the editor of your employee newsletter can work one into a forthcoming issue. Or perhaps the public relations department can prepare a release for industry trade publications.

Essential elements: This kind of internal office communication should include:

1. The new employee's name and position.
2. The new employee's responsibilities and working relationship with other employees.
3. The new employee's background.
4. A request for company employees to make the new person feel at home.

Sample:

E-mail

From: Fred Guterola <president@fictionalfirm.com>
Date: Monday, April 12, 20XX
To: New York Office Staff <undisclosedrecipients@e-maildomain.com>
Subject: New employee

Starting next Monday, Randy Starks will be joining our New York office as advertising manager.

Randy will be responsible for all marketing communications activities, except for trade shows (these will still be managed by Ben Buffett). Randy is the person to see when you need a new ad or brochure, and he will report directly to me. Please go through Randy for any advertising or collateral needs.

Randy comes to the New York area from our Wichita, Kansas, location, where he held the position of technical writer for five years. Since he's used to the wide-open plains of Kansas, anything we can do to make him feel more at home here in the Big Apple will be appreciated (I suggest a Friday night trip to the Village for Frank's Pizza!).

[Automatic e-mail signature should appear here; see the sample signatures in Chapter 2.]

> ## E-Mail Empowerment Tip
>
> It would be ideal to have an e-mail distribution list set up within your e-mail address book for the desired recipients of this e-mail, whether they are members of your department or a broader group. You would then not need to type in all of your recipients' e-mail addresses or names individually.

Other employment correspondence

There are a few other instances when you may need to write letters regarding employment. These include writing a letter to ask someone to be your mentor, to refuse a request for a letter of recommendation, and to recommend a job applicant.

Request for a mentorship

Background: Being mentored by a person whose background and experience match your professional goals can help you to secure the career to which you aspire. The sample provided is an actual letter that author Robert Bly sent decades ago to a direct marketing writer, asking him to be his mentor.

Essential elements: When you write a letter asking someone to be your mentor, be sure to include:

1. An introductory piece of information that shows the person you've been following his or her work and career with admiration.
2. An offer to do something useful for the person in exchange for the opportunity to be in a mentor relationship.
3. A request for a response.

Sample:

> December 2, 1981
> Re: Your recent article in *Direct Marketing* magazine
>
> Dear Mr. _____,
>
> I enjoyed your recent article in *Direct Marketing*, "How to Write Copy That Sells." I'm an advertising manager for an engineering firm but a complete novice in direct mail. Frankly, I find your niche of letter writing fascinating, which is why I am writing this letter.
>
> Perhaps from time to time when you take on clients selling technology and business products you find that doing the research to write these

letters is time-consuming. This is where I can help. Consider allowing me to explain the technology in lay language to these customers, so you can spend less time translating and more time writing your usual sizzling sales letter. I would do this free of charge, hoping, in turn, to learn direct mail copywriting from a master (I am thinking about becoming a freelancer specializing in direct marketing of high-tech and industrial products). How does this sound to you?

Sincerely,

Bob Bly

Refusal of a request for a recommendation letter

Background: When someone asks you for a letter of recommendation, are you obliged to write it, even if you had problems with the person in the past? This is a hard personal decision you have to make, but it would be dishonest to make a positive recommendation if it may hurt a potential employer. This course is better than agreeing to write the letter and then saying negative things.

Tell the person who requested the recommendation why you can't oblige, without name-calling or baiting. State the facts as you see them in a gentle but firm tone. Doing so, you have fulfilled your obligation to the request in an honorable fashion.

Essential elements: When you write a letter to refuse a request for a letter of recommendation, you should include:

1. A cordial greeting.
2. Your refusal to write the recommendation.
3. A reason for your refusal. This can be a detailed account (while remaining professional and factual), or it can be a simple statement that says you do not share the same business philosophies.
4. A suggestion for finding a positive recommendation.

Sample:

Dear Will:

Thanks for your letter. It was good to hear from you again. I wish I could be of some help, but unfortunately, after giving it careful consideration, I feel I can't in good conscience write the letter of recommendation that you requested. You are competent on the technical side of the business. But you and I had (and have) a completely different perspective on being a team player. I appreciate your desire to have time for creative thought and contemplation, but my feeling is, on a project team, you can't do so at the expense of meeting deadlines. Other team members can't proceed to meet their milestones if you haven't met yours.

While you were at this company, you worked for a number of other people with whom you may have had a better relationship. I'm sure that one of them would be glad to write you a positive letter of recommendation.

Sincerely,

Recommendation letter 🚫

Background: The key to this letter is unabashed enthusiasm. The reader knows you're a fan of the applicant; you wouldn't be writing this letter if you weren't. Don't pretend neutrality and then gush praise. Instead gush praise, and admit you're an unabashed promoter of the applicant. Let your enthusiasm shine through.

Also, go with the standard business letter format for this type of correspondence. It will help the subject of the recommendation to have a hard-copy backup for his or her files, and a signed, formal letter will appear more professional and credible to the recipient than an e-mail might.

Essential elements: To write a convincing letter of recommendation, include:
1. A statement of wholehearted recommendation.
2. Exemplary adjectives.
3. Detailed examples of positive work habits.
4. A wish to retain the person in your own employ.

Sample:

Dear Mr. Keyes:

Because you're considering hiring Bonnie Denny as a customer service representative, let me do something I rarely do—recommend this former employee wholeheartedly.

I have seen customer service reps come and go, and their quality varies. But Bonnie is the cream of the crop. Her skills are superb. In addition to being friendly, helpful, and articulate, she knew both our products and our buyers inside and out. By being an advocate for the customer, she is a champion of the company and firmly cements its relationship with the buyer.

After Bonnie moved east with her husband, who was relocated, a number of customers called me directly and complained that she was no longer available to talk to. If I had an office in your area, I would do anything I could to retain her as an employee and hire her away from you. But I don't, so she's yours to hire.

Sincerely,

4

Corresponding With Colleagues

You likely have many colleagues—from fellow members of trade associations to other businesspeople who work out at the same health club you do. Your relationship with them may be professional, personal, or both. But unlike coworkers, they don't work for the same company you do. Therefore, your communication with them must not assume knowledge of the products, services, or organization with which you are involved. Furthermore, unless you've crossed the line from colleague to best friend, your correspondences with these colleagues should always remain professional. This chapter shows you how to craft such messages.

E-mail works well for much of the correspondence described in this chapter. The samples provided in this chapter have been designed so that you can simply adapt the actual message portion of the samples to the format and structure of e-mail. (However, whenever the sample given would need more detailed tweaking to work with e-mail, we've provided a specific e-mail sample.) As always, though, be on the lookout for the ⊘icon, indicating correspondence for which e-mail is not suitable.

Business greetings

Corresponding with professional colleagues is a terrific way to network. Don't miss out on this opportunity when you have the chance. This section will help you write correspondence that will introduce you to a colleague, express your desire to keep in touch with a new acquaintance, and request a meeting or get-together.

Introduction to a colleague

Background: In today's teamwork-oriented, outsourced business world, you will be supervising and/or working with or for people you don't even know.

A simple letter of introduction is a good way to gain cooperation and start the relationship off on the right foot.

Essential elements: Saying hello is easy. Just follow these four steps:

1. Introduce yourself and mention something positive about your relationship with this colleague.
2. Detail some positive aspect of your work or a project you share with the colleague.
3. Invite the recipient to contact you.
4. End on an upbeat note.

Sample:

Hello, Mr. Bly:

I am the special sales coordinator at Financial Publishing Company and will be marketing *The Six-Figure Consultant*. I am looking forward to some great results—especially with the associations and companies listed in Appendix D of the book.

I called the American Seminar Leaders Association and spoke with June Davidson—she's very excited about the book and wanted me to say hello for her. She will probably be contacting you soon to talk about the book and about possibly writing an article for their newsletter and doing a speaking engagement. I have sent her a copy of the book and will be following up with her soon to discuss some potential sales. It certainly sounds like a great opportunity for us!

Please feel free to contact me if you have questions or suggestions and leads for possible book sales. [*If mailing a standard letter, state your contact information here. If using e-mail, include a statement that directs attention to your e-mail signature.*] This book has wide-range appeal for many audiences, and I'm expecting great results!

Robert Hammersmith,
Special Sales Coordinator

Follow-up after an initial meeting

Background: When you meet someone with whom you have the potential to enjoy a mutually beneficial business relationship, be sure to send a follow-up note. Not only does this give the person a reminder of your name and phone number, but you can use it to address any unresolved issues or queries left from your meeting. Even better, it always gives you an "excuse" to send product literature, catalogs, or other extraneous material you may want your new colleague to have.

Essential elements: When you initiate contact, do it very soon after your initial meeting (while your name still rings a bell) and be sure to include:

1. "It was a pleasure to meet you."
2. A reminder of a conversation you had at your meeting.
3. A helpful tip or lead.
4. A reason to make contact again in the future.

Samples:

Fax

> **To:** John Aristotle
> **Fax:** 123-456-7890
> **From:** Bob Bly
> **Re:** Ad agencies, business-to-business
>
> Dear John:
>
> It was a pleasure meeting you this weekend. I'm going to be traveling this week, so it will take me a little time to find the Business Marketing Association membership directory I promised to send you.
>
> In the meantime, a business-to-business ad agency I think highly of is Zinhalf & Cedar here in New Jersey. They do a lot of work for Climate Builders. The contact is Joe Alan, 123-456-7890. If you call, tell him that I sent you!
>
> All the best,
> Bob Bly

E-mail

> **From:** Regina Anne Kelly <reginaannekelly@reginakelly.net>
> **Date:** Tuesday, March 19, 20XX
> **To:** Gloria Shaheen <writer@fictionalfirm.com>
> **Subject:** Medical writing resources
> **Attachments:** AMAworkshopschedule.doc
>
> Hi, Gloria:
>
> I really enjoyed meeting you at the American Medical Association (AMA) style course over the weekend. I've attached the AMA writing workshop schedule you

were interested in. I'm planning to attend the afternoon session on writing for scientific journals on April 14 in Manhattan. If the same session interests you, why don't we meet for dinner? It will give us a chance to continue our discussion about those new footnote styling guidelines that baffle us!

In the meantime, another great resource for medical writers is the American Medical Writers Association (AMWA). Its Website is *www.amwa.org*. Its upcoming annual conference will be held in October. A former staff member, Lily, is a good friend of mine and stays up-to-date on AMWA's educational offerings. She can be reached at 123-456-7890 or lily@e-maildomain.com. If you contact her, tell her I referred you.

All the best,
Regina Anne Kelly
[*Automatic e-mail signature should appear here; see the sample signatures in Chapter 2.*]

E-Mail Empowerment Tip

For this type of e-mail, limit your number of attachments to one. You don't want to overwhelm your new colleague with reading materials and clog his or her inbox, and there will be plenty of time to share information as your relationship develops.

Arrangement to meet

Background: A nice perk of business travel is that it puts you in proximity to friends, associates, colleagues, potential customers, and other contacts, all at your company's expense. When you know you will be in an area and will have some extra time, e-mail or fax a note to arrange a meeting.

Essential elements: To arrange a meeting with a colleague, write a letter that includes:

1. When you will be in the area.
2. What you would like to talk about at the meeting.
3. A request for a response.

Sample:

Dear Patty:

I will be in Houston on June 22 giving a customer service seminar at the Hilton. You and I talked about getting together if I was ever in town so that I could get a better feel for what Knight Co. is doing and you could get a better feel for whether there's a good fit between us. If you're available on the 22nd, can we have breakfast that day? The seminar is an ideal time because I will be in your neighborhood with a little extra time on my hands (and the seminar company is paying for travel costs, although I'll spring for the coffee and waffles).

Please let me know whether this sounds good to you so that I can arrange my travel schedule accordingly. [*If mailing a standard letter, state your contact information here. If using e-mail, include a statement that directs attention to your e-mail signature.*]

Sincerely,

Requests

There are many occasions in the business world when you'll need to ask for something. You might need to ask for a favor, information, or the opportunity to speak at an upcoming event. You might need to write for permission to reproduce materials in a project or ask to serve on a committee. These are only a few of the instances in which you'll need to ask for something, but the following letters will give you a good idea how to make any request.

Request for a favor

Background: People are often willing to grant favors—sometimes generous ones—to friends, colleagues, and sometimes even total strangers. But don't assume they will. Ask. In your request letter, be cordial, direct, and clear about what you want. If there is a reward or benefit to the reader for complying with your request, state it if you feel he or she needs extra convincing.

Essential elements: A letter that is intended to request a favor should say so right up front. There's no point in trying to mask the fact. Be sure your letter includes:

1. A request for a favor.
2. Details about the project you're working on or the circumstances of your situation.
3. An explanation of why the recipient of the letter is the best person to grant this favor.
4. The exact specifications of the request (don't assume the recipient knows what you need).
5. An offer of something in return.

Sample:

Dear Charles:

I have a favor to ask.

We are currently compiling a corporate history. It will be titled *Balson Nuclear: Half a Century of Radiant Progress* and will be privately published as a limited edition hardcover book by the corporation early next year. Its main use will be as a premium and promotion.

You are a respected professor in nuclear engineering, and it was in your senior class that I learned much of what I needed to know to get hired by Balson. Would you be willing to contribute a brief (200- to 300-word) preface about the importance of nuclear energy as a current and future energy source?

The company can pay you an honorarium of $500. In addition, your preface will be bylined, so you can add the book to your list of publications. You will also get five free copies of the book. Any interest? Please let me know. We would need the preface by June 20.

Sincerely,

Request for information

Background: When you are requesting important information, it's best to do it in writing (e-mail, fax, or letter) rather than on the phone. The written request helps the reader understand exactly what you need, and it gives him or her a checklist with which to work. This kind of written correspondence is more likely to get you what you need when you need it.

Essential elements: When you need accurate information, be specific so that the reader knows exactly what you need:

1. Provide a numbered list of all the information you need.
2. Be very specific by asking questions that require detailed answers.
3. If you ask a question that requires a yes or no answer, back that up with an "If so, why (or what)?"

Sample:

Dear Pam:

I have the following questions for you, which, I hope, you will kindly answer as soon as you can:

1. What is different about this coming market crash than previous crashes? How will it differ (severity, speed, duration, and so forth)? Why? The text of our mailing needs to convey that this crash is unlike any the reader has experienced.

2. The notion that the stock market will crash is not contrarian, of course. Is there anything about your predictions for the market that is contrarian? If so, what?

3. How do we explain the recent volatility in the market? Specifically, if a person gets our mailing and sees that the Dow Jones Average went up 78 points that day, what can we say to convince him or her that it will still go down over the long run, and soon?

That's it. I'm looking forward to receiving your answers as soon as possible.

Sincerely,

Request for a speaking engagement

Background: Are you good at what you do? If so, you can earn some extra money and market your services or product at the same time by giving speeches at seminars, workshops, conferences, and so forth. The first step is to get a go-ahead to be a guest speaker. The following letter will show you how to market yourself to build a schedule of speaking engagements.

Essential elements: When you write a letter that you hope will convince someone that you have something valuable to say, be sure to include:

1. A "hook," an opening that grabs the reader's attention and makes him or her want to know more. This can be an interesting piece of research, a little-known fact, or some information that is of immediate benefit to the reader.

2. Your request, directly stating your topic.

3. The credentials that make you an expert on this topic.

4. A question asking if the reader is interested.

5. A request for a response.

Sample:

Dear Ms. Smiley:

Did you know that, according to a recent survey in *Engineering Today*, the ability to write clearly and concisely can mean $100,000 extra in earnings over the lifetime of an engineer's career?

For this reason, I think your members might enjoy a presentation I have given to several business organizations around town: "10 Ways to Improve Your Technical Writing." This presentation highlights the 10 most common writing mistakes that engineers make and gives proven strategies for self-improvement.

As the director of Plain Language, Inc., a company that specializes in technical documentation, I have worked with hundreds of engineers to help them improve their writing skills. Does this sound like the type of presentation that might fit well into your winter program schedule? I'd be delighted to speak before your group. Please phone or write so we can set a date.

Best regards,

Request to reproduce materials 🚫

Background: As a general guideline, it is permissible to copy and use up to 300 words, or 1 to 2 percent, of a work without gaining written permission from the copyright holder. Any material beyond this requires written permission. Permission is also required for reprinting any table, figure, poem, or song lyric (even as short as one line).

As authors, we are frequently asked for permission to reproduce articles we have written. With so many requests, we don't have time to write letters granting this permission. That's why we much prefer that the person making the request mail a simple release form we can sign and send back. We suggest you use such a release when seeking usage permission from a colleague, publisher, or other source. Using e-mail for this type of correspondence might be possible if you include the release as an attachment and instruct your recipient that the attachment needs to be printed, signed, and returned to you as a printed copy for your records. But because you need to make sending the release back to you as convenient as possible for the recipient, it's best to avoid e-mail, because with e-mail you are not able to provide a self-addressed, stamped envelope for your recipient. You will also have to attach scans of any supporting documents—for example, the material you are requesting permission to reproduce—and this would be inconvenient if you do not have a scanner.

Two samples are given below. The first is a more informal variety, primarily for your own records. The second sample is much more detailed and formal; this is often used when requesting permission from publishing houses.

Essential elements: Letters requesting permission should offer the recipient as much information as possible. Be sure to include:

1. A header with your name and contact information so that the recipient knows who you are.

2. The exact material you want to copy and where you saw it. You can make things easier by attaching a copy of the material.

3. Exactly what you intend to do with the material requested. State where it will be reprinted (whether it be in a newsletter, book, article, handout flyer, or otherwise), when it will be distributed, and who it will be distributed to.

4. The credit line you will include on your reprint.

5. A place for a signature of agreement and the date.

6. An easy method of return, such as a fax number or a self-addressed, stamped envelope.

Samples:

Letter #1

Dear Mr. Smith:

I read your article called "Listening Skills" at the *www._____.com* Website and was quite impressed. I will be conducting a workshop for our employees on communications skills and will have a module on listening. May I reprint your article as a handout for our training session?

We would like to distribute approximately 20 copies. If this is okay with you, please sign below and fax this letter back to me at 123-456-7890. If there are any charges, please let me know. Also, we will credit the article as bylined on the Website, unless you have an alternate credit line that you prefer we use.

Sincerely,

Approved by (signature)   Date

Letter #2

Date _____

To: _____

I am preparing a manuscript to be published by _____

Author/tentative title _____

Estimated publication date _____

Approximate number of pages _____

    I request your permission to include the following material in this and all subsequent editions of my document, including versions made by nonprofit organizations for use by blind or physically handicapped persons and all foreign-language translations and other derivative works published or prepared by the publisher or its licensees for distribution throughout the world.

Author(s) and/or editor(s) _____

Title of book or periodical _____

Title of selection _____

Copyright date _____

from page _____, line_____, beginning with the words _____

from page _____, line _____, ending with the words _____

Figure # _____, on page _____ Table # _____, on page _____

[*If necessary, attach continuation sheets.*]

    Please indicate agreement by signing and returning the enclosed copy of this letter. In signing, you warrant that you are the sole owner of the rights granted and that your material does not infringe upon the copyright or other rights of anyone. If you do not control these rights, I would appreciate your letting me know to whom I should apply.

    Thank you.

_____

Agreed to and accepted:

By _____

Signature _____ Title _____ Date _____

Credit and/or copyright notice:

_____

_____

Request that someone serve on a committee

Background: When you want someone to serve on a committee, the key is to make the invitation sound more like an opportunity than a favor. Focus on the benefits to the person, not only to the organization. Here is a letter you can use to invite a member to take a more proactive role in a professional or trade association.

Essential elements: A letter asking someone to serve on a committee should include:

1. An upbeat tone of congratulations (don't ever imply a "sorry to do this to you" attitude).
2. A flattering reason why this person is the perfect candidate.
3. A contact person or co-member.
4. A benefit the person will personally gain from making this commitment.

Sample:

Dear Patti:

It is with pleasure that I invite you to co-chair this year's Outside Speaker Committee.

Based on the great talk you gave last year, I feel speaker selection and recruitment are right up your alley. I know many of your colleagues do speaking, so here's a chance for you to showcase the best among them. As a 19-year PLT member, you know the audience's interests and needs as well as anyone.

Since we need to get started in putting together next year's programs, please let me know whether you're available to serve as co-chair. Karen Gross from Elway Technology will be your co-chair. Getting to know her well wouldn't hurt, since Elway could certainly use the types of services you offer.

Sincerely,

Thank-you correspondence

There are many occasions in everyday business where thank-you notes are appropriate—and smart. In the rush to get ahead, we often forget to look back at what someone has done for us and take the time to let that person know it was appreciated. This is, of course, good manners, but in the push-and-shove of business, it's also the perfect way to make yourself stand out as someone who's not just a user.

E-Mail Empowerment Tip

Some guidance about thank-you e-mail messages: You can certainly use them, but be aware that thank-yous printed on stationery, or expressed in a card, and cordially closed with your signature have more of a personal touch and may have greater impact and meaning to the person you want to thank. E-mail, on the other hand, is all about ease and convenience. So, if you want the object of your thank-you to really get a sense of your appreciation, take the time to type, print, and mail a letter—or perhaps handwrite your sentiments in a card.

Thank-you note for a referral

Background: People appreciate recognition when they've given your name as a referral. Conversely, if you don't acknowledge them, they'll think you're an ingrate and give the referral to someone else next time. In fact, a second follow-up thank-you a few weeks later is a nice touch if the referral works out well for you. You might even consider enclosing a small but tasteful gift with your thank-you note—perhaps a desk calendar or a pocket diary.

Fortunately, thank you can be said elegantly yet simply. The first sentence of the sample is particularly eloquent.

Essential elements: This simple letter can reap more benefits than weeks of marketing and advertising. If you use e-mail for this note, save a copy of the message in your drafts folder to use as a basis for future thank-you correspondence. If you decide to print your note and mail it, keep a copy on file on your computer. Be sure to include:

1. A statement that directly says thank you.
2. The name of the person who called as a result of the referral.
3. An assurance that you will do a good job for this person (implying you will not make your correspondent regret thinking of you).

Sample:

Dear Bob:

In this busy world of ours, it's gratifying when people take time to help others. It's for this reason that I'm writing to thank you.

At your suggestion, Paul Kamac recently called to contract my services. I really appreciate this referral. It looks like Paul and I will be doing a lot of business in the future. I'm sure he will be pleased with my work and will be happy you offered my name.

Thanks again for thinking of me.

Warm regards,

Thank-you note for a favor

Background: Thank people for favors in writing. Otherwise, they have no way of knowing you're appreciative, or even aware, of the favor they rendered. They may even assume you are ungrateful, which will unfairly remove you from their good graces.

Essential elements: A thank-you for a favor is the easiest kind of letter to put off. It crosses your mind that it was nice of someone to do something for you, but you never communicate that thought. The days go by, and soon it's an old idea. Put your thanks in words using three simple statements:

1. State specifically what you're thankful for.
2. Assure the recipient that he or she won't regret helping you out.
3. Offer to return the favor at any time.

Samples:

Letter #1

Dear Jennifer:

Just a quick note to thank you. I spoke to Jed Hasslen today. He told me that on my recommendation you hired him to do some illustrations for your customer newsletter. I'm glad to bring new business to a talented, young artist like Jed, and I appreciate that you've given him a chance. I'm sure you'll be well pleased.

If there's ever anything I can do for you to return the favor, don't hesitate to ask. Thanks again!

Sincerely,

Letter #2

Here's another thank-you letter in response to a generous contribution.

Dear Sol:

Your offer is very generous, and I accept! Our town school has a severe shortage of computers per student. Especially my son's third-grade class. Your old Mac is the perfect solution. I can pick up the Mac from you at your convenience and deliver it myself to Jason's classroom.

I know you said you have a lot of used computers around, but that doesn't make the act any less generous or helpful. I am grateful. Let me know how I can return the favor.

Sincerely,

Congratulations

The competitive environment of business can sometimes keep us from officially recognizing the accomplishments of our colleagues. When someone in your field opens a new business, accepts a new position, or wins an honor or an award, dash off a congratulatory letter. Not only is this easy to do, it is also a valuable personal and business practice that reaps future benefits in both goodwill and business gains.

Congratulations to a colleague opening a new business

Background: Whenever a colleague or anyone else you know starts a new business, send him or her a congratulations or note printed on your letterhead. Not only does this build goodwill, but it also gives your colleague a permanent record of your phone number and other contact information in case he or she ever needs you. Who knows? He or she may be a potential client, vendor, or employer for you some day in the near future. If there is any possibility of this happening, hint at it in the letter, but avoid the hard sell.

Essential elements: When you send a letter of congratulations to a colleague opening a new business, be sure to:

1. Say congratulations for beginning this new venture.
2. Offer a wish for success and personal pleasure.
3. Ask to be kept informed about the business.
4. Offer your help if needed.

Sample:

> Dear Anthony:
>
> Congratulations on your new digital prepress business! May you derive much success and pleasure from it.
>
> You know that I buy prepress services from time to time, so please keep in touch and maintain my name on your mailing list. I'd like to stay informed about your services. And if you never need anything from me, call anytime.
>
> Sincerely,

Congratulations to a colleague accepting a new position

Background: Just as for a colleague who opens his or her own business, congratulations are in order for a colleague who receives a promotion. You never know when a promotion may put a person in a better position to have a relationship with you as a vendor, customer, or employer.

Essential elements: When you write a congratulatory letter to a colleague who has just been promoted, be sure to mention:

1. A rousing congratulations.
2. Where you heard the news.
3. Your position and how it relates to the person's new position (if appropriate).
4. That you would be glad to provide any help or advice.

Sample:

Dear Cynthia:

Congratulations on your recent promotion! I read about it in the "People" column in *Technology News*. The clipped article is enclosed in case you want an extra copy.

Your new job as vice president of global marketing sounds exciting and challenging. As you know, I've been involved in direct marketing of my company's software overseas for about a year. If there's any information or resources I can share with you in your expanded role, just let me know.

Sincerely,

Congratulations to a colleague who has won an honor or award

Background: There's no real "need" to send this letter, but just do it anyway. This is a perfect way to show that your style of business does not include jealousy or backstabbing. Such a letter is also an investment in goodwill, with the potential to pay big dividends down the road.

Essential elements:

1. Congratulate the recipient, and spell out exactly what the congratulations are for.
2. Add humor if you'd like to take the edge off sounding too formal or insincere.
3. Flatter the recipient by mentioning the importance of this honor.

Sample:

Dear Siobhan:

Congratulations! I saw in *TMI Journal* yesterday that you won yet another EGGY Award! That makes six, doesn't it? As you know, I've only won once. So, you are embarrassing me terribly. If you don't stop, I'll have no choice but to tell everyone you steal all my best ideas and the awards really belong to me (although, of course, it's more the other way around!).

Seriously, congratulations again on this important honor. You are the only six-time EGGY winner I know. You should feel proud.

Sincerely,

Declining requests and invitations

Unfortunately, sometimes it's necessary to say no to colleagues who ask you to do something.

Refusal of a request

Background: A polite letter goes a long way in helping people understand why you can't comply with a request. The reason is usually lack of time. The reader understands and readily accepts this because he or she also suffers the same problem.

Essential elements: When you put together a refusal be sure to include:

1. An opening compliment. Say something positive to break the ice.
2. A definite no that leaves no doubt about your position.
3. A statement that keeps the door open to business in the future.
4. A good-luck wish for success in the venture you are refusing to join.

Sample:

Dear Danielle:

Thanks for the big notebook and the customer service book. Both are at your usual high level of excellence. Unfortunately, the answer to your question is no. I'm unable to take on any additional projects right now because I'm already too busy.

If you need further help down the line, be sure to let me know. Hopefully, my schedule will open up and allow me take on interesting work like this at a later date.

I wish you luck with the project.

Best regards,

Declining an invitation

Background: It is very rude to ignore an invitation, even when the answer is no. The *R* in "RSVP" stands for "respond." When you simply toss an invitation without a reply, it inconveniences the person making the arrangements, and it annoys the person who sent the invitation. To stay on good terms with a colleague who sends you an invitation for an event you cannot attend, write a quick note explaining your situation.

Essential elements: When you have to say no, remember:

1. Say thank you and mention exactly what the invitation was for. (Some people have more than one thing going on at a time.)
2. Mention that you value your relationship with the person.
3. Cite "prior commitment" as your reason for not attending. (Unless you choose to, there's no reason to go into the details of your refusal.)
4. Open the door to a get-together some time in the future.

Sample:

Dear Trish:

Thanks for the invitation to the Armbusters Syndicate's annual holiday bash and for the kind words regarding my consulting services. I too enjoy and value our work together.

Unfortunately, because of prior commitments, I won't be able to make it into New York City that night to attend. Perhaps we can meet when I am in the city early in the New Year?

Thanks again for the invitation. It is very much appreciated.

Sincerely,

Expressions of personal concern ⊘

Business is business, but sometimes your colleagues experience personal problems or losses that you can acknowledge through a brief note of concern. In certain circumstances, it's important to show sincere interest in colleagues as people with lives outside the office.

Because this type of letter needs to convey deep emotion and care, definitely do not send it via e-mail or fax, which would seem too convenient, cold, and impersonal.

Get-well wishes, sympathy, or similar expressions of personal concern

Background: In today's high-tech world, many people crave the personal touch. It's totally appropriate to send a letter to a business associate regarding a personal matter, if there is an established relationship between you, no matter how small. The first sample voices concern over a colleague's health problem, but you can adapt its format to other issues, such as a colleague's personal loss. The second sample is specific to expressing sympathy.

Essential elements: When you're writing to someone who has experienced a loss, whether through illness, death, or even downsizing, remember to mention:

1. Your understanding of the loss.
2. Your own experience with the same situation (if appropriate).
3. An offer of help.

Samples:

Letter #1

Dear Sharon,

I heard from Katie that you had back surgery and are out of the hospital recuperating. From my own experiences, I know how difficult being at home for an extended period can be. I hope you are feeling better and will make a full recovery soon.

If there is anything I can do to make this time easier for you, please don't hesitate to call me. I know you would do the same for me.

Sincerely,

Letter #2

Dear Don,

I've just heard about the death of your father. I wanted you to know how sorry I am for your loss. Having lost my own father only a few years ago, I understand how difficult a time this is for you.

If there is anything I can do, don't hesitate to call me. I know it can take some time to get back on track after such an emotionally draining experience.

Best wishes,

5

Corresponding With Vendors

A buyer usually has the upper hand over vendors. After all, as the adage states, "The customer is always right," and the buyer is the customer. However, miscommunicating with or mistreating a vendor will affect a buyer's bottom line. Here are some tips for more effective customer-to-supplier communications:

1. Put everything in writing. If something changes after a purchase order or contract is signed, be sure to put the changes into writing.

2. Be specific and precise. Spell out the details, terms, and conditions.

3. Don't be a difficult customer. Difficult customers are often perceived as pests. Vendors may put you at the bottom of their priority list rather than the top. You won't know they've done this—until your orders take more time to arrive.

4. Don't overestimate your importance and power. Some customers delight in making vendors jump. However, they are surprised when successful vendors, who already have plenty of business, won't fill more orders for them.

E-Mail Empowerment Tip

You can communicate with your vendors by e-mail for all the correspondence discussed in this chapter. For many of these communications, particularly those involving purchase orders, proposals, contracts, credit adjustments, requests that require detailed follow-up, and complaints for which you are asking for a specific resolution, you should e-mail your letter as an attachment (that is, a standard business letter typed on letterhead paper) that can be printed and filed, instead of typing it directly as an e-mail itself. This will better enable you to establish a paper trail of communications between you and your vendors. Whenever this approach is advisable for a particular type of correspondence, we have noted as such in the "Background" section for the correspondence; otherwise, you can just type the correspondence directly into e-mail.

Hiring vendors

To avoid misunderstandings and unexpected bills from vendors, put everything in writing. With the following sample letters, you can request proposals and sales presentations, award contracts, and notify losing bidders.

Requesting a proposal

Background: When you want to invite a vendor to place a bid on a project, you typically need to write a letter of transmittal, then include a request for a proposal (RFP) form, which invites the supplier to bid on the project and outlines the items that the supplier's proposal must address. The sample provided shows a suitable letter of transmittal. (If using e-mail, you can type this letter of transmittal into the body of your e-mail message, but attach the RFP form as a separate file.)

Essential elements: Be sure your letter includes:

1. The job you want to hire out.
2. Notification that an RFP form is enclosed (if mailing your correspondence) or attached (if e-mailing).
3. The criteria that will be used to select a proposal.
4. An invitation to call with questions or clarifications.

Sample:

Dear Richard:

We have recently won a large-scale government project to produce mobile ground-based radar stations. We want to subcontract the antenna interface design and manufacture to one or more outside contractors.

Our RFP is enclosed [*or attached*]. If you wish to bid on this project, please respond by the date indicated in the RFP. Proposals will not be accepted after the deadline date.

Price as always is an important consideration. But we are not constrained to accept the low bid. The technical solution, reliability of supply, and conformance to military specifications are also important factors in our selection of subcontractors.

If you have any questions about this, please contact me. [*If mailing a standard letter, state your contact information here. If using e-mail, include a statement that directs attention to your e-mail signature.*]

Sincerely,

Request for a sales presentation

Background: It's not difficult to get vendors to compete with one another to win your business. However, just because they'll come at the drop of a hat for a sales presentation doesn't mean such presentations are productive. Tell them why you are inviting them. Explain what they should bring and how to prepare. Be specific about the outcomes you expect. Why waste their time or yours? Make every meeting more productive.

Essential elements: When you ask vendors to present their services, ideas, or products, state in writing exactly what you're looking for:

1. Begin by complimenting their work or reputation and extending an invitation to conduct a sales presentation.
2. Make it clear that this is a sales presentation, not a paid consultation.
3. Emphasize that you are actively seeking to hire a vendor for the particular service, product, or idea about which they will present.
4. State exactly what you would like the presentation to accomplish and how to prepare for this meeting.
5. Set a date and time, or ask them to call to arrange a convenient appointment.

Sample:

Dear Mr. Smith:

We've reviewed the sample portfolio you sent us and like what we see. We'd like to invite you to meet with the marketing department and discuss ideas for new promotions.

This would be a preliminary meeting, not a paid consultation. But we have an urgent need to improve response rates on mailings for more than a dozen products. If you like us and we like you, chances are good that you'll walk away with an assignment to do a major package for us.

I've enclosed control mailings for six of our most critical products. Based on your review of these mailings, we'd be interested in hearing which product you feel you could be the most successful with—and why. We want to know how you would propose to beat mailings that have worked well and that are only tiring recently.

We're hoping you're available sometime next week, preferably Tuesday, Wednesday, or Thursday. Please let me know your availability so we can set a firm time and date. [*If mailing a standard letter, state your contact information here. If using e-mail, include a statement that directs attention to your e-mail signature.*]

Sincerely,

Acknowledgment of a sales presentation or proposal

Background: It takes time and energy for vendors to follow through on proposals and sales presentations. Waiting for your response can be agonizing for them. Your company can "outclass" others by simply sending off an acknowledgment of the vendors' work and offering an estimated response time.

Essential elements: After you receive a sales presentation or a proposal, send a letter that includes the following:

1. A thank-you for the presentation.
2. A statement of how many vendors are being considered.
3. An assurance that no more proposals are being accepted.
4. An estimate of when you will choose a vendor and an assurance that all vendors will be notified of your decision.
5. A thank-you for showing interest in your company.

Sample:

Re: RFP #48508934 [*Include this in the "subject" field if sending an e-mail.*]

Dear Mr. Hasse:

Thanks for your proposal in response to our RFP.

We are reviewing proposals from you and four other vendors. No further proposals will be accepted.

Our decision will be made within two to three weeks. We will inform all bidders of their status by mail once a contractor or contractors are selected. Thanks again for your interest in Talbot Industries and the AMC-400 project.

Sincerely,

Awarding a contract

Background: A contract award is happy news for the vendor. The award is also made with great hopes, so let your enthusiasm set the tone. If you have questions or reservations, it's best to bring them up before you award a contract, not after.

Essential elements: This is the kind of letter that keeps vendors in business. They are happy to get the news and need only a simple go-ahead to get the job going. Be sure to include:

1. A congratulatory introduction.
2. The exact job for which you are awarding the contract; include the RFP number (vendors have many bids out at one time).
3. A request for a meeting to finalize the contract details. (This can also be done through a telephone conference.)

Sample:

Re: RFP #48508934 [*Include this in the "subject" field if sending an e-mail.*]

Dear Mr. Hasse:

Congratulations! We are pleased to announce that we have selected your firm as the sole subcontractor for the AMC-400 project.

We suggest a meeting within the next week or so to work out particulars so that we can draw up a contract for your signature. Please call to set up an appointment. [*If mailing a standard letter, state your contact information here. If using e-mail, include a statement that directs attention to your e-mail signature.*]

Once again, congratulations!

Sincerely,

Notifying losing bidders

Background: Every sales presentation and proposal requires a response, even when it's a negative one. Use the sample provided to notify firms who didn't get the business. You can keep it on file on your computer (if using e-mail, in your "drafts" folder) and fill in the blanks when you need to send out notifications to losing bidders.

Essential elements:

1. An assurance that the proposal has been carefully reviewed.
2. A compliment about the quality of the company's work.

3. A statement of rejection.
4. A thank-you.
5. A promise to consider the company for future projects.

Sample:

Re: RFP #_____ [*Include this in the "subject" field if sending an e-mail.*]

Dear _____,

Your proposal for the _____ project has been carefully reviewed.
Although you are an impressive vendor, we have chosen to go with another subcontractor.
I thank you for your proposal effort. Your products might be right for some of our other contracts, and I will keep your company's name on file for consideration for future projects.

Sincerely,

Placing and receiving orders

You can pick up the phone and order just about any service you want. But, again, to avoid miscommunication and unexpected bills, put everything in writing. In this section, you'll find several samples to use when placing and receiving orders with your vendors. The following samples include a quick order request, a sample purchase order, and other letters to place an order, as well as letters to refuse a shipment, to cancel an order, and to report damages to an insurance carrier.

Purchase order

Background: Many companies use standard purchase orders to buy goods and services. If your company doesn't already have a purchase order form, you can use the sample provided or a version of it.

Sample:

[*Insert your company name and address.*]
Purchase Order
Date:
Authorized by:

Issued to:

Ship via:

Ship to attn.:

Telephone number: Ship by (date):

Description   Price

Purchase order number must appear on all invoices and correspondence. Please sign and return second and third copies.

Signed: Date:

E-Mail Empowerment Tip

If you would like to use e-mail to send a purchase order to a vendor, attach the electronic file of your completed purchase order form to your e-mail message, and state briefly in your message that you are placing an order and that a purchase order (state the purchase order number) is attached. Explain that the form must be signed and returned to you, and draw attention to the address in your e-mail signature to which the signed form should be sent.

Placing an order

Background: Small businesses that don't use purchase forms or have computerized accounting systems often use simple letters to place orders or confirm telephone orders. When you know exactly what you want and who you want it from, dash off these easy kinds of order requests.

When using e-mail, attach your order request as a separate file, typed as a standard letter on letterhead, that you can print for filing and record-keeping.

Essential elements: The basic elements of a letter placing an order include:

1. Your company name and address (presumably on your letterhead).
2. A clear, numbered list of the items you're ordering, including exactly what you need and how many you need.
3. When you need your order fulfilled.
4. How you want the order shipped.
5. How you will pay.
6. How and when the vendor should confirm receipt of the order.

Samples:

Letter #1: Standard order request

To whom it may concern:

Please send the following items to the above address via Fast Express Next-Day Air:
Catalog No. 675-XS, toner cartridge, $80 × 4 = $320
Catalog No. 232-QP, Canary yellow card stock (case), $47 × 1 = $47
Total of order: $367.

Sincerely,

Letter #2: Quick order request

Dear Samantha:

Our publishing company is planning its annual sales meeting on June 30 in Atlanta, Georgia. Approximately 225 people will attend. While I realize that time is limited, is it possible to obtain 250 copies of your brochure "Quality Time in Quality Lives" before June 15? These can be shipped COD to my attention at the above address.

If possible, would you call my assistant, Ivan Johnson, at 123-456-7890 within the next week to let him know whether these are available? Your cooperation is very much appreciated.

Sincerely,

Refusal/return of a shipment

Background: Sometimes you will get a shipment from a vendor that needs to be returned because the contents are the wrong items, damaged, or not of the expected quality. In these cases, you can either ask the company to correct the mistake, or you can cancel the order and request a refund. In either case, explain clearly in writing why you are returning the items and what you expect the vendor to do.

If you would like to use e-mail to send this correspondence, definitely attach it to your e-mail as a separate file, typed on letterhead, so that you can print it and properly document your refusal of the shipment.

Essential elements: When refusing a shipment, state exactly what items you're returning. You should:

1. Give your order number and enclose (if mailing your letter) or attach (if using e-mail) a copy of the original purchase order, if you had one.
2. Explain your reason for returning the items.
3. State what you want the vendor to do: either correct the order or refund your money.
4. Give a date by which you expect the correction or the refund.
5. End with a cordial thank-you.

Sample:

Dear Mr. Millington,

I am returning with this letter a recent shipment of 500 imprinted golf balls (order #3345) along with a copy of our original purchase order. As stated, the logo should be reproduced in our corporate color, which is green. The logos on the golf balls you sent are bright blue and therefore unacceptable.

Please make the necessary corrections and send another shipment of 500 golf balls (with the logo in our corporate green) by the 15th of this month. We need them for a company-sponsored event that starts the first of next month.

Thanks for your prompt attention to this matter.

Sincerely,

Canceling an order

Background: There are many reasons you might cancel an order after you've placed it. You might get tired of waiting for delivery. Or, if the product was not a special order just for you, you might cancel it if you find the material for a lower price elsewhere or if you decide you don't need it any more. For whatever the reason, your cancellation should be made in writing.

If you would like to use e-mail to send this correspondence, attach it to your e-mail as a separate file, typed on letterhead and signed (you can scan your signed version and attach it to your e-mail). Again, this will better allow you to create a paper trail than casually typing your correspondence into an e-mail message. You could also fax this letter and follow up with a hard copy, if you so chose.

Essential elements:

1. Give your order number.
2. State the reason you are canceling your order.

3. Make it clear that because you did not accept delivery of the items, you do not expect to receive a bill.

Sample:

Re: Order #794556

Dear Mark:

After a six-week wait, we have not received the connectors we ordered from your company.

At this point, we can't wait any longer without the risk of missing our production deadlines. I am buying the connectors from a local supplier and canceling my order with you.

I do not expect to receive a bill.

Sincerely,

Day-to-day contact

When you hire out work, you will often need to keep in touch with the vendors. The following sample letters will show you how to request a status update, request changes to a job, or discontinue an order.

Request for a status update

Background: A fax or e-mail is a good way to request a status update on an order or project from your vendors. Putting the query in writing helps clarify what you're asking for and shows the vendor you are serious and expect a timely response.

Essential elements: Keeping track of your vendors can keep you very busy. Make it simple with a two- or three-sentence request for a status update. Include:

1. The project you're inquiring about.
2. The date you expect to see the finished work.
3. Any information that will help the vendor meet your expectations.
4. A date by which you expect a status report.

Sample:

> Dear Sam:
>
> How is the Website coming? I know things are hectic over there, but I'm looking forward to seeing a sample of the site by Friday the 22nd. Be sure to scan in the photo I sent you last week and add the link to the publisher as we discussed. Please let me know how things are progressing by the end of this week. [*If sending a fax, state your contact information here. If using e-mail, include a statement that directs attention to your e-mail signature.*]
> Thanks.
>
> Cordially,

Request for changes to a job

Background: Another situation in which communication with vendors should be made or at least confirmed in writing is a request for changes to a job in progress.

If using e-mail, include this type of correspondence as a standard letter that is attached to your e-mail so that you can establish the proper paper trail. (A simple e-mail message might get lost in the shuffle, presenting problems if the changes you requested were not properly handled.)

Essential elements: It is important that this letter be very specific and each change be numbered. Be sure to include:

1. The name of the project you're talking about.
2. A positive comment to open.
3. A numbered and detailed list of the changes you want.
4. A date you will call to confirm that the changes are understood.

Sample:

> Dear Pat:
>
> The ad layouts look good. My comments follow, along with some input from the client:
> 1. One layout has three columns of copy; the second has only one paragraph. Because the ad is copy-heavy, I feel only the three-column copy can be used. The rest of my comments apply to that copy.

2. I do not care for the image of the hand holding the disk. My suggestion would be to either show samples of stationery printed with the program or a printer churning out letterhead. The client prefers the latter.

3. The border around the entire ad needs something, perhaps a shadow.

You've done a great job! Laura will call you tomorrow to discuss all of this.

Thanks,

Discontinuation of a vendor's services

Background: As vendors ourselves, we can tell you that we become concerned when a satisfied client suddenly stops requesting our services. "What did we do wrong?" we ask ourselves. Often, it's not that a vendor did anything wrong, it's that the client's needs, objectives, priorities, and situation have changed. If you stop using a vendor, especially one with which you have been satisfied, you should explain why. Believe us, it's comforting to know.

Essential elements: When you have to discontinue service from vendors you are satisfied with, be sure to include:

1. A positive statement about their work.
2. The fact that you will not be sending an order in the near future.
3. The reason for discontinuing the service.
4. An expectation of more orders at a later date.

Sample:

Dear Gary:

Enclosed is a summary of the interpersonal skills workshop evaluations. We are very pleased with the results, and you exceeded our expectations! Thank you for tailoring the course to meet our objectives.

Even with the good feedback, however, we will not be able to schedule another workshop with you this year. The money is simply not available. However, I hope that next year will be another story. Once again, it was a pleasure working with you!

Sincerely,

Problem situations

In any business, there are times when things don't go smoothly. When you have a problem with a vendor, be prompt about your complaint and clearly state what you need to fix the problem. The following letters will show you how to ask for a credit adjustment and clarify information on a vendor invoice.

Request for a credit adjustment

Background: Refunds or credits should always be requested in writing—and, if you really want to use e-mail, should always be attached as a formal letter typed on letterhead, preferably a signed copy that you have scanned. This gives you a written record with a date to use as follow-up if the request is initially ignored. Be sure to print and save a copy for your files.

Essential elements: If you're not happy with a service or product and want a refund or credit, your letter must be direct and firm. It should include:

1. Documented details of the problem.
2. What you expect done (discontinue, return, remove, and so forth).
3. The amount of refund or credit you expect.
4. The date by which you expect these things done.

Sample:

Dear Ms. Jordan:

On February 28, you installed a water-purification system in our office building. On the following dates, we requested service: March 3, 10, 20, 25; April 7, 14, 20, 23; May 2, 9, 10. The system is still not functioning today.

We have been more than patient with the system and your technicians' work. As I said on the phone this morning, I want the system removed immediately. Also, please issue a check for $935.35, the amount we have paid to date. Please complete the above transaction no later than May 22.

Sincerely,

Request for clarification of a vendor invoice

Background: Because this is a routine matter, many accounts payable departments have form letters for dealing with this problem when it occurs. Type the following form letter and save it on your computer, or save it as a form e-mail message in the "drafts" folder of your e-mail program, and use it whenever you encounter missing or incomplete information on a vendor's invoice. No other writing is really necessary.

Sample:

Re: Your invoice #____[Include this in the "subject" field if sending an e-mail.]
Dear Vendor:

Your invoice is being returned to you for the following reason(s):
____ No purchase order number
____ No job number
____ No Social Security or federal tax ID number
____ Amount of invoice does not match purchase order
____ No sign-off of acceptance from customer
____ No/incomplete receipt of goods
Please add any missing data and resolve any of the other issues indicated. Then resubmit your invoice for payment.

Thank-you correspondence

Sometimes a vendor is particularly good. When that happens, say so in writing. This simple communication is an excellent way to cement business relationships that benefit both the client and the vendor.

Praise of a vendor

Background: Customers are quick to complain and slow to praise. If you are happy with a vendor, say so in writing. The goodwill from such an act will make you stand out!

Essential elements: When you have something nice to say, it's not necessary to get gushy or overdo the flattery. Simply state:
1. What you like about the service or product.
2. How it has helped your business.
3. That the vendor can expect more business from you in the future.

Sample:

Dear Tiffany:

I want to tell you how much we like your DVD program *I Don't Have Customers*. We recently used it in our seminar "Interpersonal Skills for Systems Professionals." The program clearly and forcefully gets across the point to our trainees that we all have customers—even those of us who serve internal departments. One technical professional said after the course that viewing the DVD opened his eyes and changed his entire attitude for the better.

Thanks again for a great program. I'm sure your DVDs will become an essential element of our interpersonal skills courses in the future.

Sincerely,

Thank-you for extra effort

Background: In today's competitive business world, many vendors bend over backward to service, please, and retain clients. Clients know this and often demand it. The only reward for the vendor is often retention of the account.

When a vendor pulls out all the stops to serve you, the least expensive thing you can do to motivate the vendor is to thank the vendor sincerely. Few customers do it, so your note of appreciation stands out. If you don't think motivating suppliers should be a concern of yours, think again. Not all customers are treated equally; some are a vendor's favorites. Why not position yourself as a favorite customer, so when it counts, you will get the service and delivery you need?

Essential elements: You can't send a letter or e-mail of thanks to every person you do business with all day long, but when someone goes out of the way to make things work for you, be sure to say so with a letter or e-mail message that includes:

1. A strong, clear thank-you.
2. Your understanding that this was a special effort.
3. A promise of future business.

Sample:

Dear Madelyn:

What a great Orlando meeting! And we have you to thank!

The problems with the hotel could not have been anticipated. When they happen, most clients come down on their meeting planners, as I did on you. The pressure from my unhappy management made me short-tempered. But not only did you handle the situation with grace, you got things solved!

Aside from the first-day mishaps, this was our smoothest conference ever. You can be sure of our continued patronage of your meeting planning services. In fact, we should be thinking about next year soon. Give me a call after Labor Day if you don't hear from me first.

Sincerely,

6

Corresponding With Employees and Employers

These days, interoffice communications mainly take the form of e-mail. And e-mail definitely has its advantages: One click of the button and your message is routed to many people instantaneously. The style is also less formal than that found in a letter. However, many people mistakenly think that because their e-mail messages are addressed to people within their own company, not to customers, they can dash them off quickly and mar them with typos and jargon and the reader will still know what they mean. But be sure to heed Chapter 1's advice for writing business e-mails because your superiors, subordinates, and peers will judge you by the quality of your written communications, even when you're "just" using e-mail.

Be mindful that employees with diverse backgrounds may not share a common jargon and that, like you, the people you're writing to have busy schedules. A message they can't understand upon first reading—and especially one that forces them to contact you for clarification—is an annoying time-waster they won't appreciate.

Also remember that adding a personal touch to your communications is more important than ever in today's fast-paced electronic age. "Keep in touch with the people who work for you," advises John Beckley, founder of Economics Press. "When you think something pleasant or favorable about someone, make a note of it immediately, and be sure to tell them." Bringing your care, attention, and tact to the process of sending e-mails to people within your company can set you apart from the pack.

This chapter presents model e-mails, memos, and letters for employee-to-employee, employer-to-employee, and employee-to-employer communications in a variety of situations. Note that e-mails have become the standard way to communicate many of the messages that used to be the domain of interoffice memos, so you will find more model e-mails than sample printed memos here.

But even though e-mail is appropriate for most of the correspondence discussed in this chapter, as usual don't use e-mail for a particular type of message if you see the ⊘ icon.

Day-to-day communications with employees

There are many routine situations in your workday that require you to send messages to your employees in writing. Written messages take up less time, they communicate exactly what you want known, and they serve as wonderful reminders. In years past, these kinds of messages would be printed memorandums that were dropped into in-trays on employees' desks. Today, these everyday communications are commonly delivered via simple, straightforward e-mails, which can be sent to many people at once. The first six samples cover frequently encountered, basic day-to-day issues you will likely need to address via e-mail. You can adapt the structure of these samples to any e-mail messages you need to send about routine, day-to-day workplace matters. You may also consult Chapter 2, "How to Format Your Business Letter, Fax, or E-mail" for more direction.

E-Mail Empowerment Tip

Within your e-mail address book, set up a group distribution list consisting of the desired recipients of your e-mail message, and assign an appropriate name to this group of contacts (for example, Alpha Team Members or Capselle Employees). This strategy will eliminate the need to type in your recipients' individual e-mail addresses over and over whenever there's a need to send a message to that group.

E-mail rescheduling a meeting

Sample:

From: Allen Cvelic <acvelic@fictionalfirm.com>
Date: Tuesday, August 13, 20XX
To: Alpha Team Members
Subject: Change of date for weekly team meeting

The meeting has been rescheduled for Friday 10 a.m. instead of the usual time on Thursday. Please let me know if you have a conflict.

[Automatic e-mail signature should appear here; see the sample signatures in Chapter 2.]

Holiday schedule notification e-mail

Sample:

From: Timothy Casey <tcasey@fictionalfirm.com>
Date: Monday, December 2, 20XX
To: Capselle Employees
Subject: Holiday schedule

This year, City plant will be open on December 26 and 27 but closed from December 28 to January 2. These days are scheduled for plant maintenance, so only maintenance supervisors and their crews will be working. The building will not be accessible to other employees.

[*Automatic e-mail signature should appear here; see the sample signatures in Chapter 2.*]

Office holiday party announcement e-mail

Sample:

From: Kevin Hancock <khancock@fictionalfirm.com>
Date: Friday, December 11, 20XX
To: Newsroom and Pressroom Staff
Subject: Office holiday party

This year's holiday office party will be held at O'Sullehbhain's Pub on December 23 starting at noon. As most of you already know, the pub is on the corner of 61st and Madison. Please remember to bring a grab-bag gift worth $15 or less.

[*Automatic e-mail signature should appear here; see the sample signatures in Chapter 2.*]

Summer hours announcement e-mail

Sample:

From: Kara Richardson <krichardson@fictionalfirm.com>
Date: Monday, May 14, 20XX
To: Agency Staff
Subject: Summer hours

From June 22 to September 4, we will be operating under summer hours. During summer hours, we will close at 3 p.m. instead of 5 p.m. on Fridays. On all other days, we will be open from 9 a.m. to 5 p.m.

[*Automatic e-mail signature should appear here; see the sample signatures in Chapter 2.*]

Expense report instruction e-mail

Sample:

From: June Barrel, CFO <jbarrel@fictionalfirm.com>
Date: Wednesday, July 26, 20XX
To: Sales Staff
Subject: Expense reports

Expense reports must be filed on or before the last day of the month. Filing your expense report after that deadline may delay reimbursement up to 30 days. For your convenience, your expense reports may now be filed electronically. Just send your completed Expense Report form to Andy Devin in accounting at andyde@it.org.

This speeds communication and helps assure our receipt on or before the end-of-month deadline.

[*Automatic e-mail signature should appear here; see the sample signatures in Chapter 2.*]

Company car policy e-mail

Sample:

From: Ed Flannery, Fleet Manager <eflannery@fictionalfirm.com>
Date: November 11, 20XX
To: Company Car Users
Subject: Company car maintenance

As our fleet of company cars ages, users have been experiencing some car problems. Checking our records, I find that 70 percent of company vehicles are not brought into the garage for maintenance according to the schedule that fleet management requires. The maintenance schedule for company cars is

> posted on our intranet at http://fictionalfirm.com/fleet. Please make sure you bring your company car in for all scheduled maintenance checks and tune-ups.
>
> *[Automatic e-mail signature should appear here; see the sample signatures in Chapter 2.]*

Routing memo/e-mail

Background: When routing printed copies of materials that require review and approval by one or more managers or professionals in your firm, you can use the memo sample shown below. It's more likely, though, that you will have your materials for review in an electronic format, such as a PDF, for which you can easily solicit comments by e-mail. In that case, attach the file(s) to your e-mail, and use e-mail sample shown below.

Essential elements:

1. When using the printed memo format, include the names of all people the routing form is being sent to. When using e-mail, set up a group distribution list consisting of the e-mail addresses for the appropriate contacts from your address book in your e-mail program.
2. State the directions clearly.
3. Indicate how and when the person is to respond.
4. Include a space for an approval signature if you are using hard copy.
5. Be sure to enclose the material you would like reviewed, as an attachment to your e-mail or fastened to your printed memo.

Samples:

Printed memo

> **To:** Joe Carr, Mary Coppeyn, Cheryl Flanart, Donna Simps
> **From:** Kathy Westerholff
> **Re:** Review of attached material
>
> Please review this story for the upcoming company newsletter. Mark any changes, sign your approval below, and fax back to me at 123-456-7890 within one week. If you have any questions or need to discuss the copy, call me at 123-456-7890.
>
> Approved by _____ Date _____

E-mail

From: Kathy Westerhoff <kathyw@fictionalfirm.com>
Date: Tuesday, October 9, 20XX
To: Newsletter Review Committee
Subject: Review of attached material
Attachments: LeadStory_FallNewsletter.pdf

Please review this story for the upcoming company newsletter. Reply with your comments or approval by October 16. If you have any questions or need to discuss the copy, my contact information is below.

[*Automatic e-mail signature should appear here; see the sample signatures in Chapter 2.*]

Action memo/e-mail

Background: Simple memos are effective for communicating with employees within your firm about projects, tasks, and actions to be taken. Today most of these are sent via e-mail, as in the second sample that follows. However, if you need a permanent record of the communication for your files, you can distribute a printed memo, like the first sample. Consult "How to determine the best medium for your message" in the Introduction for more guidance on when a message in print is the best way to go.

Essential elements:

To be effective, your action memo/e-mail should contain the following:

1. The names of all recipients (if you are using a printed memo) or the name of an e-mail distribution group (if you are using e-mail); your name; the date; and the subject matter.
2. A clear, simple statement of the information.
3. A note about what you expect the recipients to do next.

Samples:

Printed memo

To: Joe Carr, Mary Coppeyn, Cheryl Flanart, Donna Simps
From: Kathy Westerholff
Re: Training budget

We have just completed the budgeting process for next year and have established several key areas to focus on. One of those areas is skill building in customer service and communications.

To continue to improve the abilities of our employees to maximize customer service, we have decided to invest $5,000 per employee on training during the upcoming year. This is the biggest investment in training we have made in our eight years in business.

In January, I will meet with each of you individually to set goals, review your current skill level in a variety of areas, and start to identify potential training sessions you should attend.

Please stop by my office sometime next week and pick up an assessment form that we'll go over in our meeting.

E-mail

From: Kathy Westerhoff <kathyw@fictionalfirm.com>
Date: Thursday, November 5, 20XX
To: Customer Service Team
Subject: Training budget
Attachments: AssessmentForm.doc

We have just completed the budgeting process for next year and have established several key areas to focus on. One of those areas is skill building in customer service and communications.

To continue to improve the abilities of our employees to maximize customer service, we have decided to invest $5,000 per employee on training during the upcoming year. This is the biggest investment in training we have made in our eight years in business.

In January, I will meet with each of you individually to set goals, review your current skill level in a variety of areas, and start to identify potential training sessions you should attend.

An assessment form is attached. Feel free to look it over, as we will be discussing it in our meeting.

[Automatic e-mail signature should appear here; see the sample signatures in Chapter 2.]

Instruction e-mail

Background: Putting ideas and instructions in writing helps clarify them not only for the recipient, but also for the writer. In our line of work, we frequently write short e-mails to make clear requests of those with whom we work. For example, the sample that follows is an e-mail that author Regina Anne Kelly sent to her office assistant concerning the preparation of the manuscript of this book.

Essential elements: Even though they are simple, memos and e-mails of instruction have an important purpose: They detail exactly what you expect and when it must be done. Giving your employees this written record of instructions increases the likelihood that it will happen the way you want it to. Just state what you want done and the date it is to be accomplished.

Sample:

From: Regina Anne Kelly <reginaannekelly@reginakelly.net>
Date: Friday, July 17, 2008
To: Jacqueline Callas <jc@reginakelly.net>
Subject: Letter book

Within three to four weeks, I will send you the following files for the book I am coauthoring for Career Press: LETFM 1, LETCH 1-10, LETBM1. When you receive all the files, I would like you to insert page numbers in the upper right corner, print out, and send one hard copy to the proofreader at his home address, one hard copy and the electronic files to Career Press in Franklin Lakes, and one hard copy to me. Please do this within 48 hours of receiving the files. Thanks.

Best,
Regina

Announcement of a change in company policy or procedure

Background: This is a simple, straightforward communication that requires a written record. All employees must be kept up-to-date on changes and should not have to rely on the grapevine for this information. A printed memo is the ideal medium for this type of communication because, unlike just another e-mail taking up space in employees' inboxes, it will grab employees' attention. Furthermore, company policy–related issues may require printed documentation for legal reasons.

Essential elements: This memo should get straight to the point:

1. Announce the change.
2. State when the change takes effect.
3. Provide instructions outlining how the new procedures are to be followed.

Sample:

To: Shift workers
From: C.F. Kornbs
Re: Shift changes

Requests to be transferred out of the night shift must now be made in writing to Sheldon Mack, day supervisor, at least one month before the shift change can be granted. There will be no exceptions. If there are not enough positions on the day shift to accommodate all requests, transfer from night to day shift will be made on a seniority basis.

E-mail reserving a conference room

Background: This sounds like a trivial message, unless you've ever reserved a conference room only to find another group already working in it upon your arrival.

Essential elements:

1. State what room you want, as well as the date and the hours you will need it.
2. Explain why you need the room and how many people will be there.
3. Put down any special requests for equipment or refreshments.
4. Ask for a confirmation response.

Sample:

From: Wayne Robbins <wrobbins@fictionalfirm.com>
Date: Monday, August 9, 20XX
To: Stacy Spretch <sspretch@fictionalfirm.com>
Subject: Conference room reservation

I would like to reserve the Main Conference Room for the entire morning (8 a.m. to noon) of August 15. We are having the 10 regional managers in

---

for the annual sales booster meeting. Can you please arrange for coffee service throughout the morning, including perhaps some pastries or rolls?

Please reply with your confirmation of the reservation, or let me know if there is any conflict.

[*Automatic e-mail signature should appear here; see the sample signatures in Chapter 2.*]

E-mail announcing a meeting

Background: Meeting announcements can be made informally by simply talking to the people you want to attend. A written message, like the sample e-mail that follows, is most effective when you feel the meeting is important but suspect many of the key team members will choose not to attend if they can get away with it.

Essential elements: Make this message firm and to the point. Include:

1. Meeting details: date, time, and location.
2. Who will be in attendance.
3. Reason for the meeting.
4. Directive regarding what attendees should bring and how they should prepare.
5. Indication of whether the meeting is mandatory.
6. How to contact you if there are problems or questions.

Sample:

From: Martin Power <martinp@fictionalfirm.com>
Date: Friday, February 28, 20XX
To: Database Team
Subject: Project milestone review meeting

This note is to confirm that we will have a milestone review meeting for the Prospecting Database project on March 10, from 10 a.m. to noon, in the West Wing videoconference room.

At that time, we will be joined by our counterparts in the Denver office through the videoconferencing facility.

It is essential that all team members here in our office attend. Senior management has expressed concern about deadline slippage and the system's ability to provide the desired functionality.

As this is an enterprise-critical project, these issues need to be resolved so that we can confidently deliver to management our assurance (and proof) that the system will be implemented on time, within budget, and according to specification. Bring with you all documents and information that will support our position.

Attendance is mandatory. If you have any questions, please contact me.

[*Automatic e-mail signature should appear here; see the sample signatures in Chapter 2.*]

Message of confirmation

Background: If you are concerned that your discussion was not understood or that the other person won't meet his or her obligations, be sure to send a confirmation message. If it's in writing, whether by e-mail or in printed correspondence, the other person will take it more seriously. A printed confirmation memo is recommended if any money is to change hands or if important deadlines are involved. An e-mail has its advantages, too, as you can request that the recipient replied to your message with his or her agreement to the terms you have described.

Essential elements: Confirm by including:

1. A positive note.
2. Details of the facts you wish to confirm.
3. An invitation to contact you for clarification or to reply with an affirmation of the terms described.

Samples:

Printed memo

To: Jennifer Croocens

From: Jane Seey

Re: Project confirmation

Thanks for spending some time with me this morning to go over the WatchWord project. As we agreed:

1. To complete this project on time, you can hire a consultant for a fee of S 1,000.
2. The deadline remains May 14th.
3. We will meet again to check progress on May 1st.

In the meantime, please call me with any questions.

E-mail

From: Jane Seey <janes@fictionalfirm.com>
Date: Thursday, April 5, 20XX
To: Jennifer Croocens <jcroocens@fictionalfirm.com>
Subject: Project confirmation

Thanks for spending some time with me this morning to go over the WatchWord project. As we agreed:

1. To complete this project on time, you can hire a consultant for a fee of $1,000.
2. The deadline remains May 14th.
3. We will meet again to check progress on May 1st.

Please reply with an acknowledgment of your agreement to these terms.

[*Automatic e-mail signature should appear here; see the sample signatures in Chapter 2.*]

E-mail encouraging employee usage of company perks

Background: Many companies, especially large corporations, give a variety of benefits and perks that many employees don't fully use and some don't even know about. Benefits and perks are part of the employee's total compensation package, and most employees today look at perks and not just the base salary when evaluating how well you take care of them and whether they should look elsewhere for a better deal. Therefore, encouraging employees to use company services and perks not only builds goodwill, but it also aids in employee retention.

Essential elements: This e-mail should serve as a detailed announcement and a reminder. Include:

1. The perk you want to focus on.
2. The facts such as time, place, and benefit to employees.
3. Further explanation of the advantages (if appropriate).
4. A note about this perk being "special" for your employees only.

Sample:

From: Ron Matthews <rmatthews@fictionalfirm.com>
Date: Monday, June 2, 20XX
To: All Beldicite Technologies Employees
Subject: Lobby discount sale

Just a reminder: Once a month we offer our own closed-out and damaged merchandise to Beldicite employees at incredible discounts, often up to 70 percent off list price.

I encourage you to stop by and look over the merchandise displayed in the lobby at lunch hour on the last Friday of the month. You can get some incredible bargains if you're looking for a DVD player, MP3 player, cell phone, and other Beldicite electronics products. The closeouts are current models about to be replaced by next year's model; usually the difference in features is minimal. The "damaged" goods may be slightly scuffed from shipping but are otherwise new and in perfect working order. All merchandise is covered by the standard Beldicite one-year warranty (although if you work in service, you may end up repairing it yourself while at work!).

This is a great deal that is available only to Beldicite employees.

[*Automatic e-mail signature should appear here; see the sample signatures in Chapter 2.*]

E-mail offering new benefits to employees

Background: It is a pleasurable task to inform employees of new benefits. Your letter should explain the benefit, encourage its usage, and build goodwill by showing the value of what you are offering.

Essential elements: An e-mail announcing new benefits can get lost in the paper shuffle if it looks like any of the other hundred e-mails your employees receive each day. The following sample presents the benefit with an attention-grabbing headline. It then goes on to state:

1. A lead that engages the reader's interest.
2. A statement of the added benefit.
3. A few details about the benefit.
4. Directions about how to obtain more information.
5. The attachment of a brochure with more details.

Sample:

From: Ron Matthews <rmatthews@fictionalfirm.com>
Date: Monday, June 16, 20XX
To: All Beldicite Technologies Employees
Subject: Employee Mortgage Program
Attachments: MortgageBrochure.pdf

As you go through life, your housing needs change. The Employee Mortgage Program can make sure you get the cash you need to make those changes happen.

Dear Employee,

Buying a home? Refinancing a home? Don't have a clue where to begin?

Well, easy home financing starts here—with the Employee Mortgage Program from Southwest Mortgage. Through this value-added program, Beldicite employees have preferred-status access to the mortgage services of Southwest Mortgage.

With more than 20 years of home-financing experience—and 1 million satisfied borrowers nationwide—Southwest Mortgage has helped more corporate employees land the home of their dreams than any other mortgage company in the region.

If you are curious about whether you qualify for a mortgage, call Southwest Mortgage Monday through Friday, 8 a.m. to midnight at 800-123-4567, or complete the online inquiry form on their Website, *www.fictionalmortgagecompany.com*. Experienced Mortgage Advisors can tell you just how big a mortgage you can get.

The attached brochure shows you the many ways Southwest Mortgage can help you come out ahead in the housing game.

Sincerely,

[Automatic e-mail signature should appear here; see the sample signatures in Chapter 2.]

Announcement of a change in health benefits coverage

Background: When you change health benefits coverage, the change may not be universally seen as an improvement. Employees tend to feel unjustly ripped off and need an explanation about why this is happening and how it will affect them. This kind of major change should be presented on paper—not by e-mail.

Essential elements: This kind of change that directly affects each employee should be stated directly and clearly so there is no misunderstanding. Include:

1. An immediate statement that there is going to be a change.
2. A reason for the change.
3. The details of the change.
4. The benefits of this change to the employee (there must be something!).
5. An offer to explain further or answer questions.

Sample:

> **To:** All employees
> **From:** Rachel Bronkson, Employee Benefits Manager
> **Re:** Change in major medical coverage
>
> As of May 14, there will be a change in our employee health coverage.
>
> Each year our insurance broker, Senders & Johnson, performs an audit of all our policies to help control corporate health care expenses. As the result of this year's audit, we will be keeping Guardian General as carrier but switching to one of their alternative plans to prevent health costs from spiraling out of control.
>
> The coverage is nearly identical to the current plan, with one major exception: The deductible per illness has been raised from $50 to $250. Although having a higher deductible is not a positive change, there are other aspects of the change that compensate. We can afford to keep our private major medical plan with Guardian, enabling our employees to continue to be reimbursed while choosing the physicians and other health care providers they prefer. Without this plan readjustment, we probably would have been forced into an HMO or PPO, which in our recent employee survey the majority of you said you did not want. The new plan permits you to keep seeing your regular doctors and have the visits paid for.
>
> The modified coverage will be in force effective May 14. If you have any questions, call me at X5567 or e-mail me via company mail at RCHLBRON.

Communications with your employer

E-mail request for training

Background: Author Robert Bly relates this background about the following sample: "In my second corporate job, I had to handle the management of trade show displays—an area in which I had little experience. Unfortunately, my boss was not a fan of training or spending money he didn't have to. Here is the letter I sent that convinced him to spend $450 to have me attend a two-day local seminar on trade show management."

Essential elements: The trick here is to show that the time and cost of training will increase profits and productivity. Include:

1. A clear statement of what training program you want to attend.
2. An acknowledgment of the cost and a statement explaining how this cost will be recouped in improved sales, profits, productivity, and the like.
3. The reason why you need the training.
4. A direct request for the go-ahead.

Sample:

From: Bob Bly <rwbly@bly.com>
Date: Thursday, January 13, 20XX
To: Mike Olson <molson@mysecondcorporatejob.com>
Subject: Training program

Dear Mike:

Enclosed is a brochure I received on a seminar called "Trade Show University." I'd like to take this program.

I realize the tuition of $450 is not cheap. But we will spend $100,000 this year redoing our displays and exhibiting at shows. If the seminar can help me cut these costs even 5 percent, it will pay for itself more than 10 times over.

My previous experience is in booth design only. I have not managed the exhibit from start to finish. The more knowledge I have, the smarter the buying decisions I can make.

Can I go ahead and register, and have Ken in accounting cut a $450 check to Trade Show University? Please let me know. Thanks.

[Automatic e-mail signature should appear here; see the sample signatures in Chapter 2.]

E-mail request to attend a trade show

Background: Trade shows offer unique opportunities to learn, network, or just visit a nice venue for a day or so. If you want to go but aren't on the approved list, send a request to your manager.

Essential elements: Trade shows take you away from work and cost money. Show your boss that it's worth it by mentioning:

1. Your company position and a problem in your area that needs to be solved.
2. How attending a trade show will help you fix a problem in the company.

3. The cost of the show and how this money is an investment in future progress or profits.

4. A direct request to make all necessary arrangements and file receipts on an expense report.

Sample:

From: Fred Bulsara <fbulsara@fictionalfirm.com>
Date: Wednesday, October 13, 20XX
To: Bob Norman <bnorman@fictionalfirm.com>
Subject: Control and instrumentation expo

Dear Bob:

As you know, you recently reassigned me to process management. Part of the immediate task Laura has set for me is control optimization. My initial review indicates that current equipment, some of it 10 years old, can't handle the requirements we have.

Rather than visit control manufacturers individually to demo new models, I'd like to attend the upcoming Control and Instrumentation Expo. The vendors I'm interested in are all exhibiting at the show, and four of them have live demonstrations at their booths. This will enable me to evaluate four potential systems in one visit and compare them side by side.

Several manufacturers have sent me complimentary passes. My only expenses would be roundtrip travel for a day to and from Pittsburgh, which would cost around $500. I feel this is a good investment considering that the control system we select will have an expected lifetime of eight to 10 years.

Can I make travel reservations and then file the receipts with my expense report? Please let me know.

[Automatic e-mail signature should appear here; see the sample signatures in Chapter 2.]

Request to create a new position

Background: Usually you cannot create a new position without the approval of your boss or human resources, or both. Write a memo that explains the need and makes clear the necessity. (Because this type of message concerns a personnel matter, going with a printed memo is best.) Speak as the authority in the needs of your department.

Essential elements: This request asks for a major change and investment. Be convincing in your approach. Include:

1. A hook to the employer's own feelings about progress in the company.
2. The name of the position you want to create and the purpose it would serve.
3. Evidence that you have researched the idea with other employees who would be affected positively by the creation of this position.
4. A recommendation of a person from within the company who could fill the position and details about why this person is best. If no one from within is qualified, propose that a new employee be hired and state the qualifications that this person should possess.
5. An enclosed job description that shows you have thoroughly investigated and planned the new position.
6. A direct request for approval.

Sample:

To: Ruth Marker

From: Ted Strykar

Re: Creating a position for an in-house Web designer

Dear Ruth:

At our meeting last week, you agreed that we need to increase the power of our online presence. I believe one step toward meeting this need would be to create the position of an in-house Web designer.

I investigated the matter and talked with supervisors in both graphics and IT. They agree that this would be a wise move, and we all feel that Dick Young could handle the position very capably.

Dick has been with our firm in IT for only six months, but has very strong technical skills in technologies such as HTML, Java™, and Adobe® Flash® Player. In addition, he is a Web junkie and knows the Internet inside and out. Right now he is maintaining our Intranet server and, quite frankly, is bored. In this new position, he would become our in-house expert in Web design—something for which he is unabashedly enthusiastic.

Attached is a job description for the Web designer position. If this meets with your approval, I'd like to begin the process with human resources so we could create the position, establish the salary, and offer Dick the job. What do you think?

Sincerely,

Request for a pay raise

Background: This is always a tough letter to write. You have to blow your own horn without sounding conceited and at the same time be convincing about your value and worth to the company. Adapt the following letter to boost your chances of getting what you deserve. Don't use e-mail; this kind of letter needs to be confidential, and e-mail is not.

Essential elements: You cannot write this letter unless you have some indication that your supervisor is satisfied (in fact, highly impressed) with your work. That's what unscheduled raises are based on. Use that information to plead your case:

1. Identify yourself and your position in the company.
2. Right up front, state the raise you are seeking.
3. Remind the reader of his or her approval and/or satisfaction with your work.
4. State your exceptional skills, work habits, results.
5. Repeat your request.

Sample:

Dear Ms. Whitehouse:

As a CAD/CAM operator in your automotive aftermarket group, I would like to request a raise of $3,000 per year effective January 1. This would bring my annual salary up to $34,000.

You have mentioned to me that you are highly satisfied with the quality of my work and my commitment to FitForm Parts. I have been a conscientious employee and have always finished tasks in an accurate and timely manner. I'm sure you have noticed that because I treat the design teams as if they were customers, they often ask to work with me in preference to other CAD/CAM operators. You have often noted that I am a great asset to our team and have frequently complimented my professional, service-oriented manner.

Although I have been with FitForm only eight months, I am asking that my salary be increased and that my compensation be reviewed again in 12 months.

Sincerely,

Recommendation of a pay raise

Background: If you are a manager or a supervisor you may be in a position to request a raise for someone who works under you. The quality of this letter will determine if this person gets the raise or not, so it must be carefully planned. It should include all the details you would put in a letter requesting a raise for yourself (see the letter on page 119). Furthermore, because it concerns a personnel issue, it should not be sent by e-mail.

Essential elements: This letter is upbeat, positive, and strong. Make sure it includes:

1. An identification of the employee and his or her position in the company.
2. Right up front, state the raise you are seeking for this employee.
3. State your approval and/or satisfaction with the employee's work.
4. State his or her exceptional skills, work habits, and results.
5. Repeat your request.

Sample:

Dear Ms. Spadafora:

I recommend that we offer Bill Dickey, a CAD/CAM operator in our automotive aftermarket group, a raise of $3,000 per year effective January 1. This would bring his annual salary up to $34,000.

I am highly satisfied with the quality of work he produces and his commitment to FitForm Parts. He is a conscientious employee, finishing tasks in an accurate and timely manner. In addition, he treats the design teams as if they were customers; they often ask to work with Bill in preference to other CAD/CAM operators.

Although Bill has been with FitForm only eight months, I am recommending that his salary be increased and that his compensation again be reviewed in 12 months. He is a great asset to our team and should be rewarded for the quality of his work and his professional, service-oriented manner.

Sincerely,

Sharing good news

Stay on the lookout for pieces of good news that you can share with your employees. These good-news messages are a great way to keep up morale and give public credit when credit is due.

Congratulations on a work anniversary

Background: In today's information-overloaded work environment, everybody has too much to read and not enough time to read it. Yet the volume of cordial correspondence has diminished to near nothingness. Therefore, the thank-you note still stands out. You can send this note via e-mail or, to add a more personal touch, in a card or in a letter on stationery or company letterhead. (If you choose e-mail, simply model the content of your e-mail on the body of the sample message that follows, while using standard e-mail formatting as described previously.)

Essential elements: This note shouldn't be too heavy in job-performance evaluation. Keep it simple, upbeat, and congratulatory. Include:

1. The details of the anniversary (number of years in current position or total years as an employee).
2. A personal note about the person's first days (if you were there and remember).
3. An overview of the recipient's accomplishments since taking the position.
4. A toast for many more years of continued excellence.

Sample:

Dear Mary,

This week marks your fifth year of employment with Westway Pharmaceuticals. Congratulations on this important anniversary.

I can hardly believe it's been a half-decade since you walked into my office for an interview...and I spilled coffee all over your resume! Despite the awkward start, I was fortunate to make the right decision and hire you for the position. Aside from your excellent performance record, you are truly a pleasure to work with.

Here's to another rewarding and profitable five years for Westway...and the two of us!

Sincerely,

Congratulations for a job well done

Background: Don't pass up an opportunity to motivate employees and build morale. When someone has done a good job, take a few minutes to acknowledge that effort. You'll be paid back in increased loyalty and commitment. Sending this note via e-mail is fine, but a card or a letter on stationery or company letterhead would add a more personal touch. (For e-mail, simply model the content of the e-mail on the body of the sample message that follows, while using standard e-mail formatting as described previously.)

Essential elements: It's not necessary to go overboard and gush all over a person. Simply state your congratulations and appreciation. Include:

1. What it is you're pleased about.
2. Why this project/service/contribution is especially valued.
3. A word about future work.
4. A thank-you.

Sample:

Dear Lou:

I just finished reading the first draft of the Syntron manual and am very pleased with it.

What amazed me was how quickly you were able to take a mass of unorganized tech specs, memos, and assorted gibberish and edit it into a strong, cohesive introductory product guide.

I'm circulating the manual to the design team for comments now. As you know from experience, when writing about a product still under development, specs change from day to day, so I anticipate a lot of little edits and corrections, which should be easy for you to make. But the basic organization, style, and content of the document are right on target.

Thanks again for the excellent work. I value your contributions to Syntron's success.

Sincerely,

Note of thanks for an extraordinary effort

Background: You know instinctively when you have pushed your employees to deliver service and effort above the norm. When they rise to the challenge, thank them in writing. A small token of appreciation is also a good idea (and a comp day is even better). Furthermore, expressing your appreciation via e-mail is okay, but a card or a letter will seem less impersonal. (For e-mail, simply model the content of the e-mail on the body of the sample message that follows.)

Essential elements: This letter is the "pat on the back" that an employee has earned with effort that goes beyond the call of duty. Make it express sincere thanks by including the following:

1. State exactly what the employee did (he or she will probably put this in a file for future career use).
2. Acknowledge the personal sacrifices that were required.
3. Offer apologies for undue hardships (if appropriate).
4. Say thank you.

Sample:

Dear Jeff:

Thanks for your extraordinary efforts on the GoldSeek version 2.0 beta release. Without the dedication of you and other members of the team, we would never have made this impossibly tight deadline.

You clearly went above and beyond the call of duty, without letting the long hours and steady diet of late-night pizza affect your effort. In addition, I know that you have kids and there are a lot of family and school events around the holiday season. I hope the project didn't interfere unduly, although I suspect it did. And for that, you have my apologies and thanks.

Now, as the holidays approach, you can take the well-deserved rest you need.

Sincerely,

E-mail announcing a promotion

Background: We know of a colleague who went into his employee's office to criticize her handling of a project. She argued back vehemently—too vehemently, he felt, for a subordinate. He reminded her that she worked for him. However, he got a big surprise: He, in fact, worked for her! She had been promoted and the lines of reporting reversed. Embarrassed and upset, he left her office, hoping his new boss would not hold his tirade against him. That's why all employees in a department or workgroup should be told when one of them is promoted.

Essential elements: This kind of correspondence is usually distributed in an e-mail. Be sure to have a group distribution list set up in your e-mail program for the recipients of this message. Make the message short and simple:

1. State the person's full name, his or her old and new positions, and the date the promotion takes effect.
2. Detail how that promotion affects other employees and the chain of command.
3. You may add a note of congratulations if you like.

Sample:

From: Joy Robbins <jrobbins@fictionalfirm.com>
Date: Friday, May 25, 20XX
To: All Department Personnel
Subject: Promotion

Effective June 1, Sheila Anderson is being promoted from shipping clerk to director of shipping operations. She will report directly to me, and all employees designated as shipping clerks, service desk representatives, or order handlers will report directly to Sheila.

I'm sure we all join in congratulating Sheila on this well-deserved promotion.

[*Automatic e-mail signature should appear here; see the sample signatures in Chapter 2.*]

E-mail announcing a retirement

Background: This announcement is routine for you but not for the person retiring, who may have a strong emotional attachment to his or her job, workplace, coworkers, customers, or vendors. Personalizing this announcement with an anecdote or observation makes it more memorable and pleasurable for everyone reading it.

Essential elements: This message serves two purposes: It notifies all employees of the retirement, and it praises the retiree for his or her years of dutiful service. It should include:

1. An announcement of the retirement and effective date. State the person's name and position for employees who may not personally know him or her.

2. A short background history on the retiree, such as when he or she started working with the company and the positions he or she has held.

3. A personal anecdote about a positive experience with the person.

4. A brief description of the person's retirement plans if you know what they are and are sure the person won't mind having them announced.

5. If you plan any kind of retirement celebration, you can add the details to this memo.

6. End with a verbal toast, noting that the person will be missed by all.

Sample:

From: Theresa Gerardo, City Desk Editor <citydeskeditor@fictionalfirm.com>
Date: Monday, March 25, 20XX
To: Newsroom Staff
Subject: Retirement of Stu Gruben

Stu Gruben is retiring from his position as managing editor effective April 1.

Stu started with the *Herald* in the 1960s as a reporter, eventually working his way up to managing editor. When I first started here in the 1980s, I handed in an article in which I referred to a politician having "a surgical procedure." Stu circled it and wrote in the margin, "Why not just say 'surgery'?" I'm sure we've all learned similar lessons from Stu about how to be better journalists.

In retirement, Stu plans to move to Minneapolis to be closer to his children and grandchildren. He told me yesterday he also plans to pursue the novel he has wanted to write. We wish him well.

We are having a retirement party at lunch this coming Friday to honor Stu Gruben as he retires from our staff. A buffet lunch will be served, and we'll all toast to a wonderful and productive retirement for a top editor whom we will all miss.

[*Automatic e-mail signature should appear here; see the sample signatures in Chapter 2.*]

E-mail expressing appreciation for a suggestion

Background: A colleague employed by a large computer company was paid a bonus of $100,000 for a simple suggestion he put into a suggestion box. Your reader isn't expecting $100,000 from you, but a simple message of appreciation is a nice idea.

Essential elements: It's the thought that counts. Convey your support of employee input. Include:

1. An upfront thank-you for the suggestion. (State the suggestion specifically in case the employee has submitted several ideas and needs to know which one you're talking about.)
2. State why you like the idea.
3. If you cannot implement it right away, explain why.
4. Invite the employee to continue to be involved in the implementation of the suggested idea. Or, if that is not appropriate, encourage him or her to continue to share thoughts and ideas in the future.

Sample:

From: George Clark, CFO <CFO@fictionalfirm.com>
Date: Thursday, September 21, 20XX
To: Rhagu Naveen <rnaveen@fictionalfirm.com>
Subject: Thanks for your valuable suggestion

Dear Rhagu,

Thank you for your great suggestion on how to restructure the Artech Web site to give international customers access to pricing and product information specific to their country.

It's something we discussed for this year but didn't implement because of its complexity and our limited budget. Our goal was just to get basic product descriptions up on the site to create an Internet presence for Artech, which we did.

For this year, doing country-specific pages or sites is again on the agenda. We were thinking of picking one country or region as a test site.

Do you have a preference of which we do?

Sincerely,

[Automatic e-mail signature should appear here; see the sample signatures in Chapter 2.]

Announcing bad news

If you're in a position of authority, it will often be your job to be the bearer of bad news. The correspondence that conveys this news should be well crafted so that you never appear to be uncertain or weak.

Announcement of a layoff

Background: Announcing a layoff requires sensitivity and tact and is best accomplished via a printed memo. A layoff is never a happy occasion. If there is realistic hope of a quick solution to the problem, say so in your memo, but do not promise. Encourage supervisors to discuss each employee's situation with him or her separately. The more notification you can give, the better. A sudden loss of employment is always traumatic; be sure to convey that you are sensitive to this.

Essential elements: This memo must be many things at one time: It should be firm, informational, sympathetic, and hopeful. Be sure it includes:

1. An explanation of the negative financial circumstances that have recently affected the company.
2. The announcement that these circumstances (which are beyond your control) require (or may require) employee layoffs.
3. The details, if known, about who will be laid off and when.
4. Assurances that further information regarding all employee status will be forthcoming.
5. A request for continued hard work on remaining projects with the explanation that this is the way to reduce the need for further layoffs.

Sample:

To: Long Island Plant employees, Virtuen Industries
From: Sol Bier, Personnel Director
Re: Employee layoffs

Unfortunately and unexpectedly, Virtuen was not awarded the contract for the EWACS inertial navigational system for which, until recently, we thought we were a shoe-in. The customer preferred the new E-5 technology from Allied Corporation because of its compatibility with GPS-7. We could not certify such compatibility and lost the contract on that basis.

Because EWACS was projected to be a significant part of our total revenue over the next two to three years, we are enforcing a hiring freeze effective immediately and may be looking at layoffs for up to 10 percent of the plant staff within the coming months. At this time, we do not know for certain how many and which employees will be affected by the layoff. However, we want employees to be aware of this potential problem and to plan accordingly.

Supervisors wil be kept informed and will communicate the status of the Long Island plant to employees on a regular basis. Employees having concerns about employment status should see me or their supervisors.

In the meantime, we must double our efforts to implement the new GPS-7 compatible upgrades and to prepare bids for other opportunities now on the table including ELGIN and EAGLE. Even a partial win on just one of these would retain jobs potentially lost due to the EWACS disappointment.

Warning about poor employee attendance

Background: Employees have many legal rights on the job, and the law today seems stacked against the employer. For this reason, every major incident of discipline should be documented and communicated to the employee in writing (in print), with a copy for the employee's personnel file.

Essential elements: If you ever have to fire an employee because of excessive absenteeism, this memo will become an invaluable document. Craft it carefully to cover all your bases:

1. Refer to a company rule regarding absenteeism (if one exists).
2. State that there is a problem with the employee's absentee rate.
3. Give absentee dates and times and details of previous warnings.
4. State that you are very concerned about this problem.
5. Tell the employee what you expect in the future.
6. Outline exactly how all future absences must be handled (doctor notes, advanced approval, and so forth).
7. Give a warning that a copy of the memo will be placed in the employee's file.
8. State what will happen if the problem continues.
9. Instruct the employee to sign on the space provided to verify that he or she has read the letter.

Sample:

To: Bob Brook

From: Danielle Mosely, Manager

Re: Company policy on discipline for excessive absenteeism

The following documents a problem with excessive absenteeism:

On December 7, 14, and 21, you were absent from work. Each of these absences was on a day before your scheduled day off. On December 27, I counseled you about your attendance on the job. You were absent again on January 5 and 16. On January 29, I again counseled you about your attendance on the job and cautioned you that further absences would lead to formal disciplinary action.

On February 1, you called in sick. This was the day before your weekend off. When you returned to work on February 4, you told Bob Sharpe, your supervisor, that you had gone dirt bike riding in the desert. On February 7, I met with you to discuss your attendance. During this meeting, I gave you a verbal warning about your poor attendance record.

I want to be sure you understand that I am seriously concerned about your attendance record. I expect you to be at work, on time, every day you are scheduled to work unless you have a legitimate medical emergency that prevents you from coming to work or are authorized in advance to take time off.

If you are unable to come to work, you must contact Sam Rodriguez in advance. If you miss work for medical reasons, you must submit a doctor's note indicating that you are medically able to return to work before you may begin working. If you want to use some of your accumulated vacation days for time off, you should submit a request at least two days in advance.

A copy of this memo will be placed in your file. Unless you follow this directive, you will be subject to further serious disciplinary action. Please sign below and return this memo to my office before you leave work today.

I have received a copy of this memo:
Bob Brook/Date

_____

Warning about employee attitude problems

Background: The following is another discipline memo, this one documenting a poor attitude. Note how the writer took an arguably vague topic, "poor attitude," and proved it with detailed specifics.

Essential elements: Similar to other warning correspondence, this memo may become the ammunition you will need if you ever need to fire the employee. It is important to show a paper trail of warnings and efforts to help the employee improve. This memo must contain:

1. An immediate statement of disapproval for a specific act. Give the date and time and details.

2. Details about all previous training, counseling, and mentoring experiences given to the employee to teach what is expected.

3. A statement of exactly what you expect the employee to do from now on.

4. The offer of another opportunity for further training, counseling, or mentoring.

5. Notification to the employee that this letter will be placed in his or her file.

6. Explanation of what will happen if the problem continues.

7. Instruction to the employee to sign on the space provided by a certain designated time to verify that he or she has read the letter.

Sample:

To: Jim Shipman, Customer Service Representative
From: Kathy Flanders, Customer Service Manager
Re: Written warning—work performance

Your behavior and attitude toward customers are completely unacceptable, as I witnessed yesterday. As you were assisting a customer at noontime, I walked into the showroom and heard you say, "I am sick of listening to you complain about our products. Did you ever think it doesn't work because you didn't read the manual?" When I asked the customer what had happened, she said she had asked several questions about the owner's manual. She said you were impatient and rude. She said that you had talked loudly to her, almost to the point of shouting.

When I asked you what had happened, you told me, "I am tired of dealing with customers who are too lazy to read the manual." This behavior and attitude are unacceptable. When you joined our company on November 1st, you attended two weeks of customer service training. Our training program emphasizes the importance of working with our customers to meet their needs. Several of the exercises involved role-playing to show you how to work with customers under various conditions. Then, you worked beside Neil Villalos, Senior Customer Service Representative, to learn from him during your first two weeks in the department.

After all this training, you must realize that your primary job is to help customers. When you talk to customers, I expect you to listen carefully to their comments. I expect you to confirm what the customer says by using statements such as, "I believe you are asking . . . ," or "That is a good question. Let's look in the manual for the answer." When you have a problem communicating with a customer, I expect you to ask another Customer Service Representative to help you.

The Training Department is offering a new course on stress management beginning on the 15th of this month. If you would like to take the course, please see Pat Cooper to sign up for it. (I strongly suggest that you do.)

This is a written warning. It will be placed in your personnel file. You must meet or exceed the objectives outlined in the third paragraph. If you do not meet or exceed them, you will be subject to disciplinary action, up to and including termination. Please sign below and return this memo to my office before you leave work today.

I have received a copy of this memo:
Jim Shipman /Date

Notification of termination with regret

Background: When you have to fire someone, do it face-to-face in a private meeting. The letter is merely a confirmation. (The primary circumstance under which you might terminate someone via letter is for a distant employee in a branch or remote office.) The following letter is a sample of what you can say when the employee is fired because of various company circumstances, rather than poor performance, attendance, or attitude.

Essential elements: This letter is the official notification after you have discussed the news with your employee. Be sure to use official company letterhead and write a formal letter—not a memo, fax, or e-mail. It should contain all the details about the termination, benefits, and company assistance:

1. Begin with a note of regret.
2. Note that this letter confirms a previous conversation regarding termination.
3. Give the details about why the employee is being let go.
4. State the terms of termination, which include any severance pay, profit-sharing, retirement benefits, and medical coverage.
5. Explain what the company will do to help this person find new employment.
6. Include a thank-you note for good work and a wish of good luck in finding new employment.

Sample:

Dear Joe,

This is my least favorite letter to write. But here it is . . .

As we discussed on Tuesday, the severe setbacks in our corporate earnings have put a hold on our acquisitions activities. As a result, your position of Business Development Manager has, unfortunately, been eliminated.

To confirm our conversation, your employment will end effective July 22. You will receive severance pay equal to four months' salary. In lieu of profit-sharing for the year, you have agreed to accept a one-time payment of $6,000. Your retirement benefits will be retained by the company until we receive instructions from you. Your medical benefits coverage will continue until you find new coverage for up to a period of one year.

We will assist you in your search for a new job. I have provided a letter of recommendation (copy attached), and you may use me as a reference.

You can continue to use your office during your job search. And you will receive consulting assistance from Black & Change, a leading outplacement firm we have retained to help you and other employees during our current downsizing transition.

Thank you for all your many contributions to this company, and good luck in your job search.

Sincerely,

Notification of termination with just cause

Background: Sometimes an employee just cannot do the job he or she was hired to do. This situation requires a sometimes-lengthy process of verbal warnings, meetings, counseling, and warning letters. But eventually you may have to lower the ax. Firing someone should always be done in person; the letter is sent to confirm the termination and outline the details.

Essential elements: This letter is a confirmation of terms of termination already discussed. It's important to get the terms down in writing so that there can be no misunderstanding. Be sure to use official company letterhead and write a formal letter, not a memo, fax, or e-mail. Include:

1. An opening that states clearly that the person is fired effective by a certain date.
2. State the reasons for the termination with mention of any previous warnings.
3. Impress upon the recipient that this is a logical course of action because you obviously need employees who can do the job they are hired to do.
4. Give the facts about any severance pay, noting when and how it will be paid.

Sample:

Dear Bob:

As we discussed in my office this morning, your employment with Current Sales has been terminated effective March 5. You received several verbal and written warnings about your excessive absenteeism, and each time you gave me assurances that you would shape up and correct the problem. Yet, last Friday, you once again were absent without prior approval or notification. I'm sorry, Bob, but that was your last chance. I'm sure you can understand why we need an employee who is on the job during scheduled hours.

You will, of course, receive the standard two weeks' severance pay. I have already requisitioned a check for you, which will be mailed to your home within the next week.

Sincerely,

7

Communications to Get, Keep, and Satisfy Customers

It's true: The more contact you have with customers, the more likely they are to place their next order with you instead of with your competitor. The reason for this is that customers are bombarded with messages from vendors looking for an order. The more recent your last communication, the more likely they are to think of you first when a need arises.

Therefore, frequent contact with your customers, whether it be by phone, mail, e-mail, or in person, contributes to your bottom line. This chapter gives you model correspondence you can use to boost the quality and frequency of customer communication. The samples cover a wide range of situations—from announcing a product upgrade to getting buyers to renew a subscription, policy, or service agreement.

We have provided sample correspondence in this chapter largely in the form of printed letters or memos because formal letters impart a sense of conscientiousness about your relationship with your customer. However, for nearly all of the correspondence described in this chapter, e-mail is an appropriate medium. Just adapt the actual message portion of the sample letters or memos you see in this chapter to the format and structure of e-mail. (Whenever the sample we provided needed very detailed tweaking to work with e-mail, or when e-mail was the primary recommended way to send a particular message, we've provided a specific e-mail sample for your reference.) As always, be on the lookout for the 🚫 icon, indicating correspondence for which e-mail is not suitable.

Getting business

At their root, all the business letters you write are for the purpose of getting and retaining business. The following samples are ones you can use to directly market yourself, gain new accounts, and retain the customers you have.

Report on results, with price quotes

Background: This kind of letter pulls double duty: It tells prospective customers why they need your product or service and then how much it will cost them.

Essential elements: The letter that reports results and quotes prices has four parts:

1. It explains the results of industry research or of a requested estimate, a consultation, an inquiry, or any other professional information that shows the product or service is necessary.
2. It presents recommendations based on the results.
3. It states an estimate of the cost of those goods or services.
4. It asks the recipient to contact you to proceed.

Sample:

Dear Mr. and Mrs. Magin:

My dental exam of your son, Andy, shows a 1.5 mm space between the upper central incisors, as well as some crowding of the lower front teeth. I recommend the use of a removable plastic and wire appliance to take the upper right central incisor out of crossbite.

The fee for this treatment, including the previously taken diagnostic information and also including subsequent future visits until additional diagnostic data or treatment are needed, would be $600. This can be paid in the following manner: $300 initially, and the $300 balance by five monthly payments of $60 each.

Please call my office and we will answer any questions you may have. If you'd like, we'll make an appointment to fit the appliance. I look forward to hearing from you.

Sincerely,
John Trackman, D.D.S.

Request for referrals

Background: You should ask satisfied customers to refer friends and colleagues to you. Referrals from satisfied customers are just about the best leads you'll ever get. If your clients aren't giving you as many referrals as you want, this is a letter you can use to ask for more.

Essential elements: This letter should be short and sweet and include:

1. A reminder of something the customer liked about your product or service.
2. A request for a favor.
3. Simple instructions to give you the names of people who might benefit from your product or service.
4. A self-addressed, stamped envelope. (This makes it very easy for the customer to respond—but, of course, it is not necessary or even possible if you are using e-mail, because your customer can simply hit the "reply" button.)
5. A thank-you.

Sample:

Dear Joan:

I'm glad you liked the spring catalog I recently sent you. Like you, I'm always on the lookout for new business. So, I have a favor to ask: Could you jot down, on the back of this letter, the names, addresses, and phone numbers of a few of your colleagues who might benefit from knowing more about my services? [*If using e-mail, simply request that the recipient reply with a list of the names, addresses, and phone numbers.*] (Naturally, I don't want anyone whose product line is in direct competition with your own.) Then, just mail the letter back to me in the enclosed reply envelope. [*Eliminate this sentence if using e-mail.*]

I may want to mention your name when contacting these people. Let me know if there's any problem with that. Once again, thanks for the favor!

Regards,

[*If using e-mail, your automatic e-mail signature should appear here; see the sample signatures in Chapter 2.*]

Solicitation for testimonials from clients

Background: After completing a job successfully, you can use this letter to solicit a testimonial from the client. A page filled with testimonials is a very powerful addition to a promotional package and convinces prospects that you are good at what you do.

Whenever a supplier you like asks you to give a testimonial or act as a reference, do it! As one of their reference accounts, you are guaranteed superior service. Once your testimonial or name appears in their marketing materials, the vendor will go to great pains to ensure your ongoing satisfaction.

Essential elements: This letter asks for a favor that may or may not be granted. Give it your best shot by including:

1. An explanation that you are compiling a list of testimonials from satisfied customers.

2. A request for the customer's opinion.

3. Instructions about how to do this (if you are sending a printed letter). This would mean asking the customer to write on the back of the letter and return the letter using an enclosed self-addressed, stamped envelope. (If you are using e-mail, simply request that the customer reply to your message.)

4. A form at the bottom of your printed letter for the customer to sign, giving his or her permission to use the testimonial for marketing purposes, or, if you are using e-mail, a request that the customer express his or her permission in his or her reply.

Sample:

Dear Andrew:

I have a favor to ask of you. I'm in the process of putting together a list of testimonials about my services from satisfied clients like you. Would you take a few minutes to give me your opinion of my writing services? No need to dictate a letter; just jot your comments on the back of this letter, sign below, and return it to me in the enclosed envelope. (The second copy is for your files.) [*If using e-mail, simply request that the recipient reply with his or her testimonial.*] I look forward to learning what you like about my service, but I welcome any suggestions or criticisms.

Many thanks.

Regards,

You have my permission to quote from my comments and use these quotations in ads, brochures, mail, and other promotions used to market your freelance writing services. [*Eliminate this sentence if using e-mail and instead simply request that the customer's reply include a statement granting such permission.*]

Signature _____ Date _____

Request for permission to use unsolicited testimonials

Background: Some clients will send you unsolicited and glowing testimonial letters. It's rare that customers put compliments in writing without being asked to. So, when they do, grab hold of it and ask to use it to promote your business. Before you use the compliments in your promotions, get the client's permission in writing. You can use the following form letter as your base. This is good practice for preventing customer problems. If a customer gets an irate call from his boss, asking, "Why are we quoted in XYZ Supplier's brochure?" and you included a testimonial from the customer without permission, rest assured it will damage your relationship with this customer.

Essential elements: Your letter should include:

1. A thank-you for the kind comments.
2. A request to use these comments to promote your business (try to state specifically how and where you would use them).
3. Instructions to sign and date the bottom of your letter or, if you are sending an e-mail, a request that the customer reply with a statement of permission to use the testimonial.
4. A copy of the testimonial and, if you are sending a printed letter, a self-addressed, stamped envelope in which the customer can return the letter.

Sample:

Dear Ms. Hernandez:

Thank you so much for your letter of February 15 (copy attached). It's always nice to hear when things are going right!

You've said such positive things about us that I'd like to quote from this letter in the ads, brochures, direct mail packages, and other promotions I use to market my writing services . . . with your permission, of course. If this is okay with you, would you please sign the bottom of this letter and send it back to me in the enclosed envelope? (The second copy is for your files.) [*If using e-mail, simply request that the recipient reply with his or her permission.*]

Thank you once again!

Regards,

You have my permission to quote from the attached letter in ads, brochures, mail, and other promotions used to market your freelance writing services.

[*Eliminate this sentence if using e-mail and instead simply request that the customer's reply include a statement granting such permission.*]

Signature _____ Date _____

Explanation of a monthly retainer arrangement

Background: Some customers may want to establish a regular relationship with you by hiring you on a monthly retainer. Customers who request such a relationship may have no idea of what is involved or how it works, so you must spell it out for them in writing before you both enter into an agreement.

Essential elements: Of course, the details of your retainer agreements will vary from this sample, but the letter should always include:

1. Acknowledgment that the recipient either has asked for information about this arrangement or might be interested because of the amount of ongoing work you do together.
2. The monthly fee.
3. Exactly what that fee buys the customer: how much time, what result, any priority advantages.
4. Work that would not be covered by the retainer.
5. The payment schedule.

Sample:

Dear Mr. Glicksman:

You recently mentioned that you are interested in hiring me on a monthly retainer to handle your company's ongoing copywriting and consulting requirements for small projects that need quick turnaround.

My standard arrangement is a monthly retainer that covers one full day's work at our current rate of $1,600. We find that that's a sufficient amount of time to handle requirements of this type. Larger standalone projects (such as our two upcoming mailings) are quoted separately.

Retainer clients get 24- to 48-hour turnaround with priority in handling their assignments and no rush charges. If I spend more than a full day in a given month on your work, you do not get charged extra, as long as my time on your account averages a day a month. If you regularly require more or less service, we can talk about setting the monthly fee upward or downward accordingly.

There is no advanced payment required. At the end of each month, you will be billed the month's fee net 30 days. You can cancel at any time, and you just have to pay for the time spent to date that month. Does this sound like what you had in mind? I look forward to continuing this conversation.

Sincerely,

Offer of renewal at birth

Background: The next time you order something online, notice what happens when you begin the checkout process. A pop-up window may tell you there is a special, and if you order two instead of one, or if you order a companion product, you will get a discount. This is called "upselling," and it is extremely effective. One version of upselling that can be done profitably by letter is called "renewal at birth." This is essentially a brief renewal sent at the time of order. It asks the customer to order more units or a second year of service while paying for the first year or units. Eliot Schein, a direct mail expert, says that, on average, 3 to 5 percent or more of customers will respond positively to the renewal at birth offer.

Essential elements: Every time you send out an invoice, you have an opportunity to sell more products or services by including this type of letter. It should have the following elements:

1. A statement that an invoice is enclosed for a particular order.
2. A discounted offer for more units, upgraded services, new products, or extended service.
3. Instructions about how to take advantage of the offer.

Sample:

Dear Mr. Whitman:

Thanks for ordering MediCare Data Online. Your invoice is enclosed.

If you regularly consult Medicare data in your work, here's a chance for immediate savings. Check the box on the invoice for extended service and pay the amount indicated. [*If using e-mail, you can attach your invoice to an e-mail as a "writeable" document—that is, a document that can be modified—and the recipient can insert a checkmark electronically and send the same document back to you.*] You'll get an updated disk every six months for two years instead of one year. That's four disks instead of two. And you'll save $59 off the regular rate.

When you return payment of this bill, just check the box in the lower right-hand corner to take advantage of this special discount. You'll be glad you did.

Sincerely,

Renewal series

Background: When a contract, subscription, or agreement is about to expire, a series of renewal letters can be used to get customers to continue service. This series of letters can contain as many letters as you'd like to keep sending. We have provided four sample letters to give you an idea of how your letters might progress in content.

Essential elements: The first letter is typically sent four to six months in advance of the expiration date of the service or publication. It is called an "early bird" because, even though you're asking the customer to renew, he or she still has plenty of time to do so. In exchange for renewing early, offer a reward such as a discount, free bonus gift, or extra service. This is your first contact with a customer whose contract is not going to expire soon. There is no need to be too pushy. The letter should read like you're offering a favor. Include:

1. The announcement of an early-bird discount.
2. The name of your company or product and an invitation to continue being a customer.
3. The special benefit of renewing now rather than later.
4. A review of why your service or product is the best.
5. A final request to encourage the customer to take advantage of your discount offer.

The second letter is sent a month or so after the early bird. It reminds the customer that it's time to renew so that service doesn't accidentally lapse. This approach works well for insurance, subscriptions, support contracts, and health plans. It still offers a gentle reminder and a financial incentive to renew the contract. Include:

1. An attention-grabbing introductory statement.
2. The benefit from the service or product you provide.
3. A request for a renewal order.
4. A reminder that this service or product will keep the recipient on top.

The third letter is sent about a month prior to expiration. It reminds the customer that he or she is in the last month of service, and if the contract is not renewed now, service will stop shortly. This letter says, "Time's up." It allows your customer a last chance to renew the contract before it expires. It should include:

1. A boldface expiration notice.
2. An opening statement of regret and surprise that the contract has not yet been renewed.
3. A statement of concern that, as a valued customer, the recipient may miss out on valuable service.
4. A review of the quality and benefit of your service or product.
5. Instructions about how to avoid missing out on continued service.
6. A reminder that the renewal must be done immediately.

The fourth letter is sent at expiration. It is notification that the agreement has expired. It tells the customer that if he or she acts immediately, service can continue on the same terms as if the agreement had never lapsed. This is your last pitch to retain this customer. You've done your best to push a renewal; now you can make one last offer and then it's time to let go. Your letter should include:

1. An upfront "final notice" announcement.
2. A one-time courtesy offer to reactivate the expired contract.
3. An explanation that after this time the rate for signing up for your service or product will be higher.
4. One last plea to renew now and a promise that no further renewal offers will be sent.
5. A postscript, repeating that this is a final offer before the customer's name is deleted from active files.

Samples:

Renewal series letter #1

Special Early-Bird Discount Offer

Dear Mr. Smith:

Renew now and save $55!

If you are enjoying your subscription to *The Journal of Financial Management*, now is the best time to renew. Here's why:

Accept this early-bird renewal now, and you will continue to receive *The Journal of Financial Management* at our lowest rate available. Renew for two years and you save $55. Renew for one year, and save $25. Either way, you win!

This is only a one-time offer. It will not be repeated. To get these savings, you must forward us your renewal instructions right away. In today's complex markets, it's more important than ever to get the expert analytical insights, clear explanations, effective strategies, and proven techniques only *The Journal of Financial Management* provides. Now you can get it more cheaply than ever, maximizing the return on your subscription investment.

Please take advantage of these savings today! Thank you.

Sincerely,

P.S. Remember, you can save up to $55 by sending us your renewal instructions now. The subscription price on subsequent renewal notices will be higher.

Renewal series letter #2

Act Now—Before It's Too Late.

Dear Mr. Smith:

It's true. In institutional investing, financial managers who have access to the best information are the ones most likely to generate the highest risk-adjusted returns—month after month, year after year. That's why it makes sense to renew your subscription to *The Journal of Financial Management* now instead of later.

Each issue lets you pick the brains of the top experts in institutional investment management. Practical applications, innovative methods, and illustrated case studies help you maximize profits, stay way ahead of the competition, and deliver even greater value to your clients all year long.

Even better, renew now and lock in our current lowest rate on a one-year subscription, or get a discount of $35 on a two-year subscription (see the attached subscription renewal form for details). Act now and save!

Sincerely,

P.S. *The Journal of Financial Management* publishes the most relevant, challenging, practical, and significant institutional investment ideas in practice today. No institutional financial manager should be without it. Don't delay. Reply today.

Renewal series letter #3

Subscription Expiration Notice

Dear Mr. Smith:

The other day, I got some rather unexpected bad news.

My circulation manager handed me a list of *The Journal of Financial Management* readers whose subscriptions are about to expire. Despite the fact that we've sent several renewal notices, your name was on it!

I'm concerned that you may not have gotten our previous letters. Whatever the situation, your subscription ends with your next issue, and you should complete and return the attached renewal form now to continue receiving the *Journal* uninterrupted.

As you know, *The Journal of Financial Management* is written for top practitioners in the field *by* top practitioners in the field. Our authors deliver the tools you need to explore the latest theories, test your own concepts, approach traditional investment practices with a fresh perspective, and take advantage of breakthroughs in strategic financial management.

In today's complex markets, the *Journal*'s "inside information" can give you a competitive edge to help you outperform your competitors month after month.

Is this an edge you really want to do without? To ensure uninterrupted service of your subscription to *The Journal of Financial Management* and prevent any missed issues, complete and mail the attached form today.

Thanks,

P.S. To ensure on-time delivery of your next issue of *The Journal of Financial Management*, please give us your renewal instructions today.

Renewal series letter #4

Final Notice

Dear Mr. Smith:

I would like to extend the following one-time courtesy offer to you: Reactivate your expired subscription now to continue uninterrupted service and delivery of *The Journal of Financial Management*. Lock in our low renewal rate. Avoid higher prices that new subscribers will be forced to pay because of increases in printing and postage costs.

Technically, because your subscription has expired, we would normally charge you our regular rate for new subscribers. Because your subscription lapsed only a few weeks ago, I can offer you renewal at the current rate, on a one-time-only basis.

Please take a moment and mail your completed subscription reactivation form today. Your subscription will continue, as if it had never expired. But I urge you to act now. This is your last chance. After this letter, no further renewal offers will be sent. This is the last one you will receive.

Sincerely,

P.S. This is your final notice. Your name has been deleted from our active subscriber files. No further issues of *The Journal of Financial Management* will be sent unless you mail the subscription reactivation form.

Request to reactivate an inactive account

Background: Experience shows that it costs five to 10 times more to acquire a first order from a new customer than to solicit and get a reorder from an existing account. Don't let customers drop out of sight without making an effort to either get them back or find out why they left (so it doesn't happen again). When making your request, you might want to enclose a reply form (questionnaire or survey) the customer can complete and return to indicate the reasons why he or she stopped buying from you. Either attach this to an e-mail or enclose it if you're using a mailing. In some cases, you will be able to overcome the customer's reasons for not continuing with your services and get the business back. But your chances of reactivating a dissatisfied account are slim unless the customer tells you what's wrong.

You may also consider giving a bribe—for example, you can include a catchy phrase upfront, such as *INSIDE: A shameless bribe to get you back* on the front of an envelope or *For a shameless bribe to get you back, keep reading!* at the beginning of an e-mail. Then offer a discount certificate or a free gift to the customer if he or she orders.

Essential elements: You don't want to be too pushy in this situation, but a polite request for an explanation is good business. Your letter should include:

1. The fact that you haven't heard from this valued customer in a certain period of time.
2. An assurance that his or her business is important to you and valued.
3. The simple question "May we still call you a 'customer'?"
4. Instructions to jot a response on the back of the letter and return it in the enclosed self-addressed, stamped envelope (if you are using a printed letter for this correspondence), or a request to simply reply to your e-mail.

Sample:

"We miss you, and we want you back!"

Dear Mr. Smith,

It's been more than 18 months since you last favored us with an order. Did we do something wrong? Your business is important to us, so we would like to know why you haven't been in touch. Could you take a moment to let us know whether we can still call you a customer?

There is no need to dictate a letter. Simply jot your reply on the back of this letter and return it to me in the postage-paid envelope enclosed. [*If using e-mail, simply request that the recipient reply.*] Thank you for your time and effort.

Sincerely,

Daily business transactions

Every day your business success requires communication with your customers. Most rather routine correspondence is offered in this section. You can use these letters, e-mails, or memos as guides to help you with all the occasions you need to say something important to the people who keep you in business.

Follow-up on a sales discussion

Background: After an in-person or telephone discussion with a prospect concerning his or her needs, reiterate your strengths and methods in a follow-up note.

Essential elements: This is a letter that says: "You told me what you needed. Here's how I can help." It should include:

1. A reminder of your sales discussion and the topic discussed.
2. Agreement that the person's needs are vital and that your company can meet them.
3. The details of what you can do for this customer.
4. If appropriate, what the customer can expect to receive from you in the next day or two or, if corresponding by e-mail, any relevant promotional or informational attachments.
5. An offer to answer any further questions.
6. A positive concluding note expressing your pleasure in working together in the future.

Sample:

Dear Ms. Nagel:

I enjoyed chatting with you today about your plans for a new employee benefits program. It sounds exciting!

Proper selection of the right insurance carrier and coverage, of course, is critical to maximizing coverage while minimizing the premium.

That's why, as you requested, I've told ABC Insurance's regional manager in your area to put together a free, no-obligation competitive policy analysis for your review.

Based on a thorough analysis of the various plans offered by the 25 major insurance carriers covering your area, our competitive policy analysis will identify those companies and plans that give you the best value for your premium dollar. And, with our large volume and decades of experience, we are often able to design plans with "tiered" levels of coverage. This allows you to pay for basic coverage for employees, while giving them the option of buying additional insurance for themselves if they so choose.

You'll have our competitive policy analysis shortly. In the meantime, if you have any questions or need additional information, you can reach me at 123-456-7890. [*If using e-mail, draw attention to your contact information in your automatic e-mail signature.*]

We look forward to providing your employees with affordable health benefits, as we have for hundreds of companies and millions of employees (and their families) throughout the tristate area.

Sincerely,

Price estimate for a current customer

Background: When giving price estimates to existing customers, you can opt for a short letter or e-mail instead of a more formal form or proposal.

Essential elements: Current customers know your work and the value of your service. They simply need to know prices for other projects. Make it simple and include:

1. A cordial greeting.
2. A quote of your prices or fees.
3. An alternate service or product if you think the client might like a choice.
4. An estimate of the time required for the job.
5. A request for a response.
6. If appropriate, add a note indicating that you are sending an enclosure or attaching a file with additional information.

Sample:

Dear Rich:

Thanks for coming by. I enjoyed seeing you, as always. I normally charge $10,000 to $12,000 or more for a traditional annual report. The reports typically run 25 to 40 pages with art and photos reproduced in four colors.

For $5,000 to $7,500, I can design a shorter, two-color annual report similar in style and complexity to the one you did last year. I will need approximately 30 days for comps and camera-ready art on disk. Let me know what you think.

Thanks,

P.S. We are sending you separately the two-color samples and my list of recommended printers. [*If using e-mail, you can indicate that you are attaching these documents.*]

Recommendation to a specific customer

Background: While serving an account, you may encounter situations that suggest the customer needs to improve its procedures, whether internally or through the use of more outside vendors. Regardless of whether there is money in it for you or not, you can build goodwill by putting the idea in a letter or e-mail and passing it on to the client.

Essential elements: This kind of message can lead to increased orders for you either directly through your recommendations or through the goodwill you will create by taking the time to offer helpful ideas. Your message should include:

1. A mention of the work currently do for this customer.
2. A suggestion about additional ways to improve the customer's business (if appropriate).
3. A suggestion about how the customer might fix the problem.
4. A closing that makes it clear you're just trying to be of help to a valued customer and that your door is always open.

Sample:

Dear Tom:

I just spoke with Steve about the fulfillment letter and will have a draft for you next week.

Steve mentioned that we get a large number of leads from the ad but many are not qualified and most don't result in business. Based on this, I feel you need some inexpensive means to keep in touch with this database of prospects on a regular basis.

Steve mentioned doing a follow-up telemarketing script to reactivate and requalify old leads, which is a good idea. We can definitely take care of this.

In addition, I think it might help your response if you also have some sort of communication going to this prospect database, ideally once a quarter. This could be as elaborate as an online newsletter or a simple as a series of postcards. Or it could be brief letters accompanying the latest reviews and press clippings on the product. But you need something to remind interested parties that a solution to their needs exists.

Just thought these ideas might help. Let me know if you want to discuss this further.

Sincerely,

Decline of an offer to bid or to provide service

Background: Turning down jobs from existing customers can potentially offend or even anger them. The trick is to say no in a way that makes customers think you are serving their best interests rather than refusing to serve them.

Although you may not be able to help your customer, suggest a vendor who may be better qualified than you to do the job or fill the order in your letter. Or if there is a way you can fulfill part of the order or at least satisfy part of the need, suggest it and say you would be happy to do so.

Essential elements: This letter should include:

1. A thank-you for offering the opportunity to bid or provide a service.

2. A brief summary of what your company provides and what the customer is looking for.

3. Your refusal, with regret, to bid or provide services. The reason will be either that the job does not fall in line with your company's capabilities or that you are simply too busy right now to do the job up to the high standards you know the customer deserves. Note that taking the job under these circumstances would be very costly for the customer.

4. An alternative the customer should consider and how you can help them do that.

5. If appropriate, an offer to bid or provide the service if the customer insists and is willing to pay the price.

Sample:

Dear Kay,

Thanks for allowing us to quote on the "Networking Sales & Marketing Guide." I appreciate the opportunities you give us, including this one.

As you know, our specialty is marketing and promotional materials that stress persuasive selling, marketing strategy, powerful graphics, and arresting design. Your current format for the Sales & Marketing Guides leans more toward a training manual and technical information document, rather than a promotional piece. The bottom line is that while we can do this for you, it's not our strength. Consequently, we probably wouldn't do as good a job as a firm that specializes in documentation and manuals. Besides, our charges would not be competitive. We're thinking you'd be better doing this job with your in-house technical publications department or through a freelance technical writer/desktop publisher. If you need a recommendation on a freelancer, let me know and we can ask around for you. Or, if you still want us to quote on this job, let me know and we will prepare an estimate.

Sincerely,

E-mail request for an extension of a deadline

Background: Missing a deadline is bad business. It can cost you untold losses, not only because it may cost you the job or the next one, but it also hurts your reputation as a reliable businessperson. If you can see that you will not meet an agreed-upon deadline, don't let the day come and go without saying anything. Well in advance of the deadline, request an extension in writing. My advice concerning deadlines is simple and straightforward:

1. Don't miss deadlines.
2. Don't promise what you can't deliver.
3. Negotiate a reasonable deadline before you accept the order, job, or assignment. Don't forget to factor in weekends and holidays.
4. If you need a deadline extension, request it sooner rather than later. Speak up early. People hate surprises.
5. When setting a deadline, specify not only a date, but also a time of day as well as a method of delivery ("November 23, 2010, by 3 p.m. or sooner via e-mail," for example).
6. Request the deadline in writing, and follow up to confirm acceptance. Because it's an urgent request and time is of the essence, send your communication via e-mail.
7. If the need for an extension is due to factors beyond your control (for example, if someone else in the workflow chain failed to deliver and that affected your ability to meet a deadline), point it out, but don't lay blame or make excuses. Simply state the facts.
8. If there is a way you can make up time later to adjust for the current lateness, offer it. For instance, if you are late handing in a layout for a promotional flier, perhaps you can send it to a different printer who can treat the job as a rush priority, and therefore get the printed pieces delivered on schedule.

Essential elements: Don't let this letter sound like you're pointing fingers. State the facts:

1. State the name of the project and the original deadline.
2. State your reasons for needing more time.
3. Offer an alternate deadline.
4. Leave the door open to other possible solutions to the problem.
5. Ask for a response.

Sample:

> **From:** Marion Kelly <mkelly@fictionalfirm.com>
> **Date:** Wednesday, October 4, 20XX
> **To:** Cheryl Sterling <csterling@fictionalfirm.com>
> **Subject:** Deadline for XTH budget and forecast
>
> Dear Cheryl:
>
> We originally set a deadline of October 10 for delivery of the XTH budget and forecast. To date, we haven't received the figures from sales or accounting. Because normal turnaround time for the analysis is five to seven days, we need to rethink the October 10 deadline. I've asked Sherry in sales and Larry in accounting about data status, and they promise raw data to me by tomorrow at noon. If they do this, we can work over the weekend and have the report no later than October 12, and quite possibly by October 11, assuming we hit no weekend computer glitches or missing figures.
>
> Please let me know if this is acceptable to you. If it isn't, let's discuss alternative solutions.
>
> Sincerely,
>
> [*Automatic e-mail signature should appear here; see the sample signatures in Chapter 2.*]

Annual account review notice

Background: Many organizations, such as banks, credit unions, insurance carriers, phone companies, utilities, and raw materials suppliers, send customers monthly or annual statements of their accounts. If you do this annually, use the annual account review letter to resell your organization and its value to the customer. If you do it monthly, the monthly notices are an ideal place to highlight news, new products, changes in service policies, and other items of importance. Note that annual account statements should be mailed to your customer because of their importance to client recordkeeping; consequently, this letter is included in the same mailing, not e-mailed.

Essential elements: There's no end to the kind of information you can get to your customers through this kind of notice. Typically, the letter will include:

1. Notification that the annual statement is enclosed.
2. A brief summary of why your company is tops in the field and the kind of advantages you offer your clients.

3. An invitation to the client to review the information and talk with a representative to review the policy and discuss any possible changes.
4. A thank-you.

Sample:

Dear Policyowner:

Your annual Crest benefit statement is enclosed for your review. It details your policy's current financial growth and status.

Your Crest life insurance policy is one of your most valuable and affordable assets. It is designed to serve your financial and protection needs throughout your lifetime. The guaranteed cash value will increase through time, and, more important, so will your ability to earn dividends that can greatly reduce your out-of-pocket cost of insurance. For 75 years, Crest policyowners have shared in our outstanding performance and prudent leadership.

Please take this opportunity to review and assess your insurance benefits with your Crest representative in light of how your financial needs and circumstances have changed over the past year. Thank you for choosing Crest. We will strive in continuing to earn your trust and confidence.

Sincerely,

Announcement of a new product or service to customers and prospects

Background: When you have a new product or service, all current customers, inactive customers, and prospects should be notified by mail or e-mail.

Essential elements: This is both a piece of sales literature as well as a courtesy call. Make it simple and to the point, but cordial. Include:
1. A statement of a customer's needs.
2. An offer to meet those needs with a new product or service.
3. A clear listing of exactly what you are now offering to clients.
4. An acknowledgment of what is not included (if appropriate).
5. The cost or fee.
6. An invitation to call for more information or to order.

Sample:

To all of my clients:

Many of you have asked for assistance in putting together or enhancing your Websites. I am now offering this service to individual clients. It is something I have already done for more than a half-dozen corporations, including AT&T and IBM. The primary services I'm offering include:

- Content creation and copywriting.
- Website organization, design, and logical link recommendations.
- Editing, rewriting, and writing of Website content.
- Website promotion—getting prospects to visit your home page.

With most clients, Web pages can be built by scanning and modifying printed literature, so all that is required is organization, design, a home page, linkages, and some interactive functionality.

I do not do programming or graphics, but I have available resources to help you with these aspects of your Website. The fee is simple: I charge the hourly or daily rate you are currently paying me, multiplied by the amount of time we agree I should spend to help you.

Call me today at 123-456-7890 for a cost estimate on your project. [*If using e-mail, draw attention to your contact information in your automatic e-mail signature.*]

Thanks once again,

Announcement of a company name change

Background: The announcement of a company name change must catch the reader's attention. This is not junk mail; it fosters one of the most valuable things your company can own: name recognition.

Essential elements: This letter must show your best side. Use quality letterhead paper (with the new name) and perfect writing format and form. Personalize the letter by addressing it to each recipient by name so that it doesn't have a "mass mailing" feel. Include:

1. An exclamatory opening that announces a name change with enthusiasm and excitement.
2. The old name and the new name.
3. The reason for the change.
4. Assurances that quality service/products will continue.

---

5. Any changes the customer can expect.
6. A final reminder of the old and new names.

Sample:

Dear Philip Pottsen:

Important news! You're about to get the same great delivery service you're accustomed to under a new name!

Associated Delivery Service, a leader in transportation, distribution, and logistics since 1953, is now changing its name to **Global Systems** to better represent our expanding range of worldwide capabilities.

This means you get the same on-time delivery, the same fast, responsive service, and the same dedication to excellence you've come to rely on from Associated. But you also get an enhanced system—a one-stop resource with expanded capabilities—for meeting your total shipping and logistics requirements, both domestic and international.

You'll notice our name change soon on all our mailings, packaging, invoices, and promotional materials. It's still the same company, just with a new name.

Remember: Associated Delivery Service is now Global Systems.

Sincerely,

Announcement of an acquisition

Background: Customers generally view acquisitions as an advantage because they offer expanded size, economy of scale, and product or service line. Be sure to announce this good news.

Essential elements:

1. The announcement of the acquisition. Name your company and the company you are acquiring.
2. A brief statement about why this acquisition has been made.
3. An introduction to the acquired company to help your customers better recognize who they are.
4. The advantage of this acquisition to the customer.
5. An invitation to ask questions or gather more information.

Sample:

> Dear Customer:
>
> Industrial Gases is pleased to announce its recent acquisition of all the assets of Becton Industries, a leading manufacturer of valves, manifolds, and other corrosion-resistant gas distribution equipment.
>
> For the past seven years, our corporate mission has been to become the leading supplier of gas solutions for corrosive applications. Our acquisition of Becton brings us one step closer to the accomplishment of that goal. As you may know, Industrial Gases has already been distributing Becton valves in its catalogs. Not only will the acquisition reduce our pricing on these components, but Becton will begin offering custom skid-mounted solutions for Industrial Gases customers. Becton components will continue to be sold under their current model names but through the Industrial Gases sales organization.
>
> If you have any questions or comments, please contact your sales representative.
>
> Sincerely,

Confidentiality agreement

Background: If you have to learn confidential facts about a customer's business to render service or customize products, you gain access to competitive intelligence about the customer's operations. An important part of customer service is taking precautions to make sure this information does not fall into the wrong hands. Some clients may ask you to sign a confidentiality agreement saying you won't share their proprietary information with other people. If the client wants you to make such a promise but doesn't have a formalized confidentiality agreement, you can perform a valuable service by providing such an agreement. You can use the simple confidentiality memo that follows as a model.

Sample:

To: Sue Simpon, XYZ Systems
From: Regina Anne Kelly
Re: Nondisclosure agreement

To render service to XYZ Systems, I agree to the following:

1. "Confidential information" means any information given to me by XYZ Systems.
2. I agree not to use, disseminate, or share any confidential information with my employees, vendors, clients, or anyone else.
3. I will use reasonable care to protect your confidential information, treating it as securely as if it were my own.
4. I won't publish, copy, or disclose any of your confidential information to any third party and will use my best efforts to prevent inadvertent disclosure of such information to any third party.
5. The copy I do for you shall be considered "work for hire." XYZ Systems will own all rights to everything I produce for you, including the copyright. I will execute any additional documents needed to verify your ownership of these rights.

Agreed: _____   Date: _____

Taking care of customers

The correspondence covered in this section will help you stand out from the crowd. It consists of communications that are optional, but smart. They keep you in touch with your customers and let them know you care about their needs and not just your own welfare.

Client satisfaction survey (post-assignment)

Background: A good way to please and retain customers is to ask them if they have any problems with your service or product that you can solve. Try surveying your customers to see if they are pleased. If they respond, thank them and pledge to remedy their complaints. Then make sure you do so.

Essential elements: This survey should give you information you need to better service your customers in ways that may be unique to your business. You can mail the survey or attach it to an e-mail as a writeable document that your recipient can complete and e-mail back to you. Areas of concern you might possibly survey include:

1. A rating for the quality of a specific product or service.
2. A rating for the overall quality of your company's service.
3. A rating to compare the quality of the product or service with the fee.
4. An opportunity to comment on the good things about your product or service.
5. An opportunity to comment on the negative things about your product or service.
6. A space for the person's name (this is optional).
7. Instructions on how to return the form.

Sample:

Dear Valued Client:

Would you please take a minute to complete and return this brief questionnaire to me? (Doing so is optional, of course.) It would help me serve you better—and ensure that you get the level of quality and service you want on every job. Thanks!

1. How would you rate the quality of the copy I wrote for you?
   ◯ Excellent ◯ Very good ◯ Good ◯ Fair ◯ Poor
2. What overall rating would you give my copywriting services?
   ◯ Excellent ◯ Very good ◯ Good ◯ Fair ◯ Poor
3. How would you rate the value received compared with the fee you paid?
   ◯ Excellent ◯ Very good ◯ Good ◯ Fair ◯ Poor
4. What did you like best about my service?

   _____

5. What would you like see improved?

   _____

Your name (optional): _____

Company _____

Please return this form to:
48 Cooper Road Suite #2
Oak Ridge, NJ 07438
[*If sending this form as a writeable document attached to an e-mail, instruct the reader to complete the form and e-mail it back.*]

Referral of a lead to a client or colleague

Background: When you get a request you can't handle, don't just turn the prospect away. Instead, figure out who in your network can help the person. Then put the two of them together. The following sample shows you how to refer an opportunity in writing.

Essential elements: When you offer a client or colleague a referral, try to be very clear about the details so that the person can judge whether this is an opportunity he or she has the time and knowledge to take on. Include:

1. An explanation of what the project is, where the work is coming from, and the offer to pass it on.
2. The reasons why you thought this person or company would be right for the job.
3. More details on the job or the source of the project (if desired).
4. Instructions on what to do next.

Sample:

Dear Tom:

Harry Nerburg, the largest independent publisher of telecommunications magazines, has recently asked me to write a book about wireless voice and data applications. I cannot take on this project right now, but I thought it might be something you'd be interested in.

This could be an excellent way to further solidify your company's leadership position in the industry ("the people who wrote the book") and educate both service providers and end users on the variety and benefits of wireless voice and data applications.

Harry Nerburg is a reputable company that can offer you many opportunities down the line as well. They publish *Computer Connections* and founded *WireCom Magazine*. They are also the number-one publisher of telecommunications books (Telecom Books).

If you're interested, give me a call and I'll hook you up with the publisher over there.

Sincerely,

E-mail suggesting a substitute product

Background: When a customer orders a product, the easiest thing to do is ship it. But what if another product would better meet his or her needs? Taking the time to suggest the substitute, rather than automatically fulfilling the original order, is a value-added service your customers will appreciate. Because this communication can delay delivery of the order, it's best to e-mail it.

Essential elements: Impart a friendly and helpful tone, not one reminiscent of a bait-and-switch sales pitch. Include:

1. An acknowledgment of the original order and its availability.
2. The suggestion that another product might better meet the customer's needs.
3. A description of the substitute product.
4. A comparison of the substitute product to the ordered product in price, quality, and function.
5. A request for further instruction about the order.
6. Mention of a guarantee, if there is one available.

Sample:

From: Patricia Bakos <pbakos@fictionalfirm.com>
Date: Wednesday, June 14, 20XX
To: Bob Donahue <bdonahue@fictionalfirm.com>
Subject: Your recent order

Dear Bob:

We do have the book you ordered, *Career Planning Guide*, in stock, and I'd be happy to send you 12 copies immediately for your outplacement program.

However, we've recently introduced a product that might be a better value for your program: Career Planner 1.0. This software package is an interactive version of the *Guide*. It includes spreadsheets for all the exercises in the book as well as a database for the job seeker to enter contact information for potential employers and networking leads. The software, which runs on Windows 95 or higher, comes with a companion book that is essentially an updated version of *Career Planning Guide*.

Career Planning Guide sells for $29.95 per copy, and Career Planner 1.0 is $49.95 for the book and diskette. But as the enclosed order form shows, our volume discount for software is higher than for books. So, for 12 units, your cost for Career Planner 1.0 is only $37.95 per copy.

Let me know whether you want to order the book or the updated software-and-book package. Your order is covered by our usual 90-day money-back guarantee, so there is no risk of any kind.

Sincerely,

[*Automatic e-mail signature should appear here; see the sample signatures in Chapter 2.*]

Vacation notification

Background: Customers depend on their vendors to be available to help them. When going on vacation, notify customers in writing, whether by e-mail or a printed mailing such as a memo or a postcard. (The sample provided is a memo; adapt it to your chosen format.) Send the notice at least two to three weeks in advance. Customers hate surprises.

Essential elements: The notice needs to be very specific about the dates of your vacation and how business will be conducted in your absence. Include:

1. The dates of your absence.
2. Your plans for keeping in touch with the office (if any).
3. How customers or clients can get in touch with you if necessary.
4. An invitation to talk before the scheduled departure.

Sample:

To: Clients
From: Regina Anne Kelly
Re: April schedule

I will be traveling and out of the office April 21 to 25. I will be in touch with the office via voice mail. (I will not be checking e-mail.) The office will be open during this period, and if you need anything, you can leave a voice mail for me at 123-456-7899, or call me directly at 123-456-7890. Let me know if you have any questions or need additional information before I leave.

Announcement of a new account representative

Background: Whenever customer service personnel change, notify customers immediately of the change. Be aware that in some industries customers tend to stick with a vendor regardless of who their representative is, while in other businesses (stock brokerages and so forth), customers commonly follow the person they're dealing with and move their business to his or her new company. In the latter case, an immediate phone call to follow up on the letter (which can be sent via e-mail if the change will take place immediately) can help reduce customer movement and loss.

Essential elements: This letter must have a very positive and reassuring tone. If the replacement is due to any internal problems, keep this information to yourself. The letter should include:

1. The announcement that the account representative has left (you can state the reasons if they are positive).
2. An introduction to the new account manager that gives his or her credentials in brief.

3. Assurance to the customer that the high level of service he or she has come to expect will continue uninterrupted.

4. If possible, an arrangement for the customer to meet the new representative in person.

Sample:

> Dear Mr. White:
>
> Joe Carr has left our account management team to become a regional manager at our California office. John Newcomb will be your new account manager.
>
> John has worked with us for 11 years in a variety of production-related positions and has a keen grasp of the technical aspects of our product line. We are pleased to assign him to your account, and I'm sure he'll do an exceptional job serving your needs, especially when it comes to training operators and handling support matters. I have been working with John for several weeks to train him in your procedures and to bring him up to date on your account.
>
> I notice you are signed up for our Advanced Process Management seminar for next month at the Hilton. I will attend and bring John with me. Perhaps we can talk and you can meet John in person over coffee in the morning or at the lunch break.
>
> Sincerely,

Keep-in-touch reminder

Background: The more frequently and recently customers hear from you, the more likely they are to think of you when they have a need for your type of product or service.

Therefore, keeping in touch is not only a sales tactic for you—but also a service to the customer. A good example is the postcard your dentist sends that says, "It's time to schedule an appointment!" The patients are reminded to get routine dental care to catch any problems early while maintaining good dental health. The dentist gets more appointments.

Periodic letters and notes to customers help keep your name before them and offer them a chance to update their literature files. This is the kind of letter that can be sent in any form you like: snail-mail, fax, or e-mail.

Essential elements: This is not a sales letter; try to make it sound friendly and helpful:

1. Open with a cordial greeting that states the purpose of the reminder to keep in touch.
2. Offer the customer something new: an updated catalog, product information, an industry news article, a business newsletter, and the like.
3. Give the customer an opportunity to ask for your product or service or information.
4. If desired, you can also give the customer an opportunity to be removed from your customer list.

Sample:

The Encyclopedia of Business Letters, Faxes, and E-Mail

To: Our valued clients
From: Bob Bly, Copywriter/Consultant, and Regina Anne Kelly, Writer
Re: FREE reprints and DVDs on improving marketing communications

This is just a cordial note to keep in touch and offer you a chance to update your files. We'd like to send you, absolutely free, a selection of recent article reprints, DVDs, and copywriting samples. To get any or all of these items, just call or e-mail us. Or, if you prefer, you can complete and mail, e-mail, or fax the form below. [*If mailing a standard letter, state your contact information here. If using e-mail, include a statement that directs attention to your e-mail signature, and attach the form as a writeable document that the recipient can complete and e-mail back to you.*]
Thanks.

Bob Bly and Regina Anne Kelly

P.S. To discuss a potential writing assignment, call us at 123-456-7899. There's no charge for a cost estimate, and no obligation of any kind.
Please send me the following free items:
Articles
____ "29 Articles You Can Use in Your Company Newsletter"
____ "Getting More Pick-Up from Your Press Releases"
New DVDs
____ 815—"How to Create Great Collateral"
____ 816—"What's Working in Direct Mail Today"

Recent Copywriting Samples

___ Direct-mail packages—business-to-business newsletters, Internet-based services, directories.

___ Direct mail packages, consumer newsletters.

___ Call me to discuss a potential assignment.

___ Please remove my name from your valued client list.

Name _____

Title _____

Company _____

Address _____

City _____

State _____

ZIP Code _____

Phone _____

Fax _____

E-mail Address _____

Website _____

Being courteous

It's always smart business to be courteous to your customers. Take the time to write any one of the following this week and watch what happens to your relationship with your customers!

New customer welcome

Background: A growing (although still not widely used) practice in business is to send a "Welcome Kit" to new customers. The benefits include increased customer goodwill and an opportunity to clearly communicate terms, conditions, ordering information, and other important information.

The kit can include standard documents (brochures, catalogs, labels, air-bills) as well as documents written specifically for the kit. The first of these is usually a cover letter as shown on page 164.

Essential elements: This letter is not a sales letter; it is a welcome letter that supplies information. It should include:

1. A thank-you for the order or business.
2. A referral to enclosed company literature.
3. An introduction to the area sales manager (if appropriate).
4. An open invitation to call for information or service.

Sample:

Dear Mr. Singer:

Thank you for your order last week. We're delighted to be doing business with you.

To give you a better feel for who we are and what we do, I've enclosed our corporate capabilities brochure and latest purchasing catalog. On page 2 of the catalog, you'll find our terms, conditions, shipping, and return policies.

Our sales representative serving your region, Joe Young, will contact you to set up an appointment. He can explain our product line more to your liking and answer any questions you may have.

In the meantime, if there's anything I can do to help serve you better, please call me directly at 123-456-7890.

Sincerely,

Thanks to a customer for a referral

Background: We can tell you from personal experience that not thanking someone for a referral irks him or her. However, most people don't even acknowledge the referrals you give them! When that happens, we assume the referral is not appreciated, and we are more likely to refer someone else the next time if an alternative vendor comes along whom we like and trust. To keep this from happening when you get referrals, use the simple letter that follows.

Enclose a small but tasteful gift as a thank-you for the referral. (When we thank someone for a referral to a writing assignment, we enclose an autographed copy of one of our books.) You should send the thank-you and the gift regardless of whether the referral results in an order. It's the thought that counts, not the result.

Essential elements: This is short and sweet, but it packs a strong message:

1. Open with the details of the job you have been contacted about.
2. Acknowledge that you know that the person you're writing to referred the work.
3. Explain why this referral is so pleasing to you.
4. Give your sincere appreciation.

Sample:

> Dear Ilise:
>
> Yesterday I received a big assignment from BWJ Advertising, and Gale Krashner, the creative director, told me that you were responsible for my getting the business.
>
> I was pleased to get the project, Ilise, but even more pleased that you thought well enough of me to recommend me to Gale. Considering the source, it's an endorsement of the highest caliber, and I appreciate it sincerely. Thank you.
>
> Cordially,

Thanks to a customer for business

Background: A.L. Williams, the life insurance tycoon, once observed that "you beat 90 percent of the competition just by being competent." Sales trainer Paul Karasik agrees: "Success means doing the little things exceedingly well." One thing businesses don't do nearly enough of is thank customers for their patronage.

It's a small thing, but if neglected, it can cause a slow-burning resentment among good customers. Done properly and frequently, it can help you beat the 90 percent of competitors who don't pay attention to these little details. The best time to thank someone for their business is immediately after they've given it to you. The recent communication makes the message seem fresher and more relevant.

Essential elements: This letter or e-mail can serve two purposes: It says sincere thanks, and it also reminds the customer of your special services or features. Include:

1. An upfront thank you for a recent order or patronage.
2. An acknowledgment of past business dealings.
3. Things you've done to ensure top-quality service or product.
4. A wish for future success.

Sample:

Dear Ms. Camico:

I want to thank you again for choosing the Atlantic Reef as your head-quarters during the five days of the Manager's Conference. It's people like you who make the hotel business rewarding and satisfying.

Of course, I know you didn't choose the Atlantic just because it was the site of the exhibit hall. You have regularly booked the Atlantic whenever you have an event in our region, and of course we are delighted to have you do business any time you visit the coast.

To make each stay the best it can be, we strive to provide you with total support for all your event management needs. For instance, we didn't add our new videoconference center just for your group's executive board, but we were thinking about your need for videoconferencing when we made the decision to build it. I'm glad you found it so helpful in linking with your Swiss office on this trip.

I hope you had a good trip back to California and were satisfied with the CD duplicates of your breakout sessions made by Sound Enterprises.

Sincerely,

Message accompanying an article sent to a customer

Background: Regularly sending articles of interest to customers, along with a short note, is a great customer communication strategy. Your customers will appreciate the fact that you're thinking of them. In addition, people like getting articles on topics related to their business. We have had many prospects and customers tell us that the articles we send are appreciated and made them think of us when they needed to buy what we were selling. The best articles to send are those by or about you. But any article related to the reader's business, products, markets, or industry will be of interest. Try sending articles. It works!

Essential elements: This is neither a sales letter nor a request for business, nor is it an opportunity to pitch a new product. Rather, it is a random act of kindness that shows you are thinking about your customers and what they are interested in. Make it simple. You can attach your article to an e-mail as a link or a PDF and include:

1. A statement that says you saw this article and thought the reader might be interested.
2. A comment about why you know this is a subject of interest.
3. A wrap-up wishing the reader well.

Sample:

Dear Mr. Martin:

I saw the attached article in this month's *Business Magazine*, and I thought it was something you'd be interested in reading. We've talked in the past about the difficulty resellers have when choosing a leasing company. This article gives a few very helpful tips. I hope you find it useful.

Best regards,

Letter accompanying a gift to a customer

Background: You want to make your customers happy. People like to get presents. By sending an occasional inexpensive and tasteful gift, you go a long way toward building goodwill—and your customers will fondly remember your name. A simple letter that accompanies the free gift is all that is necessary.

Essential elements: There's not much to say here besides:

1. The gift is to say thank you.
2. You look forward to working together more in the future.

Sample:

Dear Ms. Roth:

The enclosed gift is our way of saying "thanks" for the business you gave Jane Edleman Associates last year. We look forward to servicing your needs in the future. Enjoy!

Sincerely,

Personal congratulations to a customer

Background: Although this is a book of business letters, not every letter a businessperson writes is about business. Addressing the personal side of a customer's life on appropriate occasions is an effective technique for strengthening the bonds between you. This type of correspondence is intended for congratulating a customer on a nonwork-related achievement.

Essential elements: This has nothing to do with business, so don't use it as an occasion to sell. Simply include:

1. The event warranting congratulations.
2. The fact that you're impressed, happy, pleased, or proud.

Sample:

Dear John,

I read in this morning's *Record* that John Jr.'s soccer team, the Screaming Eagles, won the East Division Title in Sunday's game. Congratulations to John Jr. I'm sure he must be thrilled!

And congratulations to you too. I know how dedicated you are to being a team coach and the late hours you put in to accommodate this time-consuming activity around your busy work schedule. Although it's an effort I do not duplicate, I admire it immensely.

Sincerely,

Customer survey letter and form

Background: One of the best ways to find out what your customers need is simply to ask them. The customer survey form is a good idea when you're looking to add products or services to your line. When you send a survey to customers, you need to include a cover letter indicating what you are sending and its purpose. The following sample is a model letter to accompany your survey.

E-Mail Empowerment Tip

For the convenience of your customers, you might wish to send an e-mail message about the survey that contains a link for completing the survey online, if you have the technological know-how to do so. Your customers will appreciate your consideration of their time. In addition, you can improve the odds of getting a response to a survey if you offer a free gift in return for completing it.

Essential elements: You're asking someone to give you their time, so ask nicely:

1. Acknowledge that you're asking a favor.
2. Give the details about why you're interested in the customer's opinion.

3. Give instructions about how the survey should be completed and returned.

4. Flatter the reader by explaining why his or her opinion is so valuable to you.

Sample:

Dear Direct Marketer:

Would you do me a favor? Tell me about your wish list.

Right now, I'm planning a special half-day executive briefing called "Database and Direct Marketing: How to Double Your Response Rates This Year." I'll be inviting you and a select few other direct marketing professionals to attend this informative seminar without charge.

Before I finalize the program, I want to gauge your interest and find out which topics are most important to you. So, if you could please take a moment to complete the attached survey, it would be greatly appreciated. Please fax it back to me at 123-456-7890. [*If using e-mail to send an Internet link to an online survey, direct your customers to follow the link and complete the survey online.*] You are one of the best in this business, so I value your opinion. Your response will help me offer the topics that will be most beneficial to you and other direct-marketing professionals.

Sincerely,

P.S. If it's easier, you can also respond by phone. Call 800-555-5555 and ask to speak to my assistant Philip Paine at extension 1234.

A simple survey

Background: The following short-form customer survey will give you an idea of the format to use in your own survey.

Sample:

Complete and return this form today:

1. Would you be interested in attending a special FREE half-day executive briefing, "Database and Direct Marketing: How to Double Your Response Rates This Year"?

   ○ Yes ○ No ○ Possibly

2. Which of the following topics would you be most interested in discussing at the seminar? (1 = low interest, 5 = highest interest)

Choosing mailing list brokers
List selection
Testing
Saving money with net-name arrangements
Merge/purge
NCOA processing
Database marketing

3. Other Comments:

Name _____

Title _____

Company _____ Phone _____

Address _____

City _____ State _____ ZIP Code _____

Dealing with problems

If you have customers, you're going to have problems. Dealing with these problems in writing is a good way to get down the facts and offer possible solutions. The following samples will give you a guide.

Negative commentary letter

Background: Sometimes a client or customer will ask your opinion, and your answer won't be what he or she wants to hear. A letter or fax is a nonconfrontational way of presenting your response, without the awkwardness of a face-to-face confrontation. It also gives the person being criticized time to think about your comments and a response, rather than responding on the spot in a way that may be defensive, which may happen with e-mail or a phone call.

Essential elements: This letter needs to sound helpful not critical. Include:

1. A positive statement to open.
2. A statement about what's wrong.
3. A detailed explanation (or list) of problems you see.
4. A suggestion for solutions and next steps.

Sample:

To: Harry Mostly
Via: Fax
From: Bob Bly
Re: New A&B-Shield letter

Dear Harry:

Although your A&B-Shield letter is very well written, I do not think it will work. Here's why:

1. You are selling two separate things in one mailing: a Web-based upgrade to A&B-Shield, and a support program. You should sell one thing in one mailing. These offers should be promoted in two separate mailings.

2. The Web-based version should be positioned as an upgrade of the Windows product and should therefore be offered via mail order at a fixed price that represents some discount off the list price—that is, existing A&B-Shield users should get it at a deep discount of 50% or more.

3. The new Web-based version and the new partnership program are totally unrelated. I should be able to buy the upgrade for a fixed price, just as I bought my Windows version, by mail, without committing to a monthly partnership fee.

The partnership might work as a more formalized support program. However, that's a separate mailing, and we would have to give much more value and benefits than outlined here.

Follow-up after not getting a customer's order

Background: A good practice is to send a short note to customers and prospects when you do not get their order. Thank them for their consideration and then praise, rather than criticize, the decision they made. You can do this through e-mail, a fax, or a memo or letter.

This has several benefits. For one, it creates a professional image and is contrary to the sour grapes the customer might get from other suppliers (your competitors) who also didn't get the order. At the same time, you can correct wrong impressions that may have led to your not getting the job. Even though you lost this sale, you can set the stage for repeat inquiries (and eventually, a new order) from this customer.

Also, if you know whom the customer has chosen, be sure to say something good about that firm. If there was a selection factor the customer overlooked or did not know about, let him or her know about it. Perhaps you'll get called if the first supplier doesn't deliver.

Essential elements: Don't sound too disappointed—sound optimistic! Include:

1. A thank-you for the opportunity to bid (or give a sales presentation or proposal).

2. A statement saying you're happy the customer found someone qualified to do the job.

3. Add a piece of additional information that would be interesting to this client.

4. Request to be given the chance to bid on another project.

5. A small piece of flattery.

Sample:

> Dear Karen:
>
> Thanks for the opportunity to bid on the Fergeson job. I'm glad you could find someone who can meet your requirements so quickly, especially given your tight deadline.
>
> In the future, please keep in mind that we just became a dealer for a new supplier that manufactures a midrange product ideal for your work. It isn't the premium brand like the Insu-Range we normally use, but it fits your specifications and is 20 percent cheaper.
>
> Please keep us in mind for your next job. We are always glad for the opportunity to send a bid to a quality company like yours.
>
> Best wishes,

Announcement of a store closing

Background: Announcing the closing of a business is more than a formal courtesy. Often there is inventory, office equipment, real estate, or other assets that need to be disposed of. By selling them, the owner can pocket a handsome sum and avoid large losses.

The notification of closure letter can be used to promote the going out of business sale. An effective offer is to sell the remaining inventory and assets at a discount given to past customers and shoppers.

Essential elements: Whether you're happy or sad about closing your business, this correspondence should convey good news to the reader. Make sure it includes:

1. The announcement that you're going out of business.
2. If desired, the reason for closing.
3. The savings you're offering to your customers.
4. Dates of sale and store hours.
5. Final closing day.

Sample:

> Dear Preferred Customer and Friend:
>
> Al's Men's Store is quitting business. And that means a sale with our best prices ever!

After 30 years, I am retiring, and we are having an absolutely incredible "going-out-of-business" sale. Our entire inventory of men's clothing is on sale during this huge discount sale. Even the store fixtures and equipment are for sale.

Unfortunately for me (but fortunately for you) our vendors could not cancel our last orders after we notified them of our closing. This new merchandise has been shipped, and we have to unload it fast! You will probably never have a chance to buy quality clothing in these brands and styles at these incredible low prices anywhere else, ever again!

You should not miss this event! Beat the rush and shop now! As a preferred customer, you have first choice of all merchandise at rock-bottom liquidation prices. If you have a friend or relative you want to share this opportunity with, simply bring them (and this letter) with you when you come to the store.

Our going-out-of business hours are Monday through Saturday, 10 a.m. to 7 p.m. This is a wonderful opportunity to save money. We're ready to move merchandise. Everything must go (so I can go fishing in Florida).

Come now. This sale ends January 21, and then we close our doors forever!

Sincerely yours,

Response to a customer complaint

Background: One essential technique for ensuring customer satisfaction is to respond to complaints promptly and with genuine interest in solving the problem. The sample provided here is an e-mail that author Robert Bly sent to a client who wasn't happy with an ad that he wrote for him and who wanted him to adjust the bill downward. As you can see, Bob Bly complied, but he also addressed the issue more broadly to prevent recurrence.

Essential elements: When you write to a customer in response to a complaint, you must walk the fine line between keeping the customer happy and being walked all over. Include:

1. An acknowledgment of the complaint and a statement about valuing your business relationship.
2. An explanation of how you perceive your obligation to the customer in this circumstance.
3. An explanation of how you perceive the customer's obligation.
4. A request for agreement to avoid similar situations in the future.
5. A request for a response.

Sample:

From: Robert Bly <rwbly@bly.com>
Date: Wednesday, November 6, 20XX
To: Mike <mhs@fictionalfirm.com>
Subject: Deadline for XTH budget and forecast

Dear Mike:

Thanks for your memo. Obviously, I value our long-term relationship, and if you want to discuss an adjustment to this bill, I'm happy to do so. I do want to be clear about the conditions under which I work for clients. When you ask me to do an ad, letter, or other piece of copy, I guarantee your satisfaction. I do this by offering unlimited rewrites at no extra charge—something almost no other writer does. I can't guarantee anyone's satisfaction with the first draft, of course. But I can and do guarantee your satisfaction with the rewritten copy. It is my responsibility to listen and polish until you're happy.

At the same time, it's the client's responsibility to let me know if he's unhappy and to tell me where the copy didn't meet his expectations. If a client doesn't take advantage of my free rewrite service, they are then billed for the agreed-upon amount. If they later decide to have me revise, there is generally no charge, provided the request is made within a reasonable period of time. Does this sound like a reasonable way for the two of us to work together?

It would require that you let me know when you're unhappy with something. In return, I will correct any defects in a timely manner to ensure your total satisfaction. Fair enough? Let me know your thoughts.

Sincerely,

Response to complaints about price increases

Background: The best way to avoid complaints about price increases is not to raise them too frequently (once a year is enough for business products and services) or too much at one time (no more than 10 percent per increase).

You may still get complaints because no one wants to pay more. At the same time, your customers know that prices on everything go up. Most will eventually accept this if it is patiently explained. Some will not, and with every price increase, you may lose the bottom percentile of your customer base to lower-priced vendors.

Essential elements: When you raise prices, you're bound to hear complaints. Don't just ignore them, use them as an opportunity to communicate with your customers and build goodwill. Make sure you include:

1. A note of appreciation for taking the time to complain.
2. An agreement that no one likes to pay more.
3. An explanation of why prices must go up occasionally.
4. An assurance that you work hard to keep prices affordable.
5. An offer to work with this person to find a way he or she can continue to afford your product or services.

Sample:

Dear Annette:

I appreciate hearing from good customers like you about our recent price increases on components and subassemblies.

No one likes paying more, and we do not raise our prices at a whim. But when the manufacturers whose products we stock and distribute raise their prices to us, we have to pass on at least part of that cost increase to you.

Our price increases are a result of Tension Tools and other major suppliers raising their prices across the board—from 10 to 20 percent or more, depending on the item. This reflects higher production costs they incur due to increased materials prices and higher standards. If you compare our prices with other distributors, you'll find we are right in line and usually lower for the brand names listed above. Some of the biggest distributors can beat some of our prices on some orders. But as you know, our Total Supply Management Solution keeps your overall cost of goods lower when you buy from us in volume.

Our price per unit on Tension and other major brands is as low as it can be. If you need to cut component costs further, give me a call. Perhaps we can substitute compatible components from alternative manufacturers.

Sincerely,

Sample virus protection policy

Background: It is possible to lose a client if the client feels he or she may have received a computer virus from an e-mail you sent. We find that having a virus protection policy and giving every client a copy of it is a good measure.

Computer viruses can cause customers significant headaches and expense. By helping to keep their computers free of viruses, you are performing a valuable customer service.

Essential elements: If you perform a customer service that's valuable to your customers, make sure they know about it. Explain to new and existing clients in writing the steps you take to prevent the files you send from being contaminated with viruses. Here is a sample antivirus protection policy you can send via e-mail, fax, or letter.

Sample:

To: All clients and potential clients
From: Bob Bly
Re: Our antivirus policy

Because I know we are all concerned about computer viruses infecting our online business relationships, my company has outlined a virus protection policy that I wanted you to know about so you can feel more comfortable doing online business with me. Take a moment to read the policy and then be sure to give me a call if you have any further questions or concerns.

Antivirus Policy

1. We make every effort to ensure that files sent to our clients are virus-free, but we cannot guarantee it.

2. We run Carumen 3.5 VirusScan, which is the most widely used antivirus program worldwide. 50 million people, 90 percent of the Fortune 1000, and 400,000 organizations use it.

3. According to Carumen, VirusScan technology has been shown in lab tests to detect virtually every virus. These include boot, file, multiparties, stealth, mutating, encrypted, spyware, and polymorphic viruses.

4. Because new viruses crop up all the time, we routinely upgrade our VirusScan program by downloading the latest versions from the Carumen BBS (bulletin board). We recommend that clients running VirusScan do likewise.

5. Even running the latest antivirus software cannot guarantee a virus-free file with absolute certainty, because of the new viruses that are constantly launched. Clients should run the most recent version of whatever antivirus software they use.

6. If you open a file we send you via e-mail and it contains a virus, it does not mean it had a virus when we sent it from our end: Files sent via the Internet can pick up viruses in transit.

7. The only 100-percent foolproof protection against receiving a virus is to request that documents be faxed instead of e-mailed. You can't pick up a computer virus from hard copy.

8. If you have any problems with a virus in a file we send you, please notify us immediately. If you are having a virus problem in general, we can refer you to computer consultants who may be able to help.

8

Business and Consumer Complaints and Requests

According to the White House Office of Consumer Affairs, 68 percent of customers who leave a business (and never go back) do so because a manager, owner, or employee has treated them with indifference. In addition, 96 percent of dissatisfied customers don't bother to complain; they simply stop buying. Even worse, the average dissatisfied customer tells eight to 10 people about his or her negative experience with you.

In this chapter, you will find model correspondence for making and handling complaints and requests as both a businessperson and a consumer. In an ideal situation, a person makes a request and you oblige. Everybody's happy. But in the real world, you simply can't do what everyone asks you to do. When this happens, it's a good idea to put your refusal into writing so there can be no misunderstandings. The following samples will give you a good idea how to say no and yet remain on good terms.

E-mail is an appropriate medium for nearly all of the correspondence described in this chapter. Just adapt the actual message portion of the sample letters or memos you see in this chapter to the format and structure of e-mail. (Whenever the sample we provided needed very detailed tweaking to work with e-mail, or when e-mail was the primary way to send a particular message, we've provided a specific e-mail sample for your reference.) As always, be on the lookout for the Ⓢ icon, indicating correspondence for which e-mail is not suitable.

Business requests

Refusal of an unrealistic request from a customer

Background: Sometimes we cannot (or are unwilling to) do everything a customer asks us. But even when customers are at fault or their expectations are unrealistic, they may be irritated by our refusal. That's why the refusal should be made in a firm but polite message that explains your reasoning and, when possible, offers alternative solutions.

Essential elements: This is the kind of message you can write in response to returned merchandise or a refund request. The details, of course, will be different depending on your product and the customer's request, but you should include:

1. An acknowledgment of the request and an apology for the dissatisfaction the customer feels.
2. A firm statement of your policy regarding the topic of complaint.
3. The details about why the request is unrealistic.
4. If appropriate, a compromise solution.
5. An offer to talk further.

Sample:

Dear Mr. Kane:

I received the wildlife prints you returned and your request for a refund. I'm sorry you are unhappy with this merchandise. However, we offer a refund only on merchandise returned within 30 days in good condition. According to our sale records, you bought these prints more than 14 months ago. They are a discontinued series, and we no longer stock them.

In addition, the prints are wrinkled and discolored, as if they had been exposed to bright sunlight or moisture over an extended period. Therefore, even if we did still carry them, these particular prints could not be resold. Based on the condition of the merchandise and the expiration of our guarantee period, we would not normally grant a refund. But we do value you as a customer. What I can do, based on your preferred customer status with us, is give you a credit for 50 percent of the purchase price of these prints, which would equal $125.

I hope you find this solution satisfactory and fair. If you have any questions or concerns, call me at 123-456-7890 and we can talk further.

Sincerely,

Refusal of a business request

Background: The following model can be adapted easily to your needs. In this situation, a potential client asked for a memo, which typically involved a fee, to be prepared on speculation. The potential client's logic was that it offered the opportunity for the company to get new business; he did not realize that there was already more than enough business and speculative work was not needed. The model shows the reply sent in response to his e-mail:

Essential elements: Refusing a request is a sensitive area. It should be dealt with honestly, succinctly, and directly. Doing so via mail, fax, or e-mail is better than via telephone or in person, because it lets the recipient understand your reasoning before reacting. The letter should include:

1. A direct "no" (cushioned with an "I'm sorry"). Make refusals firm. Don't be ambiguous. Don't hint that you're flexible if you aren't.

2. A short explanation of your reasons (nothing too detailed; no time or no budget are usually good enough). However, don't just say what you won't do, also say what you would be willing to do to help. For example, if you can't sponsor a fundraiser, maybe you could donate some of your products as a door prize.

3. An offer to do something else (less costly or time consuming) to help.

4. A wish of good luck.

Sample:

Dear Richard:

Sorry, I can't help you on this one. Right now, I'm just not interested in convincing anyone to do direct mail. I'd rather work with clients who are already convinced. Also, my schedule does not allow me to write a proposal on spec for something that is so uncertain at this point.

To support your meeting in Denver, you are welcome to use any of my materials. Often my book on direct mail helps people decide to enter the business. If you'd like another copy, I'll be happy to send you one. Just let me know what materials you'd like and I'll send them to you via express mail.

Good luck on this project.

Sincerely,

Refusal of a request to advertise

Background: Frequently, companies are asked to advertise in media that would support a local community cause but would not be a cost-effective use of the firm's advertising dollars. You can use this short note to politely decline to participate without offending the person who extended the invitation.

Essential elements: A simple no won't do here. It can cause ill feelings and hurt business down the road. Take the time to explain your reasons and maintain a cordial relationship. Include:

1. Appreciation for the offer.
2. A regretful decline to advertise.
3. The reasons you will not be buying an ad (budget restraints or target market problems are acceptable reasons).
4. If desired, a helpful referral to more appropriate business types (best not to name a particular business).
5. A thank-you and wishes for success.

Sample:

Dear Brett:

I appreciate your invitation to purchase an advertisement in *Smalltown Annual*. Thank you.

Unfortunately, we will not be able to contribute an ad this year. Many thousands of service club books are published each year, and it is impossible for us to purchase advertising in all of them. National advertisers like us are forced to spend their money where the message gets into the hands of purchasing managers, office managers, principals, and others who buy in large quantities. Your market doesn't match these needs.

I expect that you will have to rely mainly on local community businesses to purchase space in the *Annual*. Many businesses feel a strong obligation to support worthy community activities; just having their names associated with your *Annual* is a strong incentive. Indeed, we feel the same way about *Central City*, which is our home base.

Thank you for thinking of us, Brett, and best wishes for the most successful *Annual* that has ever been published.

Cordially yours,

Decline of a request for a donation

Background: When saying no to a fundraiser, the important thing to remember is that your refusal to donate does not mean you don't support the cause. If you point out that there are limitless fundraisers competing for a limited amount of your company resources, your refusal will seem reasonable and acceptable.

Essential elements: Keep the door open to goodwill by including:

1. A thank-you for the invitation to donate.
2. An acknowledgment of the good work the organization does.
3. A statement of decline, with regret.
4. A statement keeping the door open to possible donations in the future.
5. A wish for success.

Sample:

Dear Mrs. Mintzer,

We carefully study all requests for contributions we receive and we thank you for inviting us to donate to the Anytown Symphony Orchestra.

Although we all unanimously agree that the Anytown Symphony Orchestra contributes much to the community—as well as to the performers themselves—we can't, unfortunately, provide financial support at this time.

I do hope that in the future we will be in a position to provide some funds for the Symphony. In the meantime, we wish you success with your efforts on behalf of this excellent organization.

Sincerely,

Business complaints

As a businessperson, you not only get complaints from customers, you may often find yourself in a position to be making a complaint. The following letters will help you find the words you need when things aren't going right and you want to tell someone about it.

Business-to-business complaint

Background: This is a complaint letter from one business to another. Avoid e-mail for this correspondence because of its potential to incite an immediate, defensive response from your correspondent. Additionally, using a printed letter will help you better document your complaints and their outcomes.

Essential elements: There are a thousand reasons you might write to complain to another businessperson. Use this sample as a guide to make sure you include:

1. A direct statement of your complaint.
2. Specific details of the problem (don't give a vague or general complaint).
3. An acknowledgment of the fact that you value your business relationship with this person and want to work out the problem.
4. A course of action you would like the recipient to take to resolve the problem.
5. A cordial and upbeat ending.

Sample:

Dear Richard:

I am writing because I feel that communication between us is deteriorating and will soon affect my ability to continue doing business with your firm. I have found that in the past month I cannot discuss our company sales policies without feeling very defensive, faced with your immediate negative responses.

The example that comes quickest to my mind occurred last Friday. If you remember, I simply wanted to ask if it was possible to transfer your discount credit to next month's order, but ended up arguing the value of the discount policy in general.

I value our relationship very much and I think you have a terrific service to offer. But our ability to do business suffers when our communication breaks down and we don't understand each other. If you have complaints about our overall business arrangement, please let me know so that we can get the problem out in the open. Otherwise, I need you to listen before you start arguing when I call with a question. Let's try this one again: "Is it possible to transfer your discount credit to next month's order?"

I look forward to continuing our business relationship in a positive and cordial manner.

Sincerely,

Intraoffice complaint

Background: Some businesspeople use the term *client* to refer to people within their own company. Many line managers (managers with profit and loss responsibility) view service departments within their companies (information systems, marketing, communications, technical publications, shipping and logistics, and so forth) as "vendors," and the people in the company whom these vendors serve are considered to be "clients."

This view is more accurate than ever before: With downsizing, service departments are usually the first to be cut; line managers are more likely to retain their jobs. The rising popularity of outsourcing gives managers more flexibility than ever in "farming out" computer programming, package design, technical writing, and other functions previously performed in-house. Therefore, the "clients" really do have a choice. Accordingly, the service department needs to treat them as clients, not as burdens or annoyances.

This customer-focused orientation toward internal clients will only become more critical as time goes on. Look for people who you formerly thought of as co-workers to treat you as a vendor and think of themselves as customers, as in the following sample.

Essential elements: These days, this kind of correspondence is usually sent by e-mail, but be careful of your tone if you take this route. You do not want to burn any bridges or kill working relationships, while at the same time you should get right to the point. Any intraoffice complaint should include:

1. A concise statement of the problem.
2. Any history of correspondence about this problem.
3. How this problem affects others in the company.
4. An acknowledgment of the difficulties surrounding this problem.
5. If appropriate, a statement acknowledging that the client has other options and is willing to exercise them.
6. A statement of exactly what you expect the recipient to do to remedy the problem.
7. A request for a reply.

Sample:

From: Kim Kohad <salesmanager@fictionalfirm.com>
Date: Thursday, March 4, 20XX
To: Steve Mahal <gtservicesmanager@fictionalfirm.com>
Subject: New sales automation system

Dear Steve:

When we last spoke, you promised me that 90 percent of the first pass on the new sales automation system would be ready last week. I counted on that deadline because I know you realize how much these dates affect the entire line of production. Unfortunately, last week has come and gone, and I have not heard from you.

The delayed arrival of the system is seriously compromising the performance of our field sales force, which, in turn, has a direct negative impact on the bottom line. In addition, I'm taking considerable heat from my vice president for the late delivery of the software.

I know how busy you are. But this is a deadline you promised you could make. If I were aware that you were too busy to take this job on at the beginning, I would have chosen an alternative supplier. That is still an open option. If you can't deliver a system by the end of the month, we will turn this project over to a third-party vendor.

It's preferable to have you finish what you started, but I am running out of time and options. Can you get the work done by June 30? Please let me know now.

Sincerely,

Complaint to management from an employee

Background: The key to complaining to a manager or supervisor is to frame your communication as a request rather than a complaint or demand. Explain not how you are personally inconvenienced, but how the problem adversely affects either the company as a whole or the area under the recipient's direct management.

Essential elements: Whether you're complaining about your parking space or the latest executive dictate, remember that the written word is mightier than the sword (and can be almost as deadly). Choose your words carefully so they don't come back to bite you. It's for this reason that you should avoid e-mail for this kind of correspondence; once it's out there, you can't get it back, and it can be forwarded to people you never intended to see it. Your complaint should include:

1. The topic of your complaint.
2. The exact reasons for your complaint.
3. An acknowledgment of the manager's point of view.
4. A request for a compromise solution (give the details).
5. A request for a response.

Sample:

To: Jim Burke, Group Product Marketing Director
From: Alex Freeman
Re: Ad agency services purchasing procedure

Dear Jim:

I just received the Approved Agency list. According to the memo, we may purchase creative and production services only from a list of six approved agencies.

I think this is counterproductive for several reasons:

1. These agencies are among the highest-priced vendors we use. They already charge fees that our limited budgets cannot accommodate.
2. When they learn they have a semimonopoly on our business, they'll charge even more.
3. The freelancers and graphic design vendors I currently use are familiar with our technology; they do as good or better job than the agencies on the list, and their fees are reasonable.
4. The turnaround from freelancers is much faster.

I agree that reducing the number of agencies helps create a consistent look and strategy. But can we amend the new policy so that marketing communications can continue to buy certain creative services (mainly copy, design, photography, and illustration) on an a la carte basis? What do you think about this?

Sincerely,

Complaint about the late delivery of a product

Background: The key to writing an effective complaint concerning a late delivery is not merely to restate that the delivery is late, as the recipient already knows that. Instead, you want to make him or her aware of the inconvenience you may be suffering as a result of the lateness. Use a printed memo or letter rather than e-mail so that you can establish a proper paper trail for future reference.

Essential elements: If tardy delivery is costing your business time, money, or goodwill, let the recipient know that. Make sure your letter includes:

1. The details of the problem shipment: the merchandise and the purchase order number.
2. The promised date of delivery and the actual date of delivery.

3. The internal problems this delayed shipment has cost your company.
4. The problems the delayed shipment has caused you with your customers (both in reputation and finances).
5. A positive statement about the quality of the company's products and your desire to continue ordering from the company.
6. What you need to continue doing business with this company (a promise of future promptness, a written agreement for late penalty fees, and so forth).
7. A request for an immediate response.

Sample:

Dear Mr. Travis:

We received the three linear amplifier circuits we ordered today on PO # 3456. As you know, this is six days past the promised delivery date. As a result, we have had to delay shipment of a base station to one of our most important network accounts. We also had to log considerable overtime in our shop to make up for the delay your late delivery caused.

We now have a major customer complaining about our service, not to mention a substantial loss of profit margin on this particular sale. Obviously, my management is not happy. Zarcon makes excellent amplifier circuits, which is why we favor you with substantial business. But now my boss is asking for technical bids from other companies.

I would like to continuing placing our orders with you if you can assure me that the delivery problem will be corrected on all future orders. In addition, we may want to write a cash penalty for late delivery into future contracts.

Please call me as soon as possible to discuss these terms and arrangements.

Sincerely,

Complaint about a missed deadline for a service

Background: When one person misses a deadline, the whole chain of business production falls behind. Be sure to keep a paper trail of all the dates missed and your complaints about each one.

Essential elements: Your letter should include:

1. The name of the project you're writing about.
2. The dates involved (original due date, any extension dates, and the overdue date).
3. The names of people who have been involved in setting or extending deadlines.
4. The reason the delay is not acceptable.
5. The current deadline with the details of exactly what's due.
6. A note requesting reassurance that the recipient won't let you down.
7. An offer to answer any questions.

Sample:

Dear Sheldon:

This letter will confirm our correspondence regarding the deadline for the *Handbook of Telecommunications Acronyms and Standards*. As I noted in our conversation, we expect to receive the complete manuscript, including revisions and any new text, in hard copy and on a USB drive by December 28. This deadline is an extension of the December 10 deadline that was set with Betsy Shephard on November 19.

We cannot extend the deadlines any further nor can we delay this publication any longer. Therefore, the above submission deadlines need to be met so we can meet our publication schedule.

I look forward to receiving your manuscript and USB drive on December 28. If you have any questions, please contact me at 123-456-7890.

Sincerely,

Responses to customer complaints

When someone complains to your company, don't shrug it off. This is a great opportunity for some good public relations work. Respond quickly, offer apologies, and turn a disgruntled consumer into a loyal customer.

Resolution of a customer's product complaint

Background: In this example, a woman purchased a particular flavor of ice cream and found that it did not have the usual amount of chocolate chips in it. Disappointed, she wrote the manufacturer to complain. The sample that follows is the letter she received in reply.

Essential elements: In most cases, your job is to assure the complainant that the customer is always right. Your letter should include the following points:

1. Thank the customer for contacting you.
2. Rather than evading the issue, address it directly and apologize.
3. Offer an explanation. An excuse is not necessary, but let the customer know if the problem is an exception to your normal practice.
4. Assure the customer that the problem is in the process of being resolved and that he or she could count on you in the future.
5. Offer restitution in some form (such as a gift certificate, replacement product, or credit on future orders) to replace the original purchase.

Sample:

Dear Ms. Poivre,

Thank you for your telephone call regarding your recent purchase of MochaCocoa Chip Ice Cream. We are sorry to hear that the ice cream lacked the quality you have come to expect from us. During our manufacturing process, added ingredients are mixed into the ice cream using a special feeder. In the case of your carton, it appears that we were the victims of human or mechanical error, in that the feeder failed to add the appropriate quantity of chocolate pieces to the mix. Please be assured that we have reported this incident to our quality assurance department and that they are implementing measures to ensure that this situation does not recur.

We are sorry that you were unable to enjoy your ice cream as a result. Please accept the enclosed gift certificate for one quart of our premium ice cream to replace your purchase. We hope that you will give us another chance to provide you with the quality ice cream you deserve and that all your future encounters with our ice cream bring you nothing but pleasure.

Warm regards,

Enclosure: Certificate-One Quart [*If using e-mail, this will appear as an attachment to your message.*]

Resolution of a customer's problem

Background: When a customer has a problem, fix it. When you resolve a problem promptly and fully, your relationship with that customer can actually strengthen. Part of gaining that benefit is to let the customer know what you have done for him or her, which of course, can be communicated in writing.

Essential elements: Effective problem resolution letters contain the following points:

1. Apologize for the problem.
2. Take responsibility. Use personal pronouns and the active voice rather than the passive corporate voice (for example, "We made a mistake" and not "The wrong unit was inadvertently sent by the shipping clerk").
3. Show how the situation has been corrected now and will be prevented in the future.
4. Don't make excuses. As Ben Franklin once observed, "People who are good at making excuses are seldom good at anything else."

Sample:

Dear Danielle:

I apologize for sending a Custom F-5 Module that was not produced according to your specifications. We have shipped a replacement unit that fits your specifications, via overnight freight, at our expense. It has been reviewed against your written specifications by Lanes Milstead, our senior application engineer. We'll arrange for someone to pick up the other unit—at our cost and your convenience, of course.

Again, my apologies. We made a mistake, and I've alerted our production department to ensure that it is not repeated.

Sincerely,

Consumer requests

When you need something from a business, not as a businessperson but rather as a consumer, your letter of request should still be professional and concise. The following two samples will serve as your guide.

Basic consumer request

Background: Many consumer requests are made by phone, but it's always a good idea to back up any conversation with a written request. This documents your need and the date of your request. The preferable format is a printed letter, although e-mail is acceptable as long as you make sure you print out your communications so that you don't lose track of them.

Essential elements: Whether you're requesting reservations, information, a change in policy, free samples, or whatever, letters of consumer request should include:

1. An opening statement of exactly what you want.
2. The details such as time, date, product number, size, color, and so forth.
3. If not included in letterhead, your address and phone for the response.
4. A thank-you.

Sample:

Dear Brian:

To confirm our phone conversation, I would like three copies of Regina Anne Kelly's article about solar energy from the October 2007 issue of *Home Power* magazine, as well as a set of 10 brochures about Sea Bright Solar LLC. As we discussed, these materials will be displayed at the Rahway Environmental Commission booth on "Green Homeowners Night" at the borough hall on November 3. Therefore, I will need the materials mailed to me by next Tuesday, October 28, to ensure that I receive them in time.

I've enclosed some information about the event should you decide to send a representative of your company, as you mentioned you were considering.

Thank you!

Sincerely,

Request for a refund

Background: Refund requests should be made in writing. If a seller does not supply a return/refund request form along with the packing slip that accompanied your order, you will need to write a letter instead. Be sure to enclose a copy of the receipt, bill of sale, or any other proof of purchase. If the product is defective and small, enclose it with the letter. If it is large, ask in your letter how the seller wants the product returned and where it should be sent. Also ask the seller to pay for the shipping.

Essential elements: When you ask for a refund, give all the details. Include:

1. An introduction that identifies the product you're writing about.
2. The problem with the item.

3. The reason you do not want a replacement or credit.
4. A request for a refund, stating the exact amount.

Sample:

> Dear Mr. Smathglatter:
>
> On August 8th, I purchased an NCA Dual Line Digital Phone from you over the phone. The person I spoke with was Shelley Dougan. Today I hooked up the phone and found it doesn't work. There are two major problems:
>
> 1. The phone can receive calls but not dial out. After I get a dial tone and dial, I hear silence for a few seconds, then a click, then get the dial tone again.
> 2. The LED displays random characters. It does not display the correct information for caller ID or any of the other messaging features.
>
> I needed a phone right away and could not wait for a replacement from your company. In its stead, I have purchased a new digital phone from a local electronics superstore.
>
> The defective NCA phone, along with a copy of the bill of sale, is enclosed. Please send me a refund for the purchase price of $149.50 plus $4.95 for shipping the phone back to your distribution center. Thank you.
>
> Sincerely,

Request for service or repair

Background: Your request for service or repair should be detailed so that the provider knows exactly what you need, when, and why. The style of your request will change depending on the circumstances and the level of cooperation from the provider. In any case, use a printed letter to properly document your requests and how they were handled. The following three letters will show you how your request can grow from simple asking to demanding to verging on threatening.

Essential elements: Whether you are sending your first letter requesting service or repair or your tenth one to the same company, every letter should include:

1. A description of the item needing repair or service and the date of purchase.
2. The problem that requires attention.
3. Exactly what you want done.

4. The date by which the service or repair should be completed.
5. A copy of or reference to all previous correspondences.
6. Notice of copies sent to the Department of Consumer Affairs (if appropriate).

Samples:

Letter #1: Cordial request

Customer Service:

On May 1st, I purchased a [name of car] from your dealership.

Despite repeated phone calls, there are still a few lose ends that need to be tied up:

1. I am still waiting for a copy of the bumper-to-bumper warrantee.
2. I have not yet received an itemized list of registration costs, and the exact amount of credit I received from the Department of Motor Vehicles for the canceled plates voucher.
3. I have asked for a new bill of sale that includes the payments for the alarm system and extended warrantee.

I have an appointment to have the car serviced on June 30th. I would like to have these details taken care of before that time.

Thank you.

Sincerely,

Letter #2: Forceful demand

Notice that in the second letter the writer now has the name of person to correspond with and has forwarded a copy to the Department of Consumer Affairs.

Dear Richard,

Attached is a copy of my June 8th letter to Customer Service. After having my car serviced on June 30th, the list of problems has grown. These matters need your immediate attention:

1. Although I did finally receive my copy of the warranty after waiting two months, it is not bumper-to-bumper as Mr. Schecht promised. It also requires service at your facility unless the warranty administrator waives that requirement. I purchased the car from you at a premium price with the expectation that I would have a bumper-to-bumper warranty that I could use at any dealer. I never would have bought this car from you if I knew about these limitations. I expect two things: A written waiver from the warranty administrator that allows me to have warranty service performed at any dealer, and a wrap-around warranty, provided at your cost, that turns this limited warranty into the promised "bumper-to-bumper" warranty.

2. I expect an itemized list of registration costs, and the exact amount of credit I received from the Department of Motor Vehicles for the canceled plates voucher I gave to Mr. Schecht. If there is a refund due, I expect it within 15 days.

3. I expect a proper bill of sale that itemizes and describes the payments for the alarm system and the extended warranty, and includes all the items on the original bill of sale.

4. Your mechanic was unable to locate a cause for the burning smell. The smell persists. I expect your written assurance that if and when the cause for this smell becomes known, you will repair the problem at your cost.

5. The mechanic did not repair the left front marker light, although he promised he would. Enclosed is a copy of your invoice for this repair, which wasn't made, as well as an invoice from another dealer who actually made the repair. I expect reimbursement for $22.90.

Sincerely yours,
Cc: Joe Smith, Department of Consumer Affairs

Letter #3: Forceful complaint

The previous demanding letter did get results. The consumer had all his demands met except for one very important one. To prompt the dealership to send the documents requested, the consumer mailed a complaint letter that looked like a legal notice. It worked. Within days, this consumer received the warranty requested.

To: Dave Cenoso, Manager, Anothertown Auto
From: David Afterwards

Notice of demand in the matter of failure to deliver vehicle services agreement

Whereas, A vehicle service agreement was purchased and paid for by David Afterwards, residing at 00-00 Mockingbird Lane, Anytown, USA on May 1, 0000, bearing the application number HH3104.

And whereas, Paperwork for said vehicle service agreement has not been completed, and the manufacturer has no record of entry of the information for this agreement into its computer system.

Therefore Demand Is made that: Paperwork must be completed and a validated Vehicle Service Agreement must be delivered to above-named plaintiff by the close of business on August 30.

Signed this _____ day of _____ by:_____
Witnessed by:_____

Consumer complaints

When writing complaint letters, don't rant and rave. Be direct and to the point. Spell out the action you want the company to take. To make sure the recipient gets your letter, and to gain his or her attention, you can send it certified mail, return receipt requested. (For all of these letters, for the purpose of creating a proper paper trail, it's best to use printed letters, not e-mail.)

Complaint of inferior product quality

Background: The key to writing an effective letter of complaint about a product you have purchased is to detail specific flaws and then state what you expect to be done about the problem.

Much less effective is to vent anger, lay blame, insult the seller, or make vague claims of general dissatisfaction that are not backed by specifics. Be specific, be controlled, and stick to your complaint—don't veer off into tangents.

Essential elements: When you purchase a product that does not meet your expectations, you should contact the manufacturer with a letter that states:

1. What the product is and when you purchased it.
2. The problem.

3. Your disappointment with the product.

4. If you'd like to try your luck with this company again, a request for a credit or a replacement product.

Sample:

> **To:** TeleToys, Customer Service
> **From:** Nicholas DeLorenzo
> **Re**: "Action Robot" construction set
>
> For Christmas, my 9-year-old son received the Action Robot construction set.
>
> Although he looked forward to building the robot, this didn't happen, for several reasons.
>
> The main problem is your instructions, which are incomplete, vague, and extremely difficult to follow. The box states, "For ages eight and up," but as an adult (certainly over the age of eight) I found the instructions almost impossible to follow.
>
> Also, many of the joints do not connect easily; some, not at all. None of the wheel joint caps will stay firmly on the axle, so the wheels always fall off.
>
> Perhaps the connectors are faulty. I have enclosed a parts list for our model where I have circled the connectors that do not work so that you are aware of the problem.
>
> I am very disappointed in the quality of this product (my son, as you can imagine, is even more disappointed). What do you propose to do to restore my satisfaction and faith in TeleToys?
>
> Sincerely,

Complaint of poor service

Background: Complaining of poor service is a good example of how the written word still maintains its power in today's age of images. Try this experiment: Complain over the phone. Often the person on the phone will sound sympathetic, but no action will be taken. Then try complaining in writing. You'll find that written complaints are resolved more completely and quickly.

Essential elements: When you complain about service, you must mention:

1. The location, date of the occurrence, and the person(s) involved.

2. Exactly what happened.

3. Something to indicate that you are a desirable customer.

4. An expression of disappointment.
5. Restitution of some sort, if you prefer.

Sample:

Dear Restaurant Manager:

On October 21, my wife and I had lunch at your restaurant. I had a ground beef taco.

While chewing, I bit down on something hard and sharp. In the ground beef, I found a piece of twisted metal. Fortunately, I didn't cut my mouth, or even worse, swallow the sharp metal, which would have no doubt landed me in the emergency room.

We called the waiter (whose nametag said "Jonathan") and explained what happened. He said, "I'm sorry," and that was it! There was no genuine concern. There was no offer to replace my lunch. There was no restitution. What we did get was a bill charging me full price for my meal!

When I objected, he pointed out that I had eaten the taco, which was true, and there was nothing he could do. When I asked to see the manager, he said the manager was out. You can only imagine my upset and displeasure.

My wife and I have been frequent patrons of your restaurant and have come to enjoy the excellent service. This experience has left both of us disappointed.

Sincerely,

P.S. A copy of our paid check for the lunch is enclosed.

Complaint of noncompliance with a service agreement

Background: Why are so many consumers with service contracts so unhappy? It's both the customer's and the vendor's fault. The vendor promises a lot in its sales pitch and promotional materials, but the service contract does not contain enough specifics and too many loopholes and exceptions.

The customer, in turn, doesn't read the fine print in the contract. When service rendered doesn't meet expectations and the customer complains, the vendor points to the contract the customer signed. The customer says, "I don't care about the contract; I'm holding you to what your ad (or commercial or sales rep) promised."

Often, a letter citing these specifics is an effective way to persuade the vendor to resolve the problems in your favor.

Essential elements: Service agreements are notoriously difficult to understand. But when you're not getting the service you believe you are entitled to, speak up. When writing this letter:

1. Open with a statement that acknowledges there is a problem with servicing.
2. State the product and the service contract you have.
3. Detail the problem: List dates, times, and names.
4. State exactly what you want the company to do.
5. Request an answer.

Sample:

Ralph Edwards
Acme Network Services
RE: Service Contract #29956

Dear Mr. Edwards:

I'm writing to resolve a conflict we're having in Acme's servicing of our account.

As you know, we are three months into a one-year network support contract. Although the quality of your support personnel is excellent, the response time to network outages is not what we expected. When we signed with your firm, Tom Nevins told us that you provide responses "in under four hours." Indeed, the promotional brochure he gave us makes the same statement: "Our network technicians will respond within four hours of your call for service—and often faster."

Unfortunately, "often faster" has become "usually slower." Response time continually takes the better part of a business day. Tom tells us that this promise is superseded by your contract, which he pulled out at our last meeting. He pointed to the language that said, "Best effort will be made to respond to support calls as conditions allow." He then pointed out that I had signed and read the contract.

Yes, I signed your contract, but I believe the promises that vendors make to me, and I expect them to abide by them. We are your customer, and we expect you to be our partner in network support and not our adversary.

My question is simple: Are you going to deliver the fast four-hour response you promised when you sold us the contract?

Sincerely,

Complaint about misrepresentation

Background: Complaints about misrepresentation should always be made in writing and copies of these letters retained, in case the matter escalates to the point where legal actions are needed.

Essential elements: If someone has taken advantage of you by misrepresenting a service or product, you should immediately write to complain and demand restitution if it is due:

1. Give the details of the time, place, and person(s).
2. Explain what you understood to be the case.
3. Detail how this understanding has been twisted or misrepresented.
4. Firmly state what you want the company to do next to rectify the problem.

Sample:

Jack Frome, Vice President
Big Life Insurance Company
Big City, USA
RE: Whole life policy #699959

Dear Mr. Frome:

Sometime last October, two of your independent representatives visited our home to make a presentation about whole life insurance for my spouse. At the time we were undecided, so they invited us to fill out the application, except for the signature. We filled it out, but we never heard from them again. (The application is attached.)

Last week, my new bookkeeper pointed out that, for the past two months, Big Life Insurance Company has been deducting $224 monthly premium for a whole life policy for my wife. This is $448 for insurance we do not want and did not agree to purchase. We already have low-cost term life insurance that meets all of our combined estate planning needs.

Effective immediately, I have instructed my bank not to make any further payments to Big Life. I will expect a refund check for $448 from your company within 10 days. The policy is null and void, and I do not consider my wife to be insured of your firm.

Sincerely,

Complaint about a billing error

Background: When the billing error is not simple or routine, send a letter to explain your position. Keep copies of all letters until the problem is resolved.

Essential elements: Billing department representatives don't want to hear a song and a dance; just give them the facts:

1. Provide the details right up front: Note the product or service, the date in question, and the order or customer number.
2. Note that a copy of the bill in question is attached.
3. Concisely explain why the figures on the bill are incorrect.
4. State what you want the company to do.
5. Offer to provide further information if needed.

Sample:

Dear Mr. Finagle,

I recently received a second notice for lab charges my insurance company tells me I am not responsible for paying. (Copies of your letters and the insurance company's response to me are attached.)

As a preferred provider, your medical lab has agreed to provide services for those covered by my plan for "usual and customary rates." The insurance company has explained to me that I am not responsible for fees above the "usual customer rates," to which you have agreed and which they have already paid.

Please remove these charges from my account immediately and stop sending me these insulting letters.

I hope this letter clears up this matter, but if I can provide more information, please call me at 123-456-7890.

Sincerely,

Complaint about a bank error

Background: Another common complaint that can be handled by letter is a potential error in your business bank account.

Essential elements: Bank statements are not infallible. Your best defense is to keep records of all your banking transactions combined with a letter documenting the problem:

1. State that you believe there is an error in your back statement.
   Note the date of the error and your account number.

2. Detail what should have been recorded as compared to what the statement says.
3. Explain what you would like the bank to do about this problem.
4. Offer to provide further information if needed.

Sample:

Dear Ms. Jensen:

I believe I may have discovered an error in our February checking account statement. Could you please look into this and help us reconcile the discrepancy?

Our statement shows deposit of a client check (Morgan Jewelry, check #551) on February 26 for $350. Then on February 27, a check we wrote to a vendor (TheftProof Electronics, our check #1106) for $872 was returned for insufficient funds, and we were assessed a $25 overdraft fee.

According to my records, however, the February 26 deposit was actually $3,500, not $350 as the statement shows. And that amount would have more than covered our February 27 check.

Attached are copies of the check we deposited on February 26 along with the deposit slip. Perhaps the teller misread my handwriting on the deposit form.

Please call me with your assessment of this situation. Our office number is 123-456-7890. I am at extension 242.

Thanks for your helping me resolve this situation as promptly as possible. I look forward to hearing from you within the next few days.

Sincerely,

Complaint about incomplete or inadequate work

Background: When the contractor or vendor is finished with a job but the work does not meet your expectations, you gain nothing by insulting or talking down to the vendor. Write a letter that maps out the problem along with a requested course of action. A subject line is a good way of quickly identifying the project as a redo or revision rather than a request for new fee-paid services.

Essential elements: Don't rant, rave, and holler—get to the point quickly:
1. Give the details of the work that you are dissatisfied with.
2. Explain exactly what you want done to complete the job.

3. Be clear about whether you expect a further charge to complete or fix the work done so far.
4. Make sure the vendor understands that no further charge will be accepted without your prior approval.
5. Thank the vendor for his or her understanding.
6. State when you expect the work to be completed.
7. Enclose copies of paperwork relevant to your complaint (contract, agreement, invoice, canceled check, warranty, and so forth).

Sample:

Re: Watch repair

Dear Mr. Lane:

I'm returning the watch you repaired for me last month because it is still not keeping accurate time. The watch kept accurate time for about a week after I got it. Since then, it's been losing 15 to 20 minutes every day.

This seems to be the original defect I paid you to repair, and because I've already paid you, I assume you will fix the problem without further charge.

If that's not the case, let me know. I've enclosed a copy of the receipt you sent me for the original repair. It states that all repairs are guaranteed for 90 days, so as far as I can see, I am still covered by your guarantee.

If you have further questions about my watch, or need to speak with me about this matter, my daytime number is 123-456-7890. Thank you for your understanding and service. Unless I hear otherwise from you, I'll expect to receive my repaired watch from you on Friday the 23rd.

Sincerely,

Thank-you correspondence for resolved complaints

Background: Whether you are a businessperson or a consumer, if your complaint is addressed and resolved you should extend the courtesy of a thank-you note. The key message of this letter is: "Your strategy worked; by resolving the problem as I requested, you retained me as a customer."

Well-written thank-you notes carry a strong message. They give the recipient motivation to continue to please you in the future.

Essential elements:

1. Say "thank you" and explain why.
2. Acknowledge that your problem/complaint was addressed to your satisfaction.
3. Assure the recipient of future business.

Sample:

Dear Ms. Lieb:

Just a short note to say "thanks" for your courteous letter and for sending a replacement amplifier cover so promptly.

In today's pressured world, many customers (including myself) are quick to criticize and slow to praise. This is a letter of praise.

Your response was fair and exactly what I wanted. You have resolved my problem, transformed dissatisfaction into satisfaction, and assured continued future orders from me. Both of us got what we want.

Thank you.

Sincerely,

9

Credit and Collection Correspondence

Credit and collection are sensitive topics—on many levels. Denying or limiting a buyer's credit, or reminding him or her that he or she owes money, is a potential emotional powderkeg. Your goal is to remain professional and neutral and get or protect your money, while retaining customer goodwill.

For all of these reasons, credit and collection issues are the domain of snail mail, not e-mail.

Correspondence regarding credit ⊗

These letters will give you the words you need to ask for credit, check on your own credit, offer or deny credit to others, and make changes to your existing credit policy.

Request for credit

Background: Credit is part of the American way of life today. According to Studebaker Worthington, a leasing company, more than 35 percent of cars, 30 percent of computers, and 40 percent of copiers and office equipment are sold through leasing. More and more sellers these days are prepared to grant credit, making the process faster and easier.

Essential elements: Different sellers will need different information to grant credit approval, but you can expedite the process by including the basics in your initial request. Your letter should include:

1. What you want to purchase and the total price of it.
2. The terms of credit you would like.
3. Very brief background information about your company.
4. A list of two or three credit references (companies you regularly buy from on credit).

5. An offer to provide further information if needed.
6. Banking information, including your bank's name, address, phone number, and account number.

Sample:

Dear Mr. Hale:

We are looking for a supplier of quality dyestuffs for our dye house operations. After seeing your ad in *Textile World*, we sent for your catalog and were impressed with the breadth of your line.

We would like to purchase an initial inventory of one unit each of #1055, 1058, and 1070. At $800 each, this would be an initial order of $2,400. We would like to purchase these materials on net 90-day terms.

XYA was established seven years ago and since that time we have grown very rapidly. Our practice is to favor a limited number of suppliers with the majority of our orders. In turn, we look for volume discounts, favorable terms, and the kind of first-rate service others have told me you supply.

Other vendors and credit references include:

VelTech, 8496 Stave Avenue, El Paso, TX 56049, ATTN: Jim Pascal

FabelCorp, 584 Fourth Street, Middletown, NJ 07410, ATTN: Nancy

Watson Chemical Supply, 670 Bergen Avenue, Vernon, NH, ATTN: Dave George

If you need additional financial information, I will be glad to supply it. Or you can contact our bank directly: First Local Bank, Washington Avenue, Anytown, USA, phone 123-456-7890, account #15886798. You can talk to the branch manager, John Sullivan.

Sincerely,

Request for a credit report

Background: One of the most basic credit communications is a request for your own credit report. The following sample shows a form letter you can send to credit agencies to get that information. To get a copy of your credit report, write to the credit agencies listed below:

EquiFax Information Service
Customer Correspondence
PO Box 105873
Atlanta, GA 30348
800-685-1111

Experian
PO Box 2106
Allen, TX 75013
800-392-1122

TransUnion
PO Box 390
Springfield, PA 19064
800-916-8800

Sample:

> To Customer Service:
>
> I would like a copy of my credit report. Please send my report to the following address:
> [Your full name (include middle initial and any Jr. or Sr.)]
> [Your address]
> [Your Social Security number]
> [Your year of birth]
> You will also find enclosed documentation verifying my identity. Thank you for your cooperation.
>
> Sincerely,

Dispute of a credit report

Background: If your credit report contains errors, you must notify the credit-reporting agency in writing. But don't rant and rave and spend ink explaining how their error has cost you time and money.

Essential elements: Be sure to provide all the information the credit bureau will need to make the change quickly. Include:

1. A statement that there has been an error that needs to be corrected.
2. What that error is.
3. What the correct information is.
4. How this information can be verified.
5. A request for the correction to be made within 10 days.
6. A request for a copy of the corrected version.
7. Include your phone number and Social Security number at the end of the letter.

Sample:

Dear Customer Service:

Please correct the following error in my credit report:

The loan account number listed for Citizens Bank on the report reads: "137547899." This is incorrect. The correct account number is 137557899.

To verify this information call my branch manager, Len Dane, at 123-456-7890.

This correction should change the report by deleting the erroneous statement that says I have twice been 60 days late in making payments.

Please update my credit report and send me the corrected, clean copy within the next 10 days.

Yours truly,

Request for credit information from a potential customer

Background: Another routine credit correspondence is requesting information from a potential credit account so you can perform a credit check.

Essential elements: You want to keep the order, but you also want to protect yourself. Be sure your letter includes:

1. An opening "thank you" for the customer's interest in your company or product.
2. A request for the information you need to process the credit application. This may include credit references, bank account numbers, bank statements, statements of ownership, and so forth.
3. A promise to expedite the order as soon as the requested information is received and the credit application is processed.

Sample:

Dear Ms. Porter:

Thank you very much for your interest in our SP-500 digital writer. This instrument was designed with the needs of the small to midsize photofinisher in mind, and your choice of this model makes good sense.

I also appreciate your request to lease. The credit references you supplied to our sales rep on your order form will be very helpful. Thank you.

Would you please send me a copy of your most recent statements of ownership and results of operations? We also need a copy of your latest business bank statement. As soon as we have the information we need, we'll process your request for financing. We're eager to help increase your profitability with the SP-500 digital writer. We'll do our best to expedite credit approval, shipment, and installation.

Sincerely,

Credit referral check on a potential customer

Background: Credit and collections take less time and are more efficient when you develop a library of routine correspondence for handling the most frequent communications. The following letter can be sent to any credit references given to you by a potential customer on whom you are running a credit check.

Sample:

Dear Ms. Macadam:

We have received a request for credit from Greta Freytag at XYA Company in Anytown, USA. Your company was listed as a credit reference. I would be grateful if you would supply the following information about this customer:

1. Credit terms extended to the customer, including limits.
2. A brief statement about the customer's promptness in meeting obligations.
3. Your reservations, if any, about the customer's financial condition and general reliability.

A reply envelope is enclosed for your convenience. I assure you that the information supplied will be treated as confidential.

Cordially yours,

Credit approval

Background: When you accept or reject a request for credit, do it in writing. The following is an example of a letter granting it. To customize this letter, put this letter on file in your computer and use it exactly as is, changing only the addressee each time you need it.

Essential elements: This letter has four simple parts:

1. State that the customer's application for financing has been approved.
2. State the product or service you are now happy to provide.
3. Briefly review the terms of the credit agreement.
4. Close by stating that you are looking forward to a continued business relationship in the future.

Sample:

Dear Ms. Porter:

Your application for financing on the acquisition of your new SP-500 digital writer has been approved. Your order for one SP-500 with continuous sheet feeder will be shipped within five days by truck.

As the enclosed lease documents indicate, your monthly lease payment is $1,870. Since your lease covers the entire purchase, including "soft" costs, installation and training are completely covered, with no additional fee or payment required.

We look forward to serving you and hope you will call upon us for service, support, and supplies. Please keep in touch and let us know how the SP-500 is working to improve sales and customer service in your shop.

Sincerely,

Credit denial

Background: On occasion you will have the unpleasant task of denying credit to a potential buyer. This refusal should be handled with tact and diplomacy.

Essential elements: This letter should include:

1. A thank-you for wanting to do business.
2. A positive word about the company and their products or services.
3. A regretful denial of credit and the reason.
4. An open invitation to talk further to create a gradually increasing credit line (if this is reasonable).
5. A reminder that cash purchases are always welcome.
6. A positive ending wishing the customer well.

Sample:

Dear Mr. Colson:

Thank you for your application for credit at Barrow's. We appreciate your interest.

Your personal references are exceptionally good, and your record of hard work indicates that your business prospects are good for the near future.

Unfortunately, at the present, your financial condition only partially meets Barrow's requirements. We cannot extend the $5,000 open credit you requested.

Please call me at your convenience. I am sure we can set up a program of gradually increasing credit that will benefit both of us. Meanwhile, remember that deliveries on cash purchases are made within two days.

Let me hear from you soon. We are interested in your business venture.

Sincerely,

Limited credit approval

Background: Another situation that must be handled sensitively is granting credit, but not in the amount the customer wants.

Essential elements: Make this letter short and to the point. Include:

1. A thank-you for the order.
2. A statement of the line of credit you are able to offer.
3. An explanation of the balance required to deliver the entire order.
4. An invitation to further discuss extending the credit limit (if appropriate).
5. An ending that assures the customer you value your business relationship and are appreciative of the opportunity to work together.

Sample:

Dear Mr. Smith,

We appreciate receiving your order for 1,000 XTM-500 linear circuit amplifiers.

Our credit department has approved your firm for a credit line of $10,000. Because the total on your current order exceeds this limit, we need at least partial payment (half up front) to ship the goods to your factory.

If you anticipate more purchases of this size, call me and we'll see what we can do about extending your limit. We value your business, hope this is a satisfactory solution, and thank you for the opportunity serve you.

Sincerely,

Credit suspension

Background: One of the toughest business decisions is whether to put an account on hold, especially a large volume customer. The best course is to establish a firm credit policy, stick with it, and suspend credit for buyers who fail to meet criteria for receiving credit. Do not criticize, insult, or blame the customer in anyway. Do not request payments due; this should be done in a separate collection letter as outlined later in this chapter.

Essential elements: The letter should explain why the decision to put credit on hold was made and what the customer can do to restore credit status. Include:

1. An opening that says you value this customer.
2. An explanation how late payments affect your company.
3. An assurance that you want to continue doing business.
4. An explanation that you require payment with future orders until past debts are paid.
5. An invitation to open a credit card account (if appropriate).
6. An assurance that the customer will return to the original credit status when the account becomes current.
7. An invitation to talk further about this problem.

Sample:

Re: Your account #58589922

Dear Ms. Jones:

We value you as a customer. But for us to offer you quality goods at competitive prices, we depend on on-time payments from our accounts. And lately your payments have been late and your account seriously past due.

We still want to provide you with the connectors and fasteners your business needs. And we won't cut off shipments. But until your account is made current, we require payment with future orders.

A review of your account shows frequent purchases with an average order of $250. For your convenience, you may pay by credit card. Just call our

Credit Department at 123-456-7890. Ask for Sheila or Sam and give us your credit card number and expiration date. We'll immediately set you up as a credit card account.

You may go off credit card status and return to a billing arrangement as soon as your account is current. If you prefer another arrangement, please call us and we will work with you to find an alternative payment method that works for you.

Sincerely,

Credit restoration

Background: This letter not only notifies the customer that credit has been restored but offers thanks and praise to the customer for improving the payment record. If there is a perk you can tie to the restored credit status, such as an extended credit line, do it in this letter.

Essential elements: Don't assume your customers know that credit terms are restored after a required payment. Notify them in writing (they may need this for their records). Include:

1. A thank-you for payment.
2. The announcement that the credit line is now restored.
3. A positive change in the terms of credit (if appropriate and desired).
4. A final closing mentioning your appreciation.

Sample:

Re: Your account #58589922

Dear Ms. Jones:

Thanks for your recent prompt payments. Our records reflect your account is now current.

Given these circumstances, I am happy to restore your full credit line. In fact, your recent payment record enables me to extend your credit line from the previous $5,000 to $8,000. This will enable you to stock the added inventory you need to accommodate the growing demands of your customers.

On a personal note, I admire your cooperation and appreciate your sincere efforts. You have made my job easier, and I appreciate it.

Sincerely,

Collection notices

It's one thing to give your customers credit—they like "free money." However, it's another to actually collect the money due. These collection letters need to be firm, yet understanding (to a point), to convince your credit customers to write out the check today.

Model invoice

Background: Firms that extend credit must bill customers. You should have a standard form invoice you use to bill credit customers. But if not, here's a format you can use:

Sample:

Invoice #

Reference: Purchase order #

From:[name, address, phone]

To:[person's name, company name, address, phone]

For:[product or service you are billing for]

Amount: $_____

Terms:[for example: net 30 days]

Notification of credit terms and conditions

Background: A bill should never be a surprise to a customer. If you attach financial penalties to your business terms, such as a doctor's office charging patients for missed appointments, these conditions must be communicated to the client in advance. Written communication is the best way to do this.

Essential elements: This letter should state the changes you are implementing and reasons for the change. It should include:

1. A positive statement about appreciating the customer's business.
2. An explanation of why you find it necessary to change the terms of your credit policy.
3. A direct statement of the change.
4. The benefit to the customer of this change.
5. An invitation to discuss the change further.

Sample:

To all clients:

Each account is of utmost importance to me. I strive to fill all orders quickly and efficiently and to extend to qualified customers satisfactory terms of credit.

However, because of an excessive backlog of overdue accounts, I find it necessary to make the following change in the terms of my credit policy effective May 1:

1. All accounts 30 days overdue will be assessed a 2 percent late fee.
2. All accounts 60 days overdue will be assessed a 3 percent late fee.
3. All accounts 90 days overdue will be referred to a collection agency.

The only way I can continue to offer reasonable rates to each of you is if I am assured payment for the products I supply. I'm sure you can understand the necessity for these changes in credit terms. If you would like to discuss these terms, please feel free to contact me.

Thank you,

Refusal of a partial payment plan

Background: When a customer offers a partial or monthly payment plan, it's generally a good idea to accept. Not doing so causes ill feelings and often results in no payment at all. However, there are cases where the customer's proposition is simply not acceptable. Your job is to say no politely but firmly.

Essential elements: This is a letter of compromise. It should include:

1. An acknowledgment of the customer's interest in making payment.
2. A review of the customer's account.
3. An explanation of why you must refuse the suggested payment plan.
4. An offer of an alternative compromise plan.
5. An invitation to discuss the terms further.

Sample:

Dear Mr. West:

Thanks for your letter. We appreciate your sincere attention to your account balance.

Given your balance of $1,600, we feel that a $50-a-month payment would take too long to bring this account current. Let me suggest an alternative: $100 a month, with the option to skip one month per year without penalty if you need to.

To discuss this further, you can reach me at 123-456-7890.

Sincerely,

Collection letter series

Background: It's a sad fact of business life: Many customers won't pay their bills on time. Some won't pay them at all.

Milt Pierce, author of *How to Collect Overdue Bills*, says that for the typical small business, 10 to 70 percent of assets are usually tied up in accounts receivables at any given time.

Here is a collection series that you can use to collect past-due bills. All of these letters can be stored on your computer as is and used as form letters when you need them. Just fill in the blanks. After the fifth letter, consider using a collection agency to shake the payment loose. See "Collection Tips" on pages 218–222 for the details.

Samples:

Collection letter #1
The first collection letter is the softest in tone.
It is a reminder and nothing more:

Dear

Just a reminder that payment of Invoice # _____ for [insert name of product or service] is now past [number of days/weeks] due. (See copy of invoice attached.)

Would you please send me a check today? A self-addressed, stamped reply envelope is enclosed for your convenience.

Regards,

Collection letter #2
The second collection letter is just as polite as the first, but it is a little firmer in requesting payment. It also sets a time frame for responding.

Dear

I haven't received payment for Invoice # _____ yet. Did you receive my original bill and follow-up letter?

Is something the matter? Is there some special reason why you have not paid? Did you receive our earlier invoice? If you need more time, don't hesitate to ask. Otherwise, please send me a check for $_____ within five business days.

Thanks,

Collection letter #3
The third letter is more insistent in tone. It says you either need payment or a good reason why payment hasn't been sent.

Dear

This is the third notice I've sent about Invoice # _____ (attached), which is now [number] weeks past due. Let me assure you that this bill will not be forgotten. Please, for the sake of your good credit rating, make every effort to clear up this problem right now. If payment cannot be delivered within five business days, call to discuss extending the terms.

Sincerely,

Collection letter #4
From this point on, the letters you send should become increasingly more insistent and urgent. Be firm. Do not make payment seem optional; make clear it is mandatory. This letter should be sent by certified mail.

Dear

Despite three previous notices about Invoice # _____ (attached), it remains unpaid. I haven't heard from you, and you haven't responded to my letters.

Unless you act within the next five days, your invoice will be referred to an outside collection agency. I have made every effort to collect payment, and still you have ignored every opportunity to pay this bill. You now have only five days to clear up this matter before more drastic action is taken.

I do not like turning accounts over to a collection agency, but you are leaving me little choice.

Sincerely,

Collection letter #5
The final letter makes clear that the grace period is over and you expect to be paid. You have to strike a balance between sounding serious and not being overly threatening. After five days, it's time to give this final notice.

You have left us no choice. We must now proceed with every legal means of collection. There is only one way that you can put a halt to our next legal action.

Dear [Name]:

If there is some good reason that you would like to discuss regarding your unpaid bill, you have only one final opportunity to put a halt to the legal action that we plan to take in your area. *Please call me right now at this number: 123-456-7890.*

Unless I hear from you within the next 48 hours, I shall institute every legal means for the collection of the amount of money that you owe.

You must act immediately. This is a serious problem.

Very truly yours,

Collection courtesy

When a customer responds to your request for payment for an overdue bill, it's a good idea to send a follow-up thank-you note. You should also respond in writing if you have made an accounting error and wrongly sought to collect money not owed.

Thanks for payment

Background: When a customer makes a payment in response to your requests for payment, thank him or her. In your letter, stress the thank-you, not the fact that the payment was late. Compliment and praise, rather than criticize or condemn.

Essential elements: Although it's about time your customer paid, be gracious with your thanks. Write a letter that includes:

1. A thank-you for the payment.
2. An acknowledgment that the customer's business is important to you.
3. A reminder of the present credit status.
4. A gentle reminder of the next payment due to motivate the customer to keep up with the payments and not be delinquent again.

Sample:

> Dear Mr. Jordan,
>
> Thank you for your payment of $1,500. We appreciate your attention to your account status with us. Your patronage is important to us, and we thank you for responding to our payment queries.
>
> Just to bring you up to date: Your current balance is $5,000, your credit limit. A payment of $750 is due May 1. If there's any problem or question, call me at 123-456-7890. Thanks.
>
> Sincerely,

Apology for an accounting error

Background: The danger of being too tough when chasing late payments is the possibility that the payment may not really be late. Your letter and the customer's check may have crossed in the mail. Or your accounting department may have misplaced or not credited a recent payment. Clear up these mistakes at once in writing. Apologize sincerely to defuse customer annoyance and anger.

Keep in mind that if you made the error, the customer suffers the additional damage of having his or her time wasted trying to resolve a problem that was your fault. Consider compensating the customer for it. A discount on a future order is the best compensation, because it not only gives the customer real value but also encourages more purchase of your product or service.

Essential elements: This letter will reflect the particular error you have made. But the basics should include:

1. Thanks for your customer's patience, and an apology for the mistake.

2. An assurance that the problem has been corrected in the customer's records.

3. Any adjustments to or the elimination of any penalties that were implemented.

4. Compensation you will give the client to rectify the inconvenience caused (optional).

5. To close, another thank-you for patience, and another apology.

Sample:

> Dear Mr. Bindleglass:
>
> Thank you for your patience and understanding. Let me apologize for the error we made in your account statement.
>
> When you called last Friday, I said we had not yet received your last payment. It turns out we had your check, but it had not yet been posted to our system. I have credited your account $850.
>
> Our policy states that 2.5 percent interest is accrued on the last business day of the month for all credit accounts. However, we are waiving this policy from January 1 through today. This will remove late-payment interest charges of $65.78 from your balance.
>
> To offset any inconvenience you have had in reconciling your account, we will give you a 20 percent discount on your next order. This should be automatically reflected in the invoice for that order. If not, let me know and I will personally handle it.
>
> Thank you again for your patience. We value your business. Please accept my apology.
>
> Sincerely,

Collection tips

The following collection tips will help you use your collection letters (also called dunning letters) to gain the most positive response. The goal is to get the money owed to you and at the same time keep the customer—not an easy task.

A change in letterhead lifts response

Experience proves that a change in letterhead in a dunning letter series will lift responses virtually every time. One situation where such a letter works well is as a replacement for the third or fourth effort in your internal cycle—typically after you have sent a bill and two notices and have suspended shipment of further orders.

Response-boosting tips

Here are some techniques that can successfully boost response:

- Vary the dunning cycle. To extend the billing series and increase net recovery rates, progressive agencies vary the timing between efforts, typically from 14 to 28 days. This is a proven response-booster.
- Vary the text of each letter in the series. Tone should increase from soft or mild to more severe and insistent.

- ☞ Change the color of the paper the letter is printed on as well as the outer envelope. Switching from white to red or blue changes the entire tone of the effort—and can significantly increase recoveries.
- ☞ Vary the size, shape, and appearance of the outer envelope.

The key is to keep each mailing fresh so that the subscriber does not think it's the same notice he or she received before. Remember, even the most powerfully written collection effort will get no response if the envelope is not opened.

Bring the collection agency in early

How long should you try to collect the money yourself? For merchandise, the internal dunning cycle (collection letters sent directly from the company) should consist of at least four efforts sent at 30-day intervals. (See sample collection series earlier in this chapter.)

At that point, it's time to refer the account to an outside agency. As you know, the older a bill gets, the more difficult it is to collect. Getting a third party involved creates a greater sense of obligation and urgency. When the collection letters suddenly start appearing on the official-looking letterhead of a third party, instead of your organization's letterhead, the bill suddenly becomes a "real" debt to the customer—one he perceives he is obligated to pay.

Choose the right agency for the job

Finally, here are some things you need to look into when evaluating outside collection agencies:

How many years has the agency has been in business?

- ☞ Check references. Find out what clients say about the agency. Is the agency successful? Are the agents easy to work with?
- ☞ Look at sample credit reports; are they clear and easy to read? Do they provide the information you need?
- ☞ Is the agency bonded? Is it a member of the American Collectors Association, or the American Commercial Collectors?
- ☞ Are the agency's IT systems compatible with yours?
- ☞ Fees are important, but beware: The lowest-priced agency may actually cost you more if it doesn't perform. By the same token, the agency generating the highest gross recovery rates may not make you the most money if its fee is too high. You want the agency that can generate the highest net recovery rates.

Third-party or contingency arrangement?

Collection agencies typically work on two different fee arrangements: third-party letters and contingency.

In a third-party arrangement, you pay a fixed fee per collection letter mailed. This is typically $400 to $600 per each thousand collected, but can be more or less depending on volume. Keep in mind that there may be minimum volume requirements for the agency to work on such a fixed-fee basis. The third-party arrangement offers you a low, fixed cost per letter, enabling you to budget accurately and to predict returns based on projected response rates.

In a contingency arrangement, the agency's compensation is a percentage of the money recovered. This is typically 40 to 50 percent. You pay only for results, not for pieces mailed. With the contingency method, there is no initial investment, no risk, and no out-of-pocket cost. You can initiate this type of program at any time because it does not require you to have a budget for back-end collections. The agency assumes all cost risks, and the program generates the agency's fee.

Whether it is better for you to use third-party or contingency collections on your first effort depends on your situation. The contingency arrangement reduces risk, because there's no out-of-pocket exposure. It also allows you to test a new collection agency for free.

On the other hand, if you have reason to think that response to the first external effort will be high, the third-party arrangement can net you more cash. You can determine the return on investment at different response rates through a simple break-even analysis based on the agency's fee and the average dollar balance of the accounts. Traditionally, the first external effort generates the highest recovery rate in the series, so it's where you are most likely to recoup your investment in a third-party mailing.

Approve collection letter copy

Review all agency letters before they are mailed. Question any language you find inappropriate for any reason.

The tone of your collection letters should be consistent with the philosophical or customer service approach of your company. Because most businesses are concerned with image, your collection letters shape your customers' perception of your organization as much as your service or product does. What works for the phone company in a billing series may not necessarily work for a landscaper.

At the same time, don't err on the side of being too soft or conservative in tone. Remember, your customer placed an order and then did not pay for it, despite repeated requests to do so. Firmness is required. Remember that the first effort in the external dunning cycle must be at least as firm as the last effort of your internal cycle.

Many businesspeople worry that the external collection cycle will upset or "turn off" unpaid accounts, alienating them from making future purchases. Experience shows this fear is largely unwarranted. Author Milt Pierce notes, "A customer who owes you money and is not responding to dunning will not place another order with you." To have a good business relationship, bills must be paid.

Any level of customer sensitivity can be dealt with, and if the agency carefully tailors the collection letters to your product, offer, company, and readership in a professional manner, complaints will be few and far between. Properly written external collection letters are never offensive. And they always protect the customer's right to dispute the invoice.

Have your agency share information with you

Make sure that information gathered by your agency's customer service and special correspondence response departments is shared with you. This information alerts you to problems.

For example, are there shipping delays? Do your sales reps make the terms unclear or mislead prospects about their obligation? Are your collection efforts evoking any ill will? In the external dunning cycle, your agency gets this information first-hand from dealing with your no-pay subscribers. Make sure they share it with you.

Find out the reason why buyers are not paying. Some will tell your agency they never received your product or received it but wrote "cancel" on the bill and returned the goods. Other excuses range from "I paid already" to "I don't like your product." Be sure to discuss with your agency how you want it to react to these kinds of responses.

Keep on top of collection results

An external collection cycle proceeds quickly, with only two to four weeks between efforts. So it's important to keep on top of results on a timely basis. Your agency should provide statistical reports on external collection recoveries in an easy-to-read format. The agency should also have the ability to check the status of any account on an online basis. The purpose of the report is to track external collection results and monitor agency performance. A collection agency report should show, for each month's referrals, the following information:

- Number of accounts referred to the agency.
- Beginning total amount to be collected for these accounts.
- Average dollar balance.
- Payments made both directly to you and to the collection agency, both full and partial.
- Number and percentage of bad addresses (nixes) and "skips" (customers who have moved without leaving a forwarding address).
- Credits and adjustments.
- Remaining number of accounts to be collected and total dollars owed.

Ideally, your agency should also be able to provide not only a summary of the above information for each month, but also a detailed report showing the activity for each account, sorted by ZIP code, source, or any other variable you desire.

Don't give up too early

Many outside collection agencies use only one or two letters to collect past-due accounts. But they may be giving up too early.

You want an agency that isn't just content to collect the "easy" receivables but that also goes after those hard-to-collect delinquent accounts. Testing by the agency may suggest that additional efforts are beneficial. For instance, although a one- or two-letter external series is common, some progressive agencies are achieving profitable recoveries with an extended letter series. Ask for these details before you hire a collection agency.

Practice customer retention, not just collection

The goal of your dunning cycle is not just to collect the money owed you but also to retain the customer—and her goodwill. You are not just a collector but a customer service representative as well. The by-product of good service is payment.

Here are some ideas on how your collection agency can help you improve customer service:

1. The external letter copy must acknowledge that not every customer the agency duns actually owes you money (for instance, it's possible a customer is being billed in error). Letters should not only seek payment but also encourage customers to call or write and explain why they have not paid or feel they do not owe the money.

2. Once the customer pays, it's your responsibility to start shipping his orders to him again promptly. Make sure your agency or accounting department can transfer payment information to your shipping department on a timely basis and in a convenient format so pay-ups can be quickly fulfilled.

3. Promptly acknowledge and resolve every nonpayment and partial payment response. Your collection agency should have a special correspondence response department whose job it is to communicate with customers who dispute invoices, make partial payments, or have other out-of-the-ordinary responses.

4. Be sure your agency employs a courteous and professional staff that treats your customers with dignity and respect at all times.

Legal action?

What about legal action? Small dollar balances make going to court impractical in most cases. However, an attorney demand letter (collection letter on law firm stationery) may prove profitable in many cases.

10

Sales Communications

Sales communications are intended to persuade, inform, alert, or perform another sales-related function. However, they are not, strictly speaking, "direct mail." They are:

- ▤ Designed to generate an inquiry, present a quotation, follow up on a proposal, or perform some sales or other persuasive task.

- ▤ Personalized and sent to a single prospect or customer at a time.

- ▤ Often contrived because of their repeated use; a sales letter is often customized to a particular prospect from a prewritten template stored on computer.

Because of the tendency to use prewritten templates, some sales letters sent by e-mail, particularly promotional letters, may be looked upon as yet another piece of spam or junk mail. Therefore, you will see the ⊘ icon frequently in this chapter, because printed letters are preferable for much of the sales correspondence here.

However, when it is appropriate to use e-mail, you can show that you have spent time crafting your message and tailoring it to its recipient (instead of simply jettisoning off a prefabricated "form" e-mail) by attaching the file of a formally written, personalized letter to your e-mail message, rather than using the body of the e-mail message itself as your letter. If you choose this route, your cover e-mail can be a brief, friendly note explaining to the recipient what you have attached.

A writing formula that sells

Most sales letters follow a pattern known to professional letter-writers simply as "AIDA," for "Attention, Interest, Desire, and Action." This simple but effective formula, first discovered by advertising writers, lets you cut through jargon and messy language to create straightforward writing that works.

Why do we need a formula for persuasion? Shouldn't we be able to simply state our proposition directly and get the action we desire? The obstacle is the glut of similar messages in your prospect's inbox, fax machine, and mailbox. A recent TV commercial informed viewers that the U.S. Post Office handles 300 million pieces of mail every day. That's a lot of letters.

But how many letters actually get their messages across and motivate the reader? Surprisingly few. In direct mail marketing, for example, a 2 percent response rate is high. A manufacturer who mails 1,000 sales letters will expect that fewer than 20 people will respond to the pitch. If high-powered letters written by ad agency copywriters produce such a limited response, you can see why letters written by busy business executives (who are not professional writers) may not always accomplish their objectives.

Failure to get to the point, technical jargon, pompous language, or misreading the reader are the poor stylistic habits that cause others to ignore the letters we send. Part of the problem is that many managers and support staff don't know how to write persuasively. The solution is AIDA, a sequence of psychological reactions that happen in the mind of the reader as he or she is sold on your idea. Briefly, here's how it works:

- **Attention.** First, the letter gets the reader's attention with a hard-hitting lead paragraph that goes straight to the point or offers an element of intrigue.

- **Interest.** Then the letter hooks the reader's interest: The hook is often a clear statement of the reader's problems, needs, or wants. For example, if you are writing to a customer who received damaged goods, acknowledge the problem.

- **Desire.** The letter should create desire and demand. Your letter is an offer of something—a service, a product, goodwill, an agreement, a contract, a compromise, a consultation. Tell the reader how he or she will benefit from your offering. That creates a demand for your product.

- **Action.** Finally, the letter states a call for action. At this point, you should ask for the order, the signature, the donation, the assignment.

What follows is an example of how each of these steps can be used to create one persuasive business letter.

Attention

Getting the reader's attention is a tough job. If your letter is boring, pompous, or says nothing of interest, you'll lose the reader—fast!

One attention-getting technique used by successful writers is to open with an intriguing question or statement—a "teaser" that grabs the reader's attention and compels him or her to read on.

Here are two types of attention-grabbing openers:

> Is *freelance* a dirty word to you?
>
> It really shouldn't be. In public relations, with its crisis-lull-crisis rhythm, good freelancers can save you money and headaches. Use them when you need them. When you don't, they don't cost you a cent.
>
> Use me. I am a public-relations specialist with more than 20 years of experience in all phases of the profession. My services are available to you on a freelance basis.

Even if you hate freelancers, you can't help but be curious about what follows. And what follows is a convincing argument to hire the writer:

Another freelance writer succeeded with a more straightforward approach:

> Dear Mr. Mann:
>
> Congratulations on your new business. May you enjoy great success and receive much pleasure from it. I offer my services as a freelance public relations writer specializing in medical and technical subjects.

Here, the writer gets attention by opening with a subject that has a built in appeal to the reader, namely, the reader's own business. Most of us like to read about ourselves. (And just about everybody would react favorably to the good wishes expressed in the second sentence.)

Interest

Once you get the reader's attention, you've got to provide a "hook" to create real interest in your subject and keep him or her reading. This hook is a promise to solve problems, answer questions, or satisfy needs:

> To stay ahead, you need aggressive people willing to take chances. People who are confident, flexible, and dedicated. People who want to learn and who are not afraid to ask questions.

What better way to hold someone's interest than to promise to solve his problems for him? A principal rule of persuasive writing is remembering that the reader isn't interested in you. The reader is interested in the reader. Because people like to hear about themselves, author Robert Bly cites the following letter as an example of one that would be particularly effective in gaining and holding his interest:

> As you may know, we have been doing some work for people who have the same last name as you do. Finally, after months of work, my new book, *The Amazing Story of the Blys in America*, is ready for printing, and you are in it!
>
> The Bly name is very rare and our research has shown that less than two one-thousandths of 1 percent of the people in America share the Bly name....

Desire

Get attention. Hook the reader's interest. Then create the desire to buy what you're selling. This is the step in which many businesspeople falter. Their corporate backgrounds condition them to write business letters in "corporatese," so they fill paragraphs with pompous phrases, jargon, clichés, and long-winded sentences.

Don't write to impress—write to express. State the facts, the features, and the benefits of your offer in plain, simple English. Give the reader reasons why he or she should buy your product, give you the job, sign the contract, or approve the budget. Create a desire for what you're offering.

With the reader's interest in hand, you can proceed to create a desire for your service or product:

> I am one of those people—one of the people you should have on your list of top freelancers. As a freelancer, I can offer you and your company many benefits. I work only when you need me. I don't require a desk in your company, nor a phone, nor stationery, nor medical benefits, nor sick or personal days. There are no "lazy" days for a freelancer: I will always hand you my very best, hoping to be hired again.

Benefits are spelled out. Anxieties are eliminated. The reader is given the reasons why he or she should hire a freelancer.

Action

If you've carried AIDA this far, you've gained attention, created interest, and turned that interest into desire. The reader wants what you're selling or at least has been persuaded to see your point of view. Now comes the last step—asking for action.

If you're selling consulting services, ask for a contract. If you want an interview, ask for it. If you're writing a fundraising letter, include a reply envelope and ask for a donation. In short, if you want your letter to get results, you have to ask for them:

> Read over the attached list of my clients and credits. It shows I can take any challenge and succeed.
>
> Then pick up the phone and call me today. Even if you have no project to assign immediately, let's talk about how my experience can help you get things done in the future.

An exchange of business letters is usually an action-reaction situation. To move things along, determine the action you want your letter to generate and tell the reader about it. Formulas have their limitations, and you can't force every letter or memo into the AIDA framework. Short interoffice e-mails, for example, seldom require this degree of persuasiveness.

But when you're faced with more sophisticated writing tasks—a memo to motivate the sales force, a mailer to bring in orders, a letter to collect bad debts—AIDA can help. Get attention, hook the reader's interest, create a desire, ask for action, and your letters will get better results!

The following is an overview of the many kinds of sales communications you may need to write—with abundant examples of how to put AIDA to work for you!

Sales series

For most firms, sales is a multistep process involving multiple communications with a given prospect. For this reason, many businesses develop a standard library of sales letters to address each stage in this multistep selling process. The following is a model series you can adapt to your own business and sales cycle.

The following series can be used for any product or service. Simply replace *computer systems* and any related language with your product or service. You can also substitute the benefits you offer (price savings, better service) for the benefits listed in the sample letters.

This is a fairly complete series. Use whatever letters fit into your selling cycle, in the order that makes sense for your business. Keep in mind that you do not have to use all the letters. Some may not apply to your product or fit your selling methods. Also, you will need to avoid e-mail for some of the more promotional letters here because of the possibility they will be categorized as spam.

Initial inquiry generator ⊘

Background: We all come across people and organizations who are a good fit for our products or services. A short, simple letter, like the one that follows, can be used to gauge their initial interest and get them to ask for more details about who you are and what you do.

Essential elements: Follow the AIDA formula:

1. Your opening should grab attention with something catchy (such as a quote, a statistic, or an interesting fact).
2. Create interest by acknowledging the reader's needs.
3. Build desire by explaining how you can meet those needs.
4. Call for action by explaining what the reader should do next.

Sample:

> Dear Ms. Gladstone:
>
> The tremendous recent improvements in hardware and software have made this adage truer than ever:
>
> "Improve your computer systems, and you improve your business systems. Improve your business systems, and you improve your business results."
>
> There's no longer any doubt: In today's business world, if you want to improve your business results, you need to have your business fully computerized and networked.
>
> When it comes to helping you improve your computer systems, we can help. Using the latest technology and proven software, we can increase your efficiency and productivity, while giving you faster access to important data for improved decision-making and business management.
>
> For more information on how we can give your business a competitive edge through better computer systems, call us today. There's no cost to talk to us. There is no obligation of any kind.
>
> Sincerely,

Sales lead: offer of free analysis of a prospect's requirements ⊘

Background: Many prospects may be wary of meeting with a salesperson. They either are afraid of being on the receiving end of high-pressure sales tactics or don't realize how they can immediately benefit from the product or service. You can use a letter to set up an appointment by positioning the initial meeting with the customer as an opportunity to assess his or her needs and recommend a solution.

Essential elements: The key here is to make the reader believe that this is not just a ploy to get a salesperson in the door. The letter should include:

1. An opening that gains attention by requiring readers to ask themselves how they can benefit from the service or product you want to sell.
2. An answer to that question that builds interest in you.
3. The details of the analysis that create a desire to find out more.
4. Instructions telling the reader how to take advantage of this opportunity with repeat assurances that the service is absolutely free.

Sample:

Dear Ms. Johnson:

Do you think that upgrading your business computer system might make sense but feel unsure about what you need or what to do next? Our free business computing needs analysis might be the answer.

Here's how it works:

One of our business computing specialists will visit your offices and, at no cost to you, conduct a complete audit of your business processes. We'll look at your operations, what's computerized, what isn't, and which areas could be made more efficient through better computing.

Within 48 hours of our visit, you'll receive a written report that gives the results of our business computing needs analysis. It includes specific hardware and software recommendations, along with cost estimates for purchase or lease of the recommended systems and applications.

There's no cost for this free business computing needs analysis. There is no obligation or sales pressure of any kind. Even if you don't have us put in a system for you, you'll find this analysis of your business processes and computing needs interesting—and useful. Call us today.

Sincerely,

Letter preceding a sales meeting

Background: Many sales meetings are unproductive simply because the seller does not help the buyer prepare. In a quick fax or e-mail, tell your prospects how they can help you serve them better in the meeting, what you need, and by when.

Essential elements: This letter serves to both confirm that you have a meeting and also make sure that everything you need to make the meeting productive is available:

1. Open with a confirmation of the time, date, and location of the meeting.
2. List each of the things you need the other person to have prepared for this meeting.
3. Conclude with a cordial closing.

Sample:

> **To:** Joseph Jones
> **From:** Bob Allen, phone 123-456-7890
> **Re**: Our Tuesday meeting
>
> I'm looking forward to meeting you Tuesday the 5th at 9 a.m. in your office. To make our session more productive, here's a list of items it would be nice to have at hand for the meeting:
>
> 1. Sample printout, or "dummy," of the standard report.
> 2. Sample printout, or "dummy," of the gold report, including the trade area map we create from their customer data.
> 3. Brochures or other promotional materials you have on your firm and consulting services.
> 4. Testimonials from satisfied consulting clients.
> 5. Client list.
>
> Ideally, if you give me the go-ahead to create a direct mail package for you, I'd like to take as much of this as I can back with me.
>
> Thanks,

Catalog insert letter

Background: Catalog marketing is an effective way to sell a broad line of related products by mail. But catalogs—professionally typeset, colorful, with lush photos and illustrations—are a rather impersonal medium. To add warmth, personality, and selling power to their catalogs, many marketers include a cover letter with their catalog mailings. You can use the letter to talk about your company, your products, your catalog, your service, your commitment to quality, your track record, benefits you offer to customers, or your guarantee. Or you can point the reader to specific features of the catalog or bargain items on various pages.

Note that you *can* use e-mail for this kind of letter as long as your catalog is available electronically and your customer has agreed to subscribe to e-mails from you; just attach the file of your catalog or refer the customer to a link to your catalog online.

Essential elements: This letter is a friendly version of the AIDA formula. It includes:

1. An attention-grabbing opening.
2. A message that talks to the needs of the reader to gain interest.
3. Information that promises a way to help the reader meet those needs.
4. Directions explaining what the reader should do next.

Sample:

> Dear Friend:
>
> The new catalog is out with a long list of brand-new items you've never seen before. [*If using e-mail, refer the customer to an attached file of the catalog or to a link to the catalog online.*]
>
> Are you looking for a unique gift for the person who has everything? Are you redecorating and need that "just right" accent piece? Have you been meaning to replace that worn-out (but much-loved) bed quilt? Are you running out of time to browse for a gift that that's just perfect?
>
> Now you can solve all your most difficult shopping dilemmas, without ever leaving the comfort of your favorite armchair. Browse through the pages of this new catalog, and you'll see high-quality products at prices that make them among the best values in the marketplace today. This is why shopping at XYZ is always a pleasure and not a chore. Our money-back guarantee assures you that if your selection does not meet your expectations, you can return it, postage-paid, with no questions asked.
>
> Send us your order today. You can call the toll-free number 24 hours a day or fax or mail the order form enclosed. [*If your catalog is online, mention this and refer to your easy, online checkout process.*]
>
> Go ahead—sit back, put up your feet, and enjoy the fun of slowly browsing through our products.
>
> Happy shopping,

Encouragement to reorder

Background: Sales letters sent to existing customers often generate responses many times more than what you would get from sales letters sent to rented lists of potential customers you don't know and who don't know you. With existing clients, seeing your company name is enough to get them to open and start reading.

Sending customers letters reminding them to reorder can be very profitable—especially if you can time the letters so the customer is likely to get one when his or her supplies are beginning to run low.

Note that you can send such letters to your existing customers by e-mail if they have agreed to receive e-mails from you.

Essential elements: This letter is a kindly reminder that should include:

1. A reminder that the customer has ordered from you before and a statement of that order.

2. A statement that you appreciate the customer's business with words of encouragement to reorder before supplies run out.

3. A very simple order form that lists the products, leaves room for new products, and gives ordering instructions.

4. A statement of the company policy on warrantees and guarantees.

5. A thank-you.

6. A discount mentioned in the postscript, to encourage the customer to place the order.

Sample:

Dear Sy Ackerman:

Back in February, you ordered the product(s) listed below. We appreciate your business. Now is the best time to reorder, before your inventory is low.

All the information needed to reorder is preprinted below. [*If using e-mail, refer to the appropriate attachment.*] Simply verify this information, make changes in quantity if necessary, even add new products. Just mail or fax this form to us, with your updated imprint samples, at 123-456-7890, or call us toll-free at 800-123-4567 and we'll take care of the rest. [*If using e-mail, you can attach a writeable document that the customer can fill out and send back via e-mail.*]

As a Business Products customer, you've recognized us for our quality products and our 100 percent satisfaction guarantee. This extended guarantee—along with our new, faster order turnaround time—separates us from any other discount professional supplier! Thank you for your continued confidence in Business Products, "Publishing's Reliable Supplier Since 1959."

Sincerely,

P.S. Now you can reorder and save 10%. All you have to do is order within 45 days from the date of this letter and use code 9801524 to receive your discount. The price on the order form already includes the discount. Thanks again for your business!

Sales proposal in memo format ⊘

Background: Writing a formal proposal is a complex writing task that takes a lot of time many of us don't have. We prefer to send proposals in memo style. It's less time-consuming, more informal, and in most instances, equally or more effective.

Essential elements: Most sales proposals include the following five sections:

1. **Overview:** This outlines the proposed project or service. It may include your objective.

2. **Concepts and methodology:** Here you map out, step-by-step, what you will do to meet the objectives set down in section 1.
3. **Assignment:** Repeat back to the client what he or she is hiring you to do.
4. **Timing:** State when the assignment will be completed.
5. **Cost:** State your fee and the other costs involved in completing the assignment.

Sample:

> **To:** Anne Chopin
> **From:** Brian Davidson, phone 123-456-7891
> **Re:** Copywriting—direct mail package for XYZ Company
>
> Dear Anne:
>
> Thanks for taking the time to chat with me. Here is the memo I promised to fax today. Questions? Call me at 123-456-7891.
>
> ### I. Overview
> XYZ Company markets credit card enhancement programs to banks, department stores, and oil companies.
>
> Sales have been primarily via telemarketing. XYZ Company is looking to develop profitable direct mail packages as an alternative. The objective is to bring in new members at a cost per order of $40 to $43.
>
> ### II. Concepts and Ideology
> Here are the steps normally involved in having me write a package for you:
> Research.
> Presentation of concepts (package outline).
> First draft of copy.
> Revisions.
>
> ### III. Assignment
> As discussed, my first choice would be to work on travel arrangements. I've done a lot of work in the travel industry and wrote a package offering a similar set of enhanced benefits to magazine subscribers.
>
> My second choice is health trends. With changes in health care today, people are uncertain about the status of their coverage. Again, almost everyone is going to use the service at least once or twice, so it will pay back its cost.

IV. Timing

If you can turn copy reviews around within a week or so, it's realistic for us to have final approved copy in November, in time to make a January mailing.

V. Cost

Copywriting: $6,500. Includes outline, copy, and revisions. Design to printer-ready disk: $2,500 to $10,000, depending on the design studio selected, package format, use of color, and photography or illustration required.

Sales lead tracker

Background: You can use this form to track sales leads generated by your various letters. The form can be stored in a file, in a three-ring binder, or on a database program to organize your follow-up efforts. A well-organized follow-up on leads is likely to increase the number of prospects who become customers.

Date_____Source of inquiry_____

Response via_____

Name_____Title_____

Company_____Phone_____

Address_____Room/floor_____

City_____State_____ZIP Code_____

Type of business:_____

Type of accounts (if an ad agency):_____

Type of projects:

For: ☐ immediate project ☐ future reference

☐ project to be started in:_____(month/year)

Status:

☐ Sent package on (date):_____

☐ Enclosed these samples:_____

☐ Next step is to:_____

☐ Probability of assignment:_____

☐ Comments:_____

Contact Record:

Date:_____Summary:_____

_____

_____

_____

Inquiry fulfillments

When you respond to an inquiry by mail, fax, or e-mail, you are usually sending the recipient information that he or she requested. This information can include fact sheets, brochures, catalogs, and other types of sales literature. The inquiry fulfillment letter is the cover letter that goes with this package.

Let's take a look at how to write an effective inquiry fulfillment piece by examining one that is ineffective. Suppose you had responded to an advertisement from a manufacturer of forged steel valves and requested more information. How would you react to this reply?

Dear Sir:

Chemical Equipment magazine has informed us of your interest in our line of valves for the chemical process industry. Enclosed please find the literature you requested. We will await with interest your specific inquiry.

Sincerely,
Joe Jones, Sales Manger
XYZ Valve Corporation

That letter doesn't call for action, build trust in the letter writer, or tell the reader why he should want to buy valves from XYZ. There's no salesmanship in it, just a blunt acknowledgment that an inquiry has been made. A fulfillment package should help move the sale along. However, this letter will not. The tragedy is that most letters mailed to fulfill business inquiries are horribly written. Too many marketers treat a cover letter as an afterthought thrown together after the pros from the ad agency have written the "important" elements of the communications program—the ads, brochures, and catalogues.

This is a big mistake. As creative consultant Sig Rosenblum aptly puts it, "Ads go through a long process of rough, layout, and finished art. But those are just devices to put ideas into the reader's mind. Your simple letters can carry powerful ideas just as easily as your complex ads."

But do they? Request more information on products and services you read about in ads or see on Websites and see for yourself. The responses you receive will include weak, dreary cover letters that rely on hackneyed expressions such as "enclosed please find," "pursuant to your request," and the ever-so-boring "as per your inquiry." That's not selling. When clichés substitute for copy that expresses a company's desire to help prospects solve problems, hot leads can quickly turn cold.

Part of the problem is that nonwriters, such as product mangers and engineers, often write cover letters. Management reasons that the advertising agent's time is better spent on ads and the like. Yet the letter provides the toughest writing challenge. It must sell on words alone, without the embellishment of color, photos, or artwork.

Tips for writing successful inquiry fulfillment letters

The key to successful cover letters? Be friendly, courteous, and helpful. Tell the reader how you will help him or her solve his or her problem better, faster, or cheaper than the competition. Here are eight letter-writing tips:

Thank the prospect for the lead

"Thanks for your interest" is a common opener. It may be becoming a cliché. However, it's still a necessary courtesy.

Highlight key sales points

Don't try to summarize your sales literature, but instead pick one or two of the important sales points and emphasize them in your letter. Letters are handy supplements to literature because they can include any recent developments that a color brochure, with its longer shelf life, may not reflect. Your letter can focus on a recent case history, a new application, a product improvement, or an addition to your manufacturing facility.

Tell the reader about the next step in the buying process

Make it easy for him or her by explaining exactly what to do next.

Write in a conversational tone

Your sales letter is communication from one human being to another—not from one corporate entity to the next. Warmth, humor, understanding, and an eagerness to be helpful are what make you the super-salesperson you are. Why not endow your letters with those same positive qualities?

Eliminate "whiskers"

One way to achieve an easy, natural style is to eliminate "whiskers" from your writing. Whiskers are those hackneyed expressions that drain life and personality from sales letters. Antiquated phrases from the vocabulary of the bureaucrat make a person (and his or her company) come across as a stuffed shirt.

Here are 10 hackneyed expressions to avoid:

1. *Enclosed please find...* The reader can find it on his or her own. Just say, "I'm enclosing," or "Here is."
2. *When time permits...* Poetic, but inaccurate. Time doesn't permit, people do.
3. *Please don't hesitate to call...* You really mean "Feel free to call."
4. *We are this date in receipt of...* Say instead, "Today we received."
5. *As per your request...* Say instead, "As you requested."

6. *Of this date...* Translation: "Today."

7. *Pursuant to your orders...* That's too formal. Just say, "As you requested" or "Following your instructions."

8. *Whereas...* Use "where" or "although."

9. *Kindly advise...* As opposed to "unkindly"? This phrase is unnecessary.

10. *Hitherto, whereby, thereby, herein, therein, thereof, heretofore...* Avoid these archaic, stilted words.

Have a "you" orientation

Good letter-writers know that the word *you* may well be the most important word in their vocabulary. A "you" orientation means thinking about what the reader wants, needs, and desires. Having a "you" orientation does not mean tooting your own horn. It means translating the technical features of a product into benefits that help the reader do his or her job, serve customers, and pleases the boss. And it means addressing the reader directly as "you." Remember, a sales letter is a personal communication, not a cold recitation of features and facts.

Be concise

Use small words and short sentences. And break the writing up into many short paragraphs. Brevity makes writing easy to read. Run-on sentences and long chunks of unbroken text bore and intimidate readers.

Make it look professional

All letters must be typed and proofread to eliminate errors in spelling, punctuation, grammar, and content.

A word on bounce-back cards

In addition to the literature and cover letter, a fulfillment package should contain a reply element. It can be a specification sheet, an order form, or a questionnaire known as the bounce-back card. Bounce-backs are postage-paid postcards addressed to you. They ask the prospect to qualify him- or herself by answering a few questions. Typically, a bounce-back questionnaire asks the prospect's name, address, and phone number, the name and size of his or her company, whether he or she specifies or recommends a particular type of product, current buying plans, applications, the names of others in the company involved in the buying decision, whether the prospect currently uses the advertiser's products or those of a competitor, whether the prospect wants a salesperson to call, and whether the inquiry is for an immediate need, a future need, or reference information only.

Bounce-back postcards may be separate from the rest of the package or they may be printed as tear-out inserts in brochures or catalogs. Some companies combine the bounce-back questionnaire, cover letter copy, and catalog information on a single sheet.

Most industrial marketing experts agree that the bounce-back is an integral part of the fulfillment package. "If you're not contacting the respondent personally, you should have a bounce-back card," says Robert L. Sieghardt, president of Professional Sales Support, a company that screens sales leads by telephone.

Sieghardt says that as many as 55 percent of prospects will respond with a bounce-back card after a series of three follow-up mailings. Some advertisers respond to inquiries by mailing a bounce-back card without any accompanying literature. They hope to avoid sending expensive sales brochures to students, competitors, brochure collectors, and other nonprospects.

But other firms criticize the practice because it delays getting information to respondents by creating an additional and unnecessary step in the sales sequence. "I think you're trying to kill responses by not sending a brochure," says Larry Whisehant, advertising manger of Koch Engineering, a manufacturer of chemical equipment. "The proper literature—what the respondent is asking for—is the most important piece of the package."

Robert Sieghardt agrees: "By trying to screen leads with the bounce-back, manufacturers are asking prospects to do some of their work for them." No two marketers agree on what makes the perfect fulfillment package. But one thing is clear: The advertiser who casually tosses a brochure in the mail with a hastily dictated cover note is wasting sales opportunities.

The entire package must be designed to generate action that leads to a sale. To accomplish this, you need three things: a clear, crisp cover letter that motivates prospects, a brochure that informs them, and a bounce-back or other reply element that makes it easy for them to respond.

Inquiry fulfillment: securing an appointment for a salesperson

Background: When a potential customer inquires about your service or product, the next logical step is to meet with the prospect to make a sales presentation. This inquiry fulfillment letter uses all the eight tips mentioned previously. E-mail is a good way to send it because it will reach your potential client sooner and allow you to schedule a meeting with him or her more quickly.

Essential elements: When someone has asked for information, you already have your foot in the door. Then it's time to sit down and visit. Your letter should:

1. Grab attention by immediately noting that the letter (and attached information, if appropriate) are being sent to respond to the reader's request.
2. Build interest by stating the reader's needs.
3. Create desire by explaining how you can solve the reader's problems.
4. Encourage action by explaining what the reader should do next.

Sample:

Dear Mr. Loman:

Thanks for asking about high-performance, tailored computer systems to run your business more efficiently and profitably. Literature describing system capabilities is attached.

The next step is to sit down and discuss your business computing requirements in detail. We'll take a look at what you have, what you need, current business processes, where computerization can help, and what hardware and software would best meet your requirements.

Then we'll provide recommendations on the system that's right for your business. We'll give you a detailed cost estimate for purchases and a low monthly lease payment quote for the system.

To schedule an appointment with one of our business computing specialists, simply give us a call. The consultation, as well as our recommendations, are free. There's no obligation to buy.

Sincerely,

Inquiry fulfillment to accompany literature

Background: A common mistake in inquiry fulfillment is to send an overly long and redundant letter that repeats product facts and features covered in the accompanying literature. Don't reproduce the text of your brochure in the letter. Rather, the letter should just hit the highlights, leaving the detail for the brochure or fact sheet to cover.

Essential elements: Your literature speaks for itself; the accompanying cover letter should move the potential customer to actually read the literature. It should include:

1. A thank-you for requesting the literature.
2. An enclosure containing the literature (or an attachment with the literature, if you are using e-mail to send it).
3. An explanation of what the literature covers.
4. A brief overview of what the service or product offers the customer.
5. An offer to discuss the service or product by phone, in person, or through an attached survey to meet individual needs.

Sample:

Dear Mr. Ramnstein:

Thanks for requesting the enclosed information on PS plumbing systems.

The enclosed literature will give you a good idea of PS's ease of use, flexibility, power, and speed. You'll also discover the many advantages of PS over conventional plumbing systems.

Your real question, of course, is "How can PS save ME time and money?"

Fortune 1000 companies worldwide have documented cost savings of 70 to 90 percent using PS. But the only way to determine the benefits to your company is to call 123-456-7890 and talk with a sales representative.

A preliminary and free phone conversation will quickly enable you to determine whether PS implementation is worth exploring further. If so, a company representative can perform a free, on-site evaluation of your current system and recommend improvements.

To find out how PS can meet your needs, simply call 123-456-7890. [*If using e-mail, refer the recipient to your contact information in your e-mail signature.*] Or complete and return the plumbing system needs assessment form attached. As always, there is no cost or obligation of any kind.

Sincerely,

Follow-ups

Making contact with customers or making a first sale is just the beginning of creating a business relationship. To bring customers in and keep them loyal you'll often have to write follow-up letters.

Follow-up after literature has been mailed

Background: It is unlikely that you will get to meet with every prospect or even the majority of prospects right away. For this reason, follow-up is key. According to a study by Thomas Publishing, publishers of the popular purchasing directory, *Thomas Directory*, 80 percent of business sales are made on the fifth follow-up, but most marketers follow up only three times or less. A series of well-crafted follow-up letters can ensure you contact prospects frequently enough to gain their attention and, ultimately, their business. E-mail is acceptable for these letters, but it is better to use a combination of printed letters and e-mail for a series of letters so as not to bombard your customer with e-mail.

Essential elements: Don't sit around waiting for potential customers to respond to your sales literature. Use the mailing as a hook that gives you line to reel them in. Follow-up letters should include:

1. Mention of the literature that was previously sent.
2. A statement about the benefit to the reader of your product or service.
3. Instructions to act now.
4. An offer to send the material again if it was not received.

Sample:

Dear Mr. Thomas:

Recently, I sent you literature describing the computer systems, services, and solutions we have created for businesses like yours. If you need to computerize your business, call us. We may be able to help you with an innovative computer solution costing much less than you'd think.

The sooner you modernize your business procedures and computer systems, the sooner you'll begin to enjoy the benefits of increased productivity, reduced paperwork, and faster access to critical information for better decision-making.

We're ready when you are. Call, e-mail, or fax us today with your requirements.

Sincerely,

P.S. If you didn't receive the information, or need additional literature, let me know. I'll make sure to send the information to you via fax or e-mail.

Follow-up after a phone conversation or first meeting

Background: This letter is sent as a follow-up immediately after a first meeting in which you have mapped out your service or product. A copy of the cost estimate, printed on a separate sheet, should be enclosed with the letter. (It is also acceptable to send this letter as an e-mail message with an attachment containing the cost estimate.)

Essential elements: This letter keeps you and your product or service on the customer's mind while he or she is making this business decision. Be sure to include:

1. Mention of your recent conversation.
2. Cost estimates of the product or service you had discussed, tailored to the customer's requirements.
3. Available financing.
4. Instructions about how the customer can take the next step.

Sample:

Dear Ms. Poplar:

It was a pleasure chatting with you today concerning your company's business computing needs. Based on our discussion, I've attached preliminary cost estimates for several different systems that meet your requirements.

As you see, our flexible financing terms enable us to tailor the low monthly lease payment to meet any budget. The system can also be purchased outright.

If these figures look good to you, the next step is to discuss the specific system configuration and options in detail. After doing that, we'll give you a final cost estimate detailing all system components, pricing, and purchase and lease options for your approval.

Sincerely,

Follow-up after a purchase

Background: Salespeople are painfully familiar with "buyer's remorse," when the customer calls the day after the purchase and says, "I'm not sure about this—maybe I made a mistake—you have a return policy, don't you?" A follow-up letter after a purchase can help assure customers they made the right decision.

Essential elements: To cut down on buyer's remorse calls, send an immediate post-purchase letter affirming the buyer's decision as a wise one to make. The letter should include:

1. Thanks for the purchase.
2. A review of all the positive features of the product.
3. A reminder of any guarantees, rebates, or other "extras" included with the product.
4. A psychological plug that assures the customer how smart he or she is for making this purchase.

Sample:

Dear Ms. Kelley,

Thanks for your recent purchase of the Axirionn-2000 laptop.

As you will discover, your Axirionn-2000's high-speed Pentium Processor, enhanced graphics board, and built-in wireless Internet give you the fastest

---

and sharpest access to the Internet you have ever experienced. As you browse, you'll experience click-through navigating and Web downloading at up to twice the speed of conventional laptops.

Your Axirionn-2000 also comes with a top-of-the-line Web navigator loaded and ready to go, with one month free through Eagle Network, the Internet Service Provider (ISP) we recommend to our local customers.

New customers also get a one-year free membership in our WebWise Users Group, which includes a quarterly Internet newsletter and discounts on our Internet seminars. A schedule of our seminars is also enclosed.

Others ride the Information Superhighway in the equivalent of a horse-and-buggy. You're doing it in a souped-up sportscar, the way it was meant to be done.

Congratulations on a wise purchase decision!

Sincerely,

Follow-up at one-year anniversary

Background: Selling does not end with purchase. The real profits in most relationships are in repeat orders and referrals. To get repeat business, you must ensure customer satisfaction with your products and services on an ongoing basis. A customer notice should be sent at least once a year to verify satisfaction and uncover any problems that require correction.

Essential elements: This is a great way to build goodwill and customer loyalty. Include:

1. A happy anniversary message.
2. A request for positive feedback (great for testimonial advertising).
3. An offer to answer questions or lend a hand.
4. An offer to solve any problems that have come up with your product.
5. An upbeat closing that looks ahead to a business relationship continuing into the future.

Sample:

Dear Mr. Towers:

I was checking my records and noticed it's been one year since you acquired your computer system from us. Happy anniversary!

If you are thrilled and delighted with your computer system, please take a moment to let me know. We always enjoy hearing from our customers about the benefits our systems have brought to their businesses.

If you have questions or need help mastering a particular application or function of your system, call us. We know the answers—and will be happy to share them with you. All you have to do is ask!

If there is a problem, if something isn't working the way you expected, or a particular business need is not being met, please call or e-mail us. We're here to help.

Again, happy anniversary! Here's to many more!

Sincerely,

Quotations and estimates ⊘

Before you begin a job or sell a product, many companies require a written quotation of cost. These quotations require a well-written cover letter that encourages the customer to sign the agreement. Because of important financials are involved that need filing and documentation and that often lead to legally binding contracts—and because you'll want to make the best impression on your potential customer—do not use e-mail for these communications. Put your best foot forward with letters printed on company stationery and professional quotation and estimate forms that display your company logo.

Quotation cover letter

Background: This letter accompanies a contract, formal quotation, or other document requiring the signature of the customer to process the order or begin the work. A duplicate of the original quotation or cost estimate should be enclosed with this letter.

Essential elements: This letter should show the customer that you want to meet his or her needs and begin a business relationship as soon as possible. It should include:

1. A statement that tells the reader a quotation is enclosed for a specific product or job.
2. A request to verify that the specs match the customer's needs and a willingness to change the quotation if necessary.
3. An encouraging note to order now while prices are in effect.
4. An explanation of how long the terms will be offered.

Sample:

> Dear Ms. Compt:
>
> As we discussed, here's a preliminary quotation for a computer system for XYZ Company.
>
> Does this reflect everything we discussed, and what you expected? If not, let us know, and we can quickly revise the quotation to reflect your needs.
>
> If the quotation is on target, tell us how you want to proceed. We can arrange a lease with low monthly payments tailored to your operating budget. Of course, the system is also available for outright purchase. But I urge you to hurry. Several of the major hardware and software vendors have announced planned price increases. When their prices go up, so do ours.
>
> We can only hold the prices in this quotation for 60 days from the date on the proposal. To ensure the lowest prices, place your order now.
>
> Sincerely,

Quotation follow-up: first reminder

Background: If after sending the contract, you don't get a response, you need to send a reminder. Enclose a copy of the original quotation. Send this letter a week or two after you mail the original quote.

Essential elements: This letter is a friendly nudge that gives the reader a reason to contact you. It should include:

1. A reminder that the attached quotation is still in effect.
2. An acknowledgment that the customer may be shopping around and looking at several different products/services.
3. An offer to requote to any new specifications.
4. An offer to answer any questions or resolve any uncertainties.

Sample:

> **Re:** Quotation and proposal for XYZ Co.
>
> Dear Ms. Compt:
>
> This is just a reminder that the terms and prices on the enclosed quotation are still good for several weeks. If you've been shopping around, you may be thinking of a system that is slightly different than the one we quoted you.

In that case, give me a call. We'd be happy to requote on your new specification. We can even provide several different quotes for various configurations, to aid you in your decision-making.

Just one other thing to keep in mind: There's rarely just "one solution" to a given business computing challenge. If you're still uncertain, please call us. We can recommend hardware, software, and service alternatives that can satisfactorily meet any requirement—and budget.

Sincerely,

Quotation follow-up: second reminder

Background: The second reminder is sent about two weeks after the first follow-up letter, again with a copy of the contract or quote enclosed.

Essential elements: This letter implies that you may be able to change your quote, but it can also mean that you can suggest substitute or alternate products/services to save money. It should include:

1. A reminder that the attached quote was submitted a while ago.
2. A request that if the customer is considering another company, he or she contact you before sealing the deal.
3. A suggestion that you can help the customer save money as compared to other companies.
4. A thank-you for the opportunity to offer a quote.

Sample:

Re: Quotation and proposal for XYZ Co.

Dear Ms. Compt:

It's been some time since we quoted you on a computer system for your business. So, I have one favor to ask. If you're considering another system, please give me a call before you sign any contract or issue a purchase order to another vendor. We may be able to provide additional ideas to save you money or enhance system performance in ways these other vendors may not know about.

Thanks again for giving us the opportunity to quote on your system.

Sincerely,

Quotation follow-up: final reminder

Background: If the prices and terms you quoted are good only for a certain period, send this letter a couple of weeks before the period is about to expire, warning the customer that after that date, the prices may be higher or the product unavailable.

Essential elements: In this letter be sure to keep your tone friendly and keep the door open to future business. Include:

1. A notice that the terms in the attached quotation are in effect for only a short while longer.
2. A request to let you know if the customer wants to go ahead.
3. A request to let you know if he or she would like a different product/service and therefore need a new quotation.
4. An offer to extend the quotation if the customer is still thinking.

Sample:

Re: Quotation and proposal for XYZ Co.

Dear Ms. Compt:

The terms and pricing on this quotation are guaranteed for only a few remaining days.

If you have made a decision in favor of our system, please let us know right away. We'll lock in the prices and begin the paperwork that moves your transaction forward.

If you think you might want a different system than is described in our quotation, no problem. Just tell us what you have in mind. We'll give you a revised quote immediately. If you are unsure as to whether you're going to go ahead right now, but think it's a possibility, call me. I'll extend the terms and prices on the enclosed quotation to you for another 60 days. That's ironclad, regardless of whether our suppliers raise their own prices to us during that time. (If they do, we'll absorb the difference.)

Sincerely,

P.S. If you have acquired a system from another vendor, we are always here to help you with software, equipment upgrades, consulting, training, service, support, supplies, or whatever else you may need-now or in the future.

Agreements ⊘

Even if a prospect agrees over the telephone to use your product or service, a formal closing of the sale should be done in writing. Agreements, even informal ones, require detailed filing and documentation because they are contractual in nature, so avoid e-mail and stick with hard copy and the post office.

Informal letter of agreement

Background: For simple uncomplicated projects, you can confirm assignments in writing with a brief letter of agreement, such as the one below. Be sure to include a second copy for the customer and a self-addressed, stamped envelope so that he or she can easily return the signed form to you. For more complex projects, you should consult an attorney who can draw up a formal business agreement.

Essential elements: This letter serves as a contract between you and your customer. Include:

1. A thank-you for being given the specified work/order.
2. A request for the signed form to be returned to you.
3. A detailed description of the service/product.
4. The fee for this service/product.
5. Any exceptions that would change the fee (overtime, revisions, changes in specs, and so forth).
6. If appropriate, the terms for payment of business expenses.
7. A payment schedule.
8. A place for the recipient to sign and date.

Sample:

Dear Mr. Jones:

Thank you for choosing XYZ Ad Agency to handle your Job #3333. The following agreement spells out the terms and conditions of this project. Please keep a copy for your records and return a signed copy to me in the enclosed envelope.

Job #3333 is a series of three capability brochures. I will write these brochures for you and provide such marketing and editorial consulting services as may be required to implement the project.

My base fee for the services I describe above is $10,000. That fee estimate is based on 100 hours of working time at my hourly rate of $100 and includes time for copywriting, editing, teleconferencing, meeting, consulting, travel, and research. Copy revisions are included in my base fee. At such time as the total time devoted by me exceeds 100 hours, I shall bill you for additional working time at the rate of $100 per hour.

> Out-of-pocket expenses, such as long-distance telephone calls, photo-copies and computer printouts, fax charges, messengers, and local and out-of-town travel incurred in connection with the project, will be billed to you in an itemized fashion.
>
> Payment of the base fee will be made as follows: One-third of the above-mentioned base fee is due upon my commencement of work, one-third due upon delivery of first draft copy, and one-third is due upon completion. Payment for expenses will be made within 10 days following receipt of invoice.
>
>
> Sincerely,
>
>
> Accepted and agreed:
>
> By:_____ Date:_____

Terms and conditions of fee structure

Background: If the pricing, fee structure, terms, or conditions are complex, they can be listed in an attachment rather than being incorporated into the body of an agreement letter.

Essential elements: This list of terms and conditions is dictated by the particular service. It should include all the terms, including hourly fees, project fees, reimbursable expenses, and contingencies such as revisions, changes in specs, overtime, and so forth.

STATEMENT OF GENERAL TERMS & CONDITIONS

1. Fee Structure

All time, including travel hours, spent on the project by professional, technical, and clerical personnel will be billed. (Travel time is billed at half-hourly fees, portal to portal.) The following approximate ranges of hourly rates for various categories of personnel are currently in effect:

Hourly Rate	Category
$400	Principal in charge
$100 to $200	Senior consultants
$40 to $75	Marketing analysts
$30 to $50	Research technicians
$15	Desktop publishing, scanning, computer entry, design

Hourly rates will be adjusted semiannually to reflect changes in the cost-of-living index as published. If overtime for nonprofessional personnel is required, the premium differential figured at time and one-half of their regular hourly rate is charged at direct cost to the project. Unless otherwise stated, any cost estimate presented in a proposal is for budgetary purposes only and is not a fixed price. The client will be notified when 75 percent of any budget figure is reached.

2. Reimbursable Expenses

a) Travel expenses necessary for the execution of the project, including rail, taxi, bus, air, rental vehicles, and highway mileage in company or personal vehicles, which will be charged at 20 cents per mile. The following expenses will be billed at direct cost:

b) Accommodations, all meals at cost.

c) Telephone/fax charges.

d) Postage and shipping/courier services.

e) In-house printing and reproduction.

f) Other project expenses: scanning, photocopying, laser printing, and so forth.

3. Art production (typed layouts, type specs, mechanical assembly)

Artist's time charged at $50/hour or estimated on project fee basis.

Correspondence about add-on support ⊗

If your product comes with a warranty or a support contract, you should be in touch when that contract is about to expire and again if it does expire. These moments are selling opportunities. It's better not to use e-mail for these letters because they, again, involve contracts.

Selling an add-on support contract

Background: One way to profit from satisfied customers is to sell more products and services to them. Here's a letter you can use to sell a service contract to customers who have bought your products and whose warranties have expired.

Essential elements: This letter should make the recipient feel he or she is getting something extra or special. It should include:

1. An opening offering to make the customer a top priority.

2. An announcement that a service/support contract is enclosed and is offered at a discounted price.

3. The benefits of the service.

4. Instructions to sign and mail to gain the coverage.

Sample:

Dear Mr. Smyth:

We can't be everywhere, all the time, for everyone. No one can.

But now there's an easy way to ensure we're always there for you, when and where you need us to be.

The attached service and support agreement spells out the various levels of service and support we offer businesses in our area. As one of our system users, you receive a discount of 30 percent off compared with what we charge for support to businesses who do not own or lease one of our systems.

You rely on computers to keep your business running and to access critical information. When the computers stop, so does business. Our service and support agreement ensures speedy repair or replacement to get you up and running with minimum downtime.

To activate your service and support, simply sign the agreement and mail it back to us. Service and support become immediately available the minute you sign. For faster service, call, e-mail, or fax us your instructions today.

Sincerely,

P.S. No need to enclose payment now. We will bill you later.

Renewal of a support contract

Background: When a customer's maintenance, service, or support contract is close to expiring, send a letter asking him or her to renew. Insert a support contract renewal for signature, and include a reply envelope.

Essential elements: This letter is sent to customers who have already shown they are interested in paying for additional support or service. Its job is to convince them that the price is worth renewing. It should include:

1. An announcement that the support contract is about to expire.
2. Instructions to sign the enclosed renewal contract to ensure uninterrupted service.
3. Assurance that payment need not be sent with the contract. You will bill the reader later.
4. The benefits of the service or support program to the customer.
5. Information about the price of the contract (and any upcoming increases if applicable).
6. Instructions to renew now.

Sample:

Re: service and support contract #87396

Dear Ms. Crocker:

Our records indicate that your service and support contract with us will expire soon. A renewal agreement is enclosed. To ensure uninterrupted service and support, please sign and return it right away. There's no need to enclose payment with your renewal instructions; we'll bill you later.

Our fast, responsive service and support keeps your critical business computing systems up and running. When there's a problem, we're there in a flash. Speedy repair or replacement minimize downtime and keep your business going.

As one of our system users, you get year-round service and support for a discount of 30 percent off what we charge to businesses that do not own or lease one of our systems.

Rising parts and labor costs will soon force us to raise our support and service fees to new customers. Renew now to lock in your current low contract rate for the next 12 months before our prices go up.

Sincerely,

P.S. To lock in the discount renewal rate and avoid paying full contract price, act now before your current contract expires. Renewing now also ensures that your service coverage will continue uninterrupted.

Renewal of support contract: second effort

Background: It is often profitable to mail several renewal notices instead of just one. With each, insert a support contract renewal for signature with a reply envelope.

Essential elements: This letter repeats the offer of the first letter and adds an additional warning. It includes:

1. An announcement that the support contract has expired.
2. An offer of a grace period during which the customer can renew the contract.
3. The benefits of renewing during this grace period.
4. A warning stating that when the grace period expires, the customer will be required to pay a higher rate than currently being charged for this service.

Sample:

Re: Service and support contract #87396

Dear Ms. Crocker:

Our records show that your service and support contract with us has expired.

For the next 30 days, we will offer a grace period during which you can renew your service and support contract.

When you renew within this grace period, your service continues uninterrupted. And you renew at the discount renewal rate, which is 30 percent less than what new service contract customers are currently paying.

If you renew after the grace period, we cannot hold the discount renewal rate, and you may be required to pay the higher standard rate for service and support.

Sincerely,

Order confirmations and "zap" correspondence

Letters that say thanks after you've made a sale open the door to future business relationships. On the other hand, sometimes it's time to "zap" an inactive customer from your files. These letters will show you how. Use printed letters, not e-mail, because contracts or reply cards may be involved.

Thank-you letter for an order, including confirmation

Background: Upon receipt of the signed contract or order, send a brief thank-you note to the customer. Include a copy of the approved quotation with any changes made from the original estimate reflected in the final order. This is a handy form letter you can file in your computer and send out easily to confirm every order you receive.

Sample:

> **Re:** Order #655321
>
> Dear Mr. Ericson:
>
> Thank you for your order.
> This is a written confirmation of the items you have requested, described in the enclosed quotation.
> If you want to make a change, please call our office immediately so we can accommodate your request. Otherwise, we'll proceed as outlined. Once again, thanks for your business.
>
> Sincerely,

Zap correspondence

Background: A "zap" letter is used to remove old names from your mailing list. If the person doesn't respond, his or her name is removed from your active database and put into an archival file.

Zap letters prevent customers and prospects from being annoyed by mail they do not wish to receive. They also remind customers that they have agreed to receive any material you are sending them, and are not sending mail without their permission.

Essential elements: This is a sales letter to someone who hasn't used your services/product in a while. It should entice him or her to renew the business relationship, but also offer the opportunity to be dropped from your mailing list. It should include:

1. An announcement that because of not ordering, the customer is about to be dropped from the mailing list.
2. A description of what the customer will lose if this happens.
3. A review of what your company offers.
4. A request for the customer to indicate (either by filling out an enclosed response card or calling) whether he or she would like to remain on your mailing list or be dropped. (Be sure to include the "favor" you're offering if the customer is not interested: you will reduce their load of bothersome advertising mail.)
5. A reminder (or warning) of what the customer will lose by not responding.
6. A final request to respond today.

Sample:

You are about to be zapped.

Don't let it happen!

Dear Mrs. Ericsson:

It's been some time since we heard from you. Unless we hear from you within the next 10 days, your name will be removed from our mailing list. You will no longer be getting exciting free offers from Studebaker-Worthington in your mailbox.

Studebaker-Worthington has a nationwide reputation for providing resellers with flexible, competitive leasing programs and free tools to help you increase sales.

But we have not heard from you in quite some time. You haven't called us about a lease. And you haven't responded to any of our recent free offers. So, we're wondering if you're no longer interested. In that case, we don't want to clutter up your mailbox.

Here's what we're asking. Let us know, either way, whether you have any interest in our leasing programs and freebie offers and whether you want to remain on our list. Simply use the handy reply card enclosed. Or call us toll-free 800-123-4567 today.

Warning: If you do not respond, you risk being "zapped" from our mailing list! To ensure that you continue to get exciting free offers from Studebaker-Worthington, including new sales aids and software upgrades, call or mail us now. Thank you.

Sincerely,

11

Direct Marketing Communications

In this chapter, we discuss how to write direct marketing correspondence, or "direct mail." Direct mail:

- Is designed to bring checks, purchase orders, credit card information, and orders (or at least an appointment with a salesperson).

- Is usually sent in mass mailings to thousands of prospects simultaneously.

- Can be mailed to existing customers and prospects, but is most often mailed to rented lists of people likely to be interested in what your company is offering.

It's worth noting that e-mail lists (or "e-lists") are used more and more in the market today, and Internet marketing has grown exponentially in popularity. The Direct Marketing Association reported that in 2007 the amount of e-mail marketing grew by more than half and e-mail marketing for the first time overtook direct mail sent via the post office. This trend is only expected to continue. At the same time, everyone has too much to read, and that's especially true with e-mail. How do you make your e-mail stand out from the crowd? The following guidelines can help.

E-mail marketing: making it work for you

How do you tell which e-lists are the quality ones? These five questions can help you determine which lists can produce profitable results for your product or service.

1. What is the Website's method for opting-in the people on its list? There are dozen of databases with fancy names and big descriptions, but after digging through the promotional information, they turn out to be nothing much.

Prospects who have not requested anything do not remember how or when they got on the list and probably will not respond. These lists might have a chance with all those free offers that have been circulating the Web, but serious direct marketers are looking for genuine Internet buyers.

For promotional e-mail, response lists are generally superior to compiled lists. In e-mail, there are numerous lists on the market compiled from Internic, which is the organization with which all Web advertisers must register their domain names. Other compiled lists consist of Internet addresses of people who visit use groups.

Response lists, by comparison, consist of Internet-enabled prospects who have either responded to an e-mail offer or registered at a particular Website. By doing so, they have actively indicated interest in a particular subject area. Another plus is that, in addition to just the Internet address, the list contains additional information as name, address, phone number, and sometimes even buying preferences and demographics.

Results from Internet marketing programs indicate that the best response is obtained using opt-in lists. The true definition of "opt-in" is that people on an e-list have registered at the site or through some other electronic or paper form and checked the option requesting additional e-mail information from other companies.

Different list owners use different definitions of "opt in," resulting in lists of varying quality. When you visit Websites and fill in guest pages, note that some Websites have prechecked the "Yes, I want to receive e-mail from other companies" option. So, when you complete and submit the guest form, you opt-in automatically.

Other Websites require the registrant to proactively check "yes" for the opt-in option. The latter is indicative of a more responsive, qualified e-list. "Make sure the opt-in language explains clearly that other companies will be e-mailing to the Internet user," advises Michelle Feit, vice president, Internet marketing, Edith Roman Associates. "If Web surfers visiting the site are not presented with the choice to opt-in, they may respond negatively to receiving e-mail from direct marketers, including you."

How can you find out what opt-in means to the e-list you are considering testing? Ask for its opt-in language. Or go to its Website and register. If an e-list owner won't give you the opt-in language or the URL address of its Website, question the integrity of the list it offers.

A number of lists use a form of "reverse opt-in." They broadcast e-mails to Internet addresses with an advertising message that includes the promise of future promotional e-mails. They state that if the recipient doesn't want to receive future e-mails, he or she must click on "unsubscribe." Therefore, these so-called opt-in lists aren't really opt-in at all, since the prospect who takes no action is considered qualified, which isn't true. (This is the electronic equivalent of mailing qualification cards for a controlled circulation publication, and considering anyone who does not send in the qualification card with a note saying "I don't want to subscribe" as a qualified subscriber.)

2. What type of relationship does the site have with the people on its list? The most responsive lists have ongoing relationships between site and registrant. "Whether they are receiving a monthly magazine, weekly newsletter, or are purchasing products from the company, look for lists of people who have an ongoing relationship with the site and are not just surfers," advises Feit. "You want to know how often the people are returning to the site, how often the site is contacting them, and the last contact date."

3. How is the e-list maintained? Well-maintained lists add new names, match e-list names to e-mail preference files, update address corrections, and remove bounce-backs and opt-outs. Thanks to the speed of the Internet, there is a lot of activity on e-lists. A inaccurate file can decrease response and increase flaming, bounce-backs, and costs. Look for e-lists that are updated monthly or more frequently and guarantee 100 percent delivery.

When you rent a quality response e-list, don't be surprised when the list owner refuses to transmit the names to you and insists on transmitting your e-mail for a fee. This is standard practice among owners of quality lists. It's the electronic equivalent of a conventional list owner who won't send his or her list directly to mailers but ships only to bonded letter shops.

For the e-lists on the market today, about one-quarter of the list owners insist on doing the transmission, while the other half will release their e-mail lists to mailers. Research shows that most of the firms who release their e-mail addresses have compiled lists.

Why do owners of quality response lists insist on controlling their lists so closely? One reason is to ensure the integrity of the list by eliminating tampering. More important, it prevents the people on the list, whose trust the owner values, from receiving unwanted offers. And it ensures that Internet users get only offers of interest—including yours.

4. What selections are available on the e-list? Selections are essential for target marketing. E-lists have two types of selections: Website data and individual data.

Site data is generated from log reports, and a "quality" e-list will have them available. Examples of site data include original registration dates, last time visited, and number of times visited.

Individual data is gathered directly from the registrant or by enhancement. Examples of individual data are consumer versus business traffic, age, gender, job title, industry, and special interests. Selections allow you to target only those Internet prospects most likely to respond to your offer.

5. Does the e-list owner offer any value-added services? Some e-lists offer value-added services that can increase the effectiveness of your marketing. You can turn your message into a personalized offer by putting the person's name in the body of your copy. Immediate "click-through" reports show how many people took the next action by clicking through to your Website. Other value-added services available include split tests for multiple messages, list owner endorsements, address corrections, e-mail address appending, data enhancements, and e-mails with graphics, to name a few. Many of these services can increase response and reduce cost per order.

Model promotional e-mail

The low cost of e-mail lets you target promotions toward different market segments. In the sample e-mail provided here, the targets were all XYZ managers with e-mail addresses. The lead of the e-mail uses this fact as the rationale why the reader should pay attention to the message received.

E-mail that promotes your business should include the same elements of direct mail–writing found in snail mail. They should:

1. Immediately attract the reader's attention by pointing out a problem or situation the reader can relate to.
2. Offer a solution to that problem.
3. Create a desire to know more about your product or service.
4. Offer proof that you are the best.
5. Tell the reader what to do next.

Sample:

From: John Johnson <mdinfo@Tech.com>
Date: Tuesday, August 13, 20XX
To: XYZ Management
Subject: Proprietary data management solutions

Dear XYZ Executive:

Attention XYZ Personnel: If you can receive and read this e-mail message, the integrity of your critical data may be at risk.

With the proliferation of distributed computing throughout the XYZ organization, more and more critical XYZ data resides on client/server networks for which no coordinated, centralized data management strategy exists.

As a result, an increasing number of XYZ systems are at considerable risk for data loss, data corruption, downtime, and other problems that can result from lack of effective data management systems.

Our company, Techo Systems, provides effective, flexible data management, storage, backup, and recovery solutions for more than 250 companies worldwide.

Within the last 12 months, Techo Systems has experienced explosive growth, increasing revenues by 70 percent and doubling customer service staff. We've recently installed systems for Sprint, GTE, Siemens, and other major telecommunications companies. *But XYZ continues to remain our best customer.*

Techo offers its XYZ customers effective, centralized data management solutions customized to meet their specific data backup and recovery requirements. Today there are more than 100 Techo systems within XYZ protecting more than 30 terabytes of XYZ proprietary information.

Special offers for XYZ only!

For a limited time, Techo Systems is making these valuable *free* offers to XYZ customers and potential customers only. Please check as many as you would like to receive: [*Note that this form would be an attachment to your e-mail message.*]

- ☐ *Free* Techo Advisor software enables you to analyze your data management needs and compare storage options costs
- ☐ *Free* TechStore98 Demo Disk and Information Kit
- ☐ *Free* no-obligation Storage Management Analysis
- ☐ *Free* Reference List of Installed Techo systems for XYZ

Name_____

Company_____

Address_____

City_____

State_____

ZIP_____

Phone_____

Fax_____

E-mail_____

You can mail or fax a printout of this reply form to:
Techo Systems, Inc.
Anytown, USA
Fax 123-456-7899
For any questions, call 123-456-7890, or e-mail mdinfo@Tech.com.

Sincerely,

P.S. These special *free* offers are available until September 15. Once they expire, they may never be available again.

Where appropriate, the direct mail sales correspondence samples provided in this chapter, including the lead-generating correspondence, can be adapted to e-mail; follow the guidelines and model e-mail we have just provided, noting that any "enclosures" would be "attachments" that your recipient would need to print out instead.

Of course, look out for the 🚫 icon.

Model direct mail

Here is an example of a direct mail letter used to generate sales leads for a chemical company. The letter, mailed to environmental engineers and consultants, generated an 11-percent response. (A typical response rate for a lead-generating letter mailed to a mailing list is 1 to 3 percent.)

Sample:

Mr. Joe Jones,
XYZ Company
Anytown, USA 00110
Dear Mr. Jones:

Do you have a potable water supply or waste stream that contains organic contaminants?

Have you considered activated carbon as an ideal treatment—but rejected it because of the cost?

Ecofilter may be the answer for you. These patented, carbon-containing precoats handle high flow rates and can be utilized at a reasonable cost for many temporary applications where a one-time cleanup of contaminated water is required. Activated carbon in Ecofilter has an extremely high adsorption capacity, so Ecofilter can readily remove many types of organic compounds.

Ecofilter's unique composition makes it all possible. In an Ecofilter precoat, discrete particles of activated carbon are attached to fibers. The result is a large exposed surface area of activated carbon for superior absorption. The open, porous structure can handle large flow volumes with minimal pressure drop across the filter. In addition to adsorption, Ecofilter can remove suspended solids, too.

Is Ecofilter right for your application? We'd be delighted to evaluate a water sample to see if Ecofiter can handle your particular requirements. To find out more, give me a call or check off the appropriate box on the enclosed reply card and mail it, today.

Sincerely,

The direct mail reply card ⊘

A business reply card should be included as part of every direct mailer you send out. If you are using a self-mailer, the bottom third portion of the trifold mailing piece should be a business reply card. The fold between this business reply card and the rest of the self-mailer should be perforated to make the reply card easy to remove. A bold dotted line can be printed horizontally across the perforated fold to graphically emphasize the fact that the reply card is designed to be torn off.

A design technique that works well is to affix the mailing label directly to the reply portion of the self-mailer, then fold the self-mailer so the label shows through a die-cut hole on the address panel. This way, the reply card is already filled in with the prospect's name and address, and you get the label back when the reply card is returned to you.

The benefit of getting the label back is that, if you are mailing to multiple lists, you can tell which list generated the response. Labels from varying lists can be assigned a key code by the list broker that identifies which list a label came from. The cost of key coding is only an additional $1 to $2 per thousand names, and it is well worth the price.

If you send out a direct mail letter, print the reply card on light blue, pink, canary, or some other brightly colored paper stock so that it stands out from the letter. Make the design as simple and clutter-free as possible.

Conventional wisdom says to make the reply element a business reply post-card, which means you, not the prospects, pay the postage (plus a small handling fee) for all cards returned to you. Your local postmaster can give you a booklet with complete instructions on how to get a business reply permit and prepare business reply cards and envelopes.

In consumer mailings, using business reply mail is clearly beneficial, because many people do not have a supply of stamps on hand (especially because the stamp rate required for postcards is not the same rate as that used for everyday mail).

In business mailings, use of business reply permits is less critical, because most businesses have postage meters, and most prospects simply run the reply card through the postage meter.

Reply cards for direct mailings generally contain these elements:

- A headline restating the key selling proposition or offer.
- A box or series of boxes where the prospect can indicate his or her desired response option.
- Space for the prospect to fill in name and address (or space to affix a mailing label, if you place the reply card so the label shows through a window on the outer envelope).
- Perhaps an optional brief questionnaire that indicates the prospect's areas of interest or that is used to prequalify leads.

The front of the card is addressed to you and contains the appropriate business reply permit number, bar codes, marks, and so on. If you elect not to use business reply mail, put your company name and return address in the center of the front panel of the card, and in the upper right corner put a box containing the words *place stamp here*. Do not place stamps for return postage on reply cards. This is a waste of money, as you'd be paying for postage on every card, yet 90 percent or more will not be mailed.

Sample Reply Card

Yes, I want to learn how Venus Software can upgrade my business!
Please send me a brochure on your Pro business software system.
Have a business computing consultant call to discuss my specific requirements.

Name_____Title_____

Company_____Phone_____

Address_____

City_____State_____ZIP_____

Business functions that I want to computerize:

☐ accounts payable ☐ accounts receivable ☐ inventory ☐ order entry

☐ general ledger ☐ others: _____

We currently use accounting software: ☐ yes ☐ no

Program used:_____

For fast service, call toll-free 800-123-4567. Or fax this form to 123-456-7890.

Direct mail sales correspondence

Selling multiple items in a single mailing

Background: In one mailing you can include any number of inserts with photos and descriptions of various items. To accompany this kind of direct mailing, you'll need a cover letter that makes the recipient want to carefully look through all of your enclosures.

Essential elements: The sample letter focuses not on the product (because there are many), but rather on the prices and the limited supply. This creates a sense of urgency and also makes the author or the letter look like the good guy who is trying to make a real effort to hold down prices for me personally. Your letter should include:

1. An attention-getting opener about a general characteristic of your products—usually price, supply, or quality.

2. An urgent message about the price, supply, or quality of the items advertised in the enclosed inserts.

3. Instructions to order now.

Sample:

Dear Mr. Bly:

My accountant tells me I am going to have to raise my prices to offset our spiraling operating costs!

But I said, "'No!" I know that customers like you, Mr. Bly, expect the best value for their money when they shop at ABC Company—and that's why I'm going to hold the line on higher prices just as long as I possibly can! So, in the next few minutes, while you're looking through the enclosed group of bargain slips, please keep in mind that I may not be able to guarantee such terrific low prices in the future.

To be sure of your selections for a week's free trial, mail your order *today* in the postage-paid envelope attached.

Sincerely,

Selling a single item by mail

Background: Here's a letter selling slippers by mail. Because slippers are an item you can buy at a store, one of the sales arguments in the letter is to convince readers they can get a better product at a better price buying direct from the manufacturer.

Essential elements: This letter does a number of things right:

1. Short paragraphs and short sentences make this long letter extremely easy to read.

2. The copywriter does a good job of building up the readers' perceived value of, and desire for, the slippers.

   Freelance copywriter Burton Pincus says that good direct mail letters "dramatize the offer in a way that dwarfs the product's or service's cost when compared to the value of what is being purchased." This letter does just that.

3. Graphic devices—indented paragraphs, words in all caps, underlines—help make the letter appealing to the eye.

4. The last two paragraphs talk about a free, no-risk trial, rather than "Buy these slippers!" The copy makes it seem like the company is loaning you a pair of slippers to try on rather than making a sale.

5. The postscript gives strong incentive to order immediately. In this case, it is a five dollar discount that will expire in 10 days.

Sample:

Dear Friend,

Are your feet tired at the end of a long day? Are they sore from walking and standing all day in stiff and unrelenting shoes? Are they cold and exposed as you pad around your home?

Your feet need slippers that pamper with a soft wool lining and genuine leather upper soles. The kind that cost you an arm and a leg at high-class boutiques and shoe stores. The kind you have probably never owned before.

But now "Comfies" can give your feet what they need to feel warm, indulged, and relaxed. In stores, you'll pay $50, $65, or even more for slippers with these "extras."

But not if you buy *direct* from **Slippers for Sale!**

See for yourself. Order at no risk. I'll rush you *on approval* "Comfies" slippers with all the style and comfort your feet deserve—for only $25.

Thanks to Comfies, your feet no longer feel pinched, cold, or sore in your own home. Instead, our soft wool lining and supported by our supple leather upper soles cradles them. You've got to feel Comfies yourself to believe the comfort.

How can we do it? All this luxury, all this comfort, *and* guaranteed fit—at your price?

By dealing with you *direct* from one central warehouse. You pay *no* middleman's markup or costly store overhead. We've been saving customers' money this way for more than 80 years now.

You risk *nothing* by trying a pair. Wear them for a full 30 days. Compare looks, comfort, and fit with *any* other slippers at *any* price. If ours aren't the most comfortable, the best value, I'll buy them back. No questions asked, regardless of wear.

Order today so I can rush your Comfie slippers by return mail. If you like, just say "charge it" to your favorite credit card.

Sincerely,

P.S. To encourage you to give us a try, I've enclosed a special coupon that gives you five dollars off your first order, in addition to the 30 to 40 percent we already save you off store prices. But it's only good for the next 10 days—so redeem it right away!

Selling a new edition/version of product

Background: Another use of direct marketing letters is to get existing customers to buy a new edition or version of a product they already own. Such a letter must make a compelling case that the old product is out of date and the new product is superior. It should also remind the buyer of his or her satisfaction with the product he or she already owns.

Essential elements: The sample letter convinces through flattery:

1. Be up-to-date.
2. Stay on the cutting edge.
3. Have the new information before the rest of the industry.
4. Have it now at a discount.
5. The cost is insignificant compared to what you gain: "changes, revisions, and new material providing thorough and up-to-date coverage on dozens of vital topics."
6. A money-back guarantee.
7. Order now to lock in the price and put yourself ahead of the pack.

Sample:

> Software technology is changing at a breakneck pace.
>
> Now *you* can be to up-to-date!
>
> Introducing the all-new, fully revised *Starset Companion: Second Edition*, the largest and most comprehensive *Starset Companion* update ever, yours for approximately half the cost of our other supplements.
>
> Dear Valued Customer:
>
> As a current subscriber to the *Starset Companion*, you need to keep current with the continual changes and improvements in available software.
>
> To keep you on the cutting edge of technology, we've substantially revised and updated the *Starset Companion*. Our new second edition is enclosed for your review.
>
> In a few weeks, we will begin offering the *Starset Companion: Second Edition* to the industry at a list price of $105.50 ($99 plus $6.50 shipping and handling).
>
> But as a current subscriber, you may keep the enclosed second edition for only $27.50 ($25 plus $2.50 shipping and handling). That's a savings of $78—a discount of 74 percent off the regular rate!
>
> Why is upgrading to the revised second edition of the *Starset Companion* for only $25 a good deal? First of all, it's only $25. Not a huge sum to

lie on the table. Especially considering your current technology investment or what you spend on a weekly basis to operate and maintain your network.

Second, look at what you get for only $25—a fully revised and expanded *Starset Companion: Second Edition*—with more than 100 pages of changes, revisions, and new material, providing thorough and up-to-date coverage on dozens of vital topics. More important, the coverage of these topics is fully updated, going beyond what we published in earlier editions and supplements.

Third, your satisfaction is guaranteed. If you are not 100-percent enthusiastic about the enclosed *Starset Companion: Second Edition*, simply return it within 30 days. When our bill arrives, tear it up, and you will owe us nothing.

To lock in your special low $25 Preferred Customer discount price and ensure that you keep up-to-date with the changes and advances in technology, keep the new manual. Simply honor our invoice when it arrives.

Sincerely,

Lead-generating correspondence

Do you ever find yourself wishing you had a steadier stream of quality sales leads? Does your business depend on a continual flow of fresh inquiries to keep the cash registers ringing? Do you ever have periods when sales leads slow down or even dry up? What would happen to your business if you didn't get the new inquiries you need every month?

Many businesses today struggle because they have difficulty with the one process that can virtually assure them all the sales they can handle: lead generation.

It's a fact: The company that can cost-effectively generate a large volume of qualified leads, rapidly and inexpensively, whenever needed, will be overwhelmed with inquiries, appointments, business, sales, and new customers, with minimal expenditure of time and money. That company will never have to fret about finicky customers, competition for new business, bad economic times, rejection, or up-and-down business cycles. When you have more leads than you can handle, your revenues stay high, without the fluctuations that keep other businesspeople up at night.

The main purpose of generating sales leads is to identify the best prospects for your product or service. By following up on those sales leads, your sales force, representatives, dealers, distributors, and others who sell your products can generate sales they might otherwise not have gotten on their own. In a survey of some of its advertisers, Penton Publications found that 88.1 percent generated direct sales of their products from sales leads. In a separate study, the Advertising Research Foundaticn found that one out of five prospects who make an inquiry eventually purchased the product.

A good lead-generating sales letter will generate response rates of between 1 and 5 percent—and sometimes higher—when mailed cold to a rented mailing list of prospect names. This response rate is for producing quality leads with a genuine and serious interest in your product or service or at least in the problem your product or service solves. Most lead-generating letters are brief. Usually, they are no more than one or two typed pages, depending on the audience and the complexity of the subject matter. Letter copy should be simple, clear, conversational, and concise.

Successful lead-generating sales letters are usually simple in style, tone, content, and proposition. Lead-generating copy is designed to accomplish only one part of the selling task: getting a qualified prospect to reply. In effect, the letter should get a customer to raise his or her hand and say, "Yes, I'm interested; tell me more."

Therefore, the copy must contain just enough information to gain attention, arouse curiosity, and generate interest. Additional information will be communicated in conversation or other sales materials requested by the prospect. The lead-generating mailer only needs to present enough information to make the prospect interested in the product or service. More detail is not required and may even serve to decrease response. After all, if there is nothing left for the prospect to find out, they have no reason to call you.

Letter generating leads for a service business

Background: Here is the sales letter author Robert Bly used to launch his freelance copywriting business in 1982. He mailed it to creative directors at 500 advertising agencies that handled industrial accounts, pulling the list from the *Standard Directory of Advertising Agencies*. He received 35 replies; a healthy 7-percent response. He mailed this letter in a business envelope with a reply card to potential clients. (Note that because this kind of letter normally involves a reply card, you would not typically use e-mail for it.)

Essential elements: This letter follows a classic formula for writing sales copy:

1. The headline grabs attention.
2. The first paragraph shows the reader that he or she has a need for freelance help.
3. The short second paragraph satisfies the need by showing the reader where to get help ("This is where I can help").
4. The rest of the letter gives reasons why the writer is the person to call when you need help.
5. The last paragraph asks for an inquiry.

Sample:

How an Engineer and Former Ad Manager Can Help You Write Better Ads and Brochures

For many people, industrial advertising is a difficult chore. It's detailed work, and it's highly technical. To write the copy, you need someone with the technical know-how of an engineer and the communications skills of a copywriter.

That's where I can help.

As a freelance industrial and high-tech copywriter and a graduate engineer, I know how to write clear, technically sound, hard-selling copy. You'll like my writing samples: ads, brochures, catalogs, direct mail, PR, and A/V. And you'll like having a writer on call who works only when you need him.

Here are my qualifications: I have an engineering background (B.S., chemical engineering, University of Rochester). I started out writing brochures and A/V scripts for the Westinghouse Defense Center. After I left Westinghouse, I became advertising manager for Koch Engineering, a manufacturer of process equipment.

In my freelance work, I've handled projects in a wide variety of industries including computers, software, chemicals, industrial equipment, electronics, publishing, banking, health care, and telecommunications. My articles on business communications have appeared in *Business Marketing*, *Computer Decisions*, *Amtrak Express*, *Chemical Engineering*, and *Audio-Visual Directions*. I'm also the author of *The Copywriter's Handbook* (Dodd, Mead), *A Dictionary of Computer Words* (Dell/Banbury), and nine other books.

I'd like to help you create ads, brochures, and other promotions. Call me when your creative team is overloaded, or when the project is highly technical.

I'd be delighted to send you a complete information kit on my copywriting services. The package includes a client list, fee schedule, biographical information, and samples of my work. Just complete and mail the enclosed reply card and the kit is yours at no cost or obligation to you.

Sincerely,

Bob Bly

P.S. Mail the reply card today and I'll also send you a free copy of one of my most popular articles: "10 Tips for Writing More Effective Industrial Copy."

Reply card for a lead-generating letter
Background: Here's what Bob Bly's reply card for this letter looked like:

Bob:

☐ Please send more information on your copywriting services.
☐ Give me a call. I have an immediate project in mind.
☐ Not interested right now. Try us again in (month/year).

Name_____ Title_____
Company_____ Phone_____
Address_____
City_____ State_____ ZIP_____
My business is:_____
Type of copy I need: ☐Ads ☐Direct mail ☐Brochure ☐A/V script ☐PR
☐Other:_____

Letter generating leads targeted to a specific industry

Background: The following is a version of the previous sales letter aimed specifically at potential clients in the software industry. It generated a response of 5 to 10 percent using various lists. (Note that because this kind of letter normally involves a reply card, you would not typically use e-mail for it.)

Essential elements: When writing your letter, keep these tips in mind:

1. Convey that there's a problem in the potential client's industry that you can solve.
2. State what it is you do.
3. Refer to other companies in the same industry you have worked for.
4. If appropriate, give proof that your service works with results you've achieved with other companies.
5. Instruct the recipient about what to do next.

Sample:

Dear Software Marketer:

"It's tough to find a copywriter who can produce results-getting copy for software, computers, and related high-tech products and services," a prospect told me over the phone the other day. Do you have that same problem? If so, please complete and mail the enclosed card, and I'll send you a free kit describing a service that can help.

As a freelance copywriter specializing in direct marketing, I've planned and written successful lead-generating and mail order copy for more than a hundred software and high-tech companies, including Computron, Hyperion Software, IBM, On-Line Software, DataFocus, Cartesia Software, Mortice Kern Systems, Yourdon, Syncsort, Samsung, Micro Logic, Citrix Systems, Plato Software, McGraw-Hill, Ascom/Timeplex, U.S. Robotics, Sony, Weka, Atech, Value Line, Medical Economics, among others.

Does my copy work?

- Convergent Solutions was getting a 1- to 2-percent response to mailings for its CS/ADS application development tool. A simple wording change to the beginning of its sales letter increased response to 5 percent—more than double what sales were before.

- Another mailing campaign, promoting disaster recovery services, pulled a whopping 56-percent response and generated an immediate $5.7 million in sales for U.S. West. (The mailing won a Gold Echo award from the Direct Marketing Association.)

- On a space ad for Chubb Institute, a computer training company, we doubled the number of inquiries produced over all previous ads, simply by changing the presentation of the offer.

- For the Novell Companion, a book and diskette product I wrote pulled double the number of orders compared with the control.

To see some of these successful ads and mailings and others more related to your product, just complete and mail the enclosed reply card today. You'll receive a complete information kit including copywriting samples, client list, testimonials, fee schedule, and more. For fastest delivery, call 123-456-7890.

Sincerely,
Bob Bly
P.S. Respond now and I'll also send you a free tip sheet, "20 Secrets of Selling Software in Print." This reprint is packed with proven techniques for increasing the selling power of your software ads, direct mail, and brochures.

Letter generating leads for an in-house corporate training seminar

Background: A friend, Dr. Gary Blake, mailed 200 of these letters at a cost of about $200 to generate leads for one of his workshops. The result was approximately $7,500 in new business. (Note that because this kind of letter normally involves a reply card, you would not typically use e-mail for it.)

Essential elements: The sample letter shows you how to include the six pieces of information that get responses:

1. A statement of a problem in an attention-getting opening.
2. An offer to solve that problem with an in-house training program.
3. A description of the program's goals and objectives.
4. A list of notable clients.
5. Instructions on what to do next to schedule the seminar.
6. An offer in the postscript of a free offer for a quick reply.

Sample:

Important news for every systems professional who has ever felt like telling an end user: "Go to —."

Dear IS Manager:

It's ironic. Today's users demand to be treated as customers of IS. Yet many systems professionals don't have the customer service skills to make the relationship work.

Our training program, "Interpersonal Skills for IS Professionals," solves that problem—by giving IS staff the skills they need to deal effectively with end users and top management in today's service-oriented corporate environment.

Presented by The Communication Workshop, a leader in teaching "soft skills" to technical professionals, "Interpersonal Skills for IS Professionals" quickly brings your team to a new level in listening, negotiating, team-work, customer service, and other vital skills for communicating complex systems ideas and technical processes to managers and end users.

For more information, including an outline of our "Interpersonal Skills for IS Professionals" program, just complete and mail the enclosed reply card, or call 123-456-7890. You'll be glad you did.

Sincerely,

Gary Blake, PhD, Director

P.S. Reply now and well also send you a free copy of our new tip sheet, "The IS Professional's Guide to Improving Listening Skills." It will answer any questions you may have about dealing with the public, by creating educated consumers who are easier and more reasonable to deal with.

Reply card for lead-generating letter

Yes, I'm interested in learning more about your on-site seminars in:

☐ "Interpersonal Skills for IS Professionals"

☐ "Technical Writing for Systems Professionals"

Name_____ Title_____

Company_____ Phone_____

Address_____

City_____ State_____ ZIP_____

☐ Call me now. Number of people requiring training:_____

☐ Call me in_____ (month/year)

For immediate information, call 123-456-7890

Or fax this card to 123-456-7899

Letter generating leads for seminar requiring paid registration

Background: Direct marketing letters can also be used to get people to attend a seminar for which there is a registration fee. The following letter, mailed to 3,000 writer's magazine subscribers, prompted 57 people to pay $99 each to attend the seminar being advertised. Mailing cost, at $600 per thousand, was less than $2,000 total. Revenue from the mailing was more than $5,600, so the mailing did almost three times break-even, making it profitable.

The response was slightly less than 2 percent. Seminar mailings typically generate registration from between one-quarter to 2 percent of the recipients, and sometimes less.

Essential elements: The sample letter gives the reader everything he or she needs to know about the seminar, as well as offering to fulfill a dream. This letter includes:

1. Attention-grabbing opening, telling the reader you share a common desire.
2. An opportunity to learn something you need/want to know.
3. The title of the seminar.
4. Bold subheads that direct the reader's attention to:

   - What will be taught.
   - Testimonials from others who have taken the seminar.
   - Biographical info about the presenter.
   - Date and location of the seminar.
   - How to register (including the cost).
   - The guarantee and cancellation policy.
   - A contact number for more information.

---

5. A registration form attached.

6. A free bonus for registering in advance.

Sample:

"How to Become a Published Author"

A one-day Saturday seminar

A personal message by Bob Bly

Ever since I can remember, I've dreamed of becoming a published author, of seeing my byline on book jackets and magazine articles. Maybe that's a dream we share. But seven years ago, I discovered the secrets professional writers use to get their works published, while others flounder on the rejection pile.

Now I want to share those secrets with you: introducing "How to Become a Published Author—The Seminar." If you live in New Jersey, New York, or the surrounding area, you can learn how to make the transition from unpublished writer to published author in my new one-day seminar.

Whether you want to publish magazine articles, essays, nonfiction, fiction, children's books, a regular column, or whatever else, this seminar reveals powerful marketing and sales techniques that professional writers use (and amateurs don't know) to break through the rejection barrier and get their writing published and into print.

What you will learn:

In my talk, you will learn tips and strategies to get your manuscript published, including:

- How to write a good article proposal without doing a ton of research.
- The five things to look for when studying potential markets for work.
- Sample query letters you can use.
- Analysis of article proposals—what works, what doesn't.
- How much of an advance you should be paid.
- How to get your book written by deadline.

Plus: How to earn an extra $20,000 a year part-time, or $85,000 a year full-time, writing material for commercial clients.

What people are saying about this seminar:

Because it was all new to me, I found it all helpful, particularly the material that had to do with fiction, which is what I'm interested in.

–Donna Box, West Orange, NJ

The marketing information was very well honed for nonfiction writers. The proposal is dynamite...

–Marilyn Nestor, Robbinsville, NJ

Comprehensive, positive manner of presentation. Good nuts and bolt... this is as much as can be absorbed in one bite.

–Marjorie Baines, Paterson, NJ

About your instructor:

Bob Bly is the author of 17 books, including *Dream Jobs: A Guide to Tomorrow's Top Careers* (John Wiley), *Ronald's Dumb Computer* (Dell), and *How to Promote Your Own Business* (NAL). His articles have appeared in such magazines as *Cosmopolitan*, *New Jersey Monthly*, *Writers Digest*, *Amtrak Express*, and *New Woman*. Monthly column in *Direct Marketing* magazine. In addition to his writings, he is also a professor of writing at New York University, a consultant to Fortune 500 corporations, as a frequent seminar leader and speaker.

Date and location:

Brook Hotel, 50 Tenney Place, Brook, NJ

Saturday, November 12, from 9:30 a.m. to 4:30 p.m.

Fee: $99 advance registration by mail ($129 at the door)

Seminar fee does not include lunch. Confirmation and directions will be sent upon receipt of payment.

Register now and save $302

To register, fill out the registration form (see reverse side) and mail with your check for $99 to: Bob Bly. If more than one person is planning to attend, write the additional name(s) and address(es) on a blank piece of paper.

Attendance is limited, so please register today to ensure admission. At-the-door registration is $129, so advance registration saves you $301.

Guarantee

If you diligently apply my advice and techniques and do not sell at least one book or article within one year after taking my seminar, I will refund your money in full.

Cancellation policy

You will receive a full refund if cancellation is received at least five days before the seminar; 50 percent refund for later cancellations.

Questions?

Call Bob Bly at 123-456-7890.

Free bonus!

Attendees who register in advance by mail receive, at no extra cost, our writer's manual #205, "How to Write a Winning Book Proposal," a seven-dollar value, yours absolutely free!

Here's the form that was included with the letter:

Registration Form

☐ *Yes*, please reserve_____ place(s) at "How to Become a Published Author" at the advance registration discount fee of $99 per person.

My check for $_____ is enclosed (made payable to Bob Bly).

Name_____ Phone _____

Address_____

City_____ State_____ ZIP _____

Detach and mail to:
Bob Bly
999 Riverview Drive
Somewhere, NJ 07000

If you've ever dreamed of becoming a published author, now you can take the next step toward making that dream come true.

Letter generating leads for a regional meeting

Background: Another use of lead-generating letters is to invite customers, prospects, and other people to regional meetings or briefings, such as a breakfast roundtable or lunchtime seminar.

Essential elements: The sample letter covers all the bases:

1. An opening that states a valuable advantage some people have over their competitors.
2. How this advantage is gained by attending the regional briefing.
3. What participants will gain.
4. How to register.
5. A note regarding limited seating, encouraging a prompt reply.

Sample:

Dear Ms. Divan:

Financial institutions whose customers travel throughout the Northeast can now gain a sustainable edge over their toughest competitors.

How? Through new electronic funds transfer (EFT) capabilities described in our upcoming Regional Briefing, "Connections: Enhancing System Performance with NYCE."

By participating in NYCE, you can reduce out-of-state ATM charges for your customers traveling in the Northeast by 10 to 20 cents per transaction compared with Plus or Cirrus.

What's more, NYCE offers a wide range of value-added services—including remote banking services, ATM terminal management, card authorization, and off-line debit card processing.

Processing almost half a billion electronic transactions a year, NYCE is the third-largest regional EFT network in the nation and the only regional EFT on the east coast with its own dedicated data center (located in Secaucus, NJ). We currently have more than 17,000 ATM and 33,000 POS locations, making us a viable alternative to other EFT providers.

At the free Regional Briefing, "Connections," you'll see how NYCE can complement your existing EFT infrastructure, reducing cost and enhancing customer service. You'll also discover new and improved NYCE capabilities that let you open new profit centers for increased revenue.

To reserve your free space at the Regional Briefing nearest you, complete and mail the attached form. Or fax it to 123-456-7890. To register by telephone, call 123-456-7899.

Sincerely,

P.S. Although attendance is free and there is no commitment, obligation, or sales pressure of any kind, seating at regional briefings is limited, so please register today.

Fundraising letter 🚫

Background: If you work for a nonprofit organization, you may use direct marketing letters for one additional purpose: to generate contributions to your organization or cause. Because there is no direct benefit to the recipient, aside from a possible tax deduction and perhaps receipt of a small gift, you have to appeal to the recipient's kindness. The following letter was sent along with a picture of an adorable young boy, to tug at the heartstrings of the reader.

It's best to send this sort of letter through regular mail so that you can include a small gift (and avoid having your message end up in a "spam" folder).

Essential elements: This letter should contain:

1. An opening that brings the reader's attention to the people who benefit from the charity (putting a face on the organization).
2. The goal of the charity.
3. What you want the reader to do to help the charity accomplish that goal.
4. The valuable deeds of the charity and its dependence on the generosity of others.
5. Instructions on how to contribute.
6. An ending that returns to the people highlighted in the opening.

Sample:

Dear Friend,

I think you'll be sad to learn that Chandler may not be going home for the holidays. You see, Chandler has been diagnosed with acute lymphocytic leukemia. We try to send the children home for the holidays. But some children are just too sick. So, we try everything possible to bring a smile to their faces.

You can help by sending a St. Agnes child a holiday card. I've even enclosed a card for you to send. I wish you could see the children's brave little eyes light up when they get a card, knowing that someone is thinking of them.

The kids at St. Agnes hospital are very special, and they need cheering up at this time of the year. They know that other kids, who aren't sick, are at home baking cookies and giving their wish lists to Santa Claus. Our kids can't. A man on staff plays Santa, but being in the hospital is never any fun. However, your gifts have given these children hope. If St. Agnes' Hospital wasn't here, few of these precious children would even be alive today. Your gifts make miracles happen.

Please send your card. It will do so much to brighten the season for a sick child. And with your card, will you send a special holiday donation a gift that can help make it possible for children, like Chandler, to spend all their holidays at home, and forget how close they came to dying too young?

We continue to count on you in this season of joy and compassion, to help a desperately sick child stay alive. I can think of no greater gift you might give.

God bless you,

P.S. Each child hangs a card on the little tree we've set up. I'm hoping that your card will be one of them. Thanks...from Chandler and me.

Letter inviting customers to visit your Website

Background: A letter or postcard can be sent to customers encouraging them to visit your Website. The letter can be used to announce a new Website or a new feature on an existing Website.

Essential elements: Similar to any piece of direct mail, this letter has to push the reader to do something to gain a personal benefit. It should include:

1. An opening that boasts the great resources available at your Website. Be sure to give the name and Web address.
2. The details of the resources found at that site.
3. Benefits of visiting that Website.
4. Instructions on how to log on (repeat the name and address).

Sample:

Dear Mr. Gahan:

You may have seen our ad in *DM News* telling direct marketers all about the great *free* resources available to them on the Roman Website at *www.roman.com.*

Resources like instant online counts from more than 30,000 different lists, a downloadable library of information-packed "how-to" articles on direct marketing, an online calculator for accurately determining the optimum size of test cells, and much, much more (see the attached ad reprint for details).

But as a Roman customer, you are automatically entitled to premium Website access, called "Gold Level."

As a Gold Level browser on the Roman Website, you can get many additional valuable resources that other direct marketers can't, including unlimited onscreen viewing and downloading of the complete and up-to-date data cards for all Roman lists.

For details, and to activate your exclusive Gold Level access, simply log onto the Roman Website right now at *www.roman.com.* But be warned: Once you see how fast, easy, and convenient it is to access list counts and data cards online at the Roman Website, you may never go back to paper data cards again.

Sincerely,

Instructions for direct marketing design

Now that we've looked at some sample letters, let's examine some of the mechanics that go into designing a successful marketing letter (whether you e-mail, fax, or mail it).

Ted Kikoler, one of the leading direct mail designers in North America, has these guidelines for designing direct marketing letters:

- Never lay out the body copy of the letter using graphic design techniques. Always wordprocess it.

- Use a serif typeface. The best is either Prestige, Times New Roman, or Courier. If you are using Microsoft Word and a laser printer, you can set the body copy in Times New Roman and the headlines and subheads in either Times Roman Bold or Helvetica Bold.

- Indent all paragraphs five characters.

- Use wide margins—long line lengths with narrow margins fill too much of the page, making it look like there's more to read than there actually is. A good line length is 6.5 inches.

- Add one carriage return of space between all paragraphs.

- Make the right-hand margin ragged right. Never justify it.

- Try to avoid paragraphs longer than six lines deep. If you have a longer paragraph, break it into two or more paragraphs.

- Indent entire paragraphs you want to highlight by 10 characters on each side.

- Typeset the headline of the letter for emphasis. If you are not typesetting the heading of the letter, set it off by putting it in a ruled box or a Johnson Box (a border around the heading), putting white space around it, or using a second color.

- The main body copy should be black, but an accent color can be used for subheads.

- Make the signature legible.

- Shorten the first name of the reader to sound friendlier and to close the gap between reader and writer. Bill sounds better than William, Tom sounds better than Thomas.

- When using a personalized letter, try to avoid using subheads, especially all caps and centered above the paragraph. Do not typeset the heading in this type of letter. Keep the logo on the front page.

- Use a blue signature.

- Underscore words that should be emphasized. A good technique is to read the copy aloud and listen to the words you emphasize. These are the ones to underscore.

- Indent the entire body copy of the postscript (P.S.) by five characters so the letters "P.S." stand out. If it's all flush left, it gets lost.

- If you are mailing small quantities (a few hundred at a time), you can print the letter without a signature, then sign each one individually with a blue pen. This creates a look and feel very close to a personal letter. Signing a stack of a few hundred letters can be done without much pain during the evening while sitting in front of the TV.

Direct-mail faxing

One of the problems with e-mail and snail mail is that there is so much of it. Consequently, it's difficult for your letter to compete for attention with all the other correspondence in the recipient's mailbox. One way to resolve this problem is to compose and transmit your letter electronically as a fax—fax machines still collect the least amount of mail in comparison to e-mail and snail mail.

Tips for effective fax broadcasting

These tips and pointers are based on the advice of Maury Kauffman, author of *Computer-Based Fax Processing*. Maury's articles on fax communication have appeared in numerous business and trade publications, including *DM News*, *Target Marketing*, *Information Week*, *Folio*, and *Voice Processing Asia*. He is active in the direct marketing industry and is a regular speaker at voice/fax and marketing conferences worldwide.

According to Maury's research, there are 86 million fax machines installed worldwide, and thousands of fax modems sold monthly. A survey by his firm showed that 90 percent of the direct marketing professionals surveyed have tested enhanced fax technology.

Fax broadcasting allows you to send a personalized document to hundreds, even thousands of different locations automatically. It's an amazingly effective, yet often overlooked, marketing tool. To increase response rates, try fax broadcasting, and:

- Personalize each and every fax; use data from customer files to communicate.

- Add a response mechanism to your fax.

- Broadcast at night when rates are lower, for maximum impact in the morning

- Keep the fax medium in mind; photos and detailed graphics will not transmit well.

- Use white paper. Colored paper does not fax well.

- Use plain paper, not rag or weave. The texture of textured paper shows up as gray marks when faxed.

- Don't overuse the fax, or you may lose the sense of urgency.

- Know the law. Read the Telecommunications Consumer Protection Act.

"I think it is very risky to broadcast fax to cold or new leads, people with whom you have not established a relationship," writes Dan Kennedy (*Marketing Briefing*). "This can and does work. You can make sales, but you will really aggravate a lot of people, and I wonder if doing that is smart, especially in a market you wish to live in for any length of time."

At time of this book's printing, cold-faxing is illegal, unless you have an established business relationship with the potential client. Although regulations change over time, as of this writing, the Telephone Consumer Protection Act prohibits the use of telephone facsimile machines to send unsolicited advertisements. Marketers should use faxes to communicate only with companies with whom they have an established business relationship and not to broadcast fax to cold prospects who don't know you. However, the "established relationship" doesn't necessarily mean the people receiving your fax are customers; they may just have made an inquiry at one time, requesting a catalog or brochure.

"Keep an internal 'Do Not Fax' list," advises Maury. "Anyone who dislikes fax messages, or who has communicated that they do not wish to receive faxes, should be taken off your fax broadcast database." He also advocates adding the following message to the bottom of fax broadcasts: "If you wish to be removed from our fax distribution list, call us."

I've found that the majority of complaints about fax broadcasts come from SOHO businesses (small office/home office). Large corporations rarely object to fax broadcasts. The reason is simple: The SOHO typically has only one fax machine. When you send unsolicited advertising, you're tying up that machine and using up the small company owner's paper, which he or she pays for out of his or her own pocket. The corporate prospect, on the other hand, has access to many fax machines and often has an assistant to send faxes. Fax broadcasting doesn't tie up his only fax or waste his time.

Here are some hints on saving money with fax broadcasting:

- Broadcast at night when the rates are lower.
- Limit graphics, as they transmit much slower than text. Use text and line art without halftones.
- Keep your fax to one page. Incorporate the recipient's information on the page to eliminate the need for a separate cover sheet.

When compiling fax lists to use for broadcasting, keep these tips in mind:

- Request fax numbers on all business reply cards and other response devices.
- Make sure fax numbers are up-to-date by verifying them periodically.
- Double-postcards should do double duty. Use them to clean your list and update fax numbers.
- Consider offering an incentive to those who mail or call with updated fax information.

- Your sales force should always update fax numbers with addresses and phone.
- Customer service should verify fax numbers when customers call in.
- Ask your mailing list house whether they can, for a fee, append fax numbers to records in your customer and prospect database that don't already contain them.
- Consider broadcasting to an association list-typically most people in your target group belong.
- If you need fax numbers immediately, use telemarketing to locate and verify.
- Once your list is compiled, be sure updates are made on an ongoing basis.

Index

About the Authors

Robert W. Bly is the director of the Center for Technical Communication, a consulting firm that helps businesspeople improve their communications and interpersonal skills. CTC presents seminars to associations and corporate clients nationwide on topics such as direct marketing, business and technical writing.

Bob Bly is the author of more than 40 books including *The Elements of Business Writing* (Macmillan), *The Copywriter's Handbook* (Henry Holt), and *Selling Your Services* (Henry Holt). Other titles include *Creative Careers* (John Wiley), *Business to Business Direct Marketing* (NTC), and *Keeping Clients Satisfied* (Prentice Hall). Bob's articles have appeared in such publications as *Computer Decisions*, *Writer's Digest*, *Business Marketing*, *Direct*, *Amtrak Express*, *Cosmopolitan*, *Science Books & Films*, *Chemical Engineering*, and *New Jersey Monthly*.

Organizations that have hired Bob as a trainer and speaker include the Cincinnati Direct Marketing Association, Thoroughbred Software, Walker Richer & Quinn, ARCO Chemical, Creative Group, Cardiac Pacemakers Inc., U.S. Army, Dow Chemical, Mail Order Association of Nurseries, Foxboro, Computron, IBM, McGraw-Hill, The Pricing Institute, and the International Laboratory DistributorsAssociation.

In addition, Bob has written sales letters, direct mail packages, and other marketing documents for such clients as Agora Publishing, Phillips Publishing, KCI Communications, Lucent Technologies, McGraw-Hill, Lane Laboratories, BOC Gases, Alloy Technology, AT&T, Intrasoft, Isogon, and Rodale. He has won several awards for letter-writing, including a Gold Echo Award from the Direct Marketing Association, an IMMY from the Information Industry Association, and two Southstar Awards. He is the editor of the magazine Bits & Pieces for Salespeople, published monthly by Economics Press.

The Encyclopdedia of Business Letters, Faxes, and E-mails

Regina Anne Kelly is a professional writer and editor with more than 15 years' experience. She is the author of a nonfiction reference book, *Energy Supply and Renewable Resources*, published in 2007, and the coauthor of three nonfiction trade books, including *Everyday Letters for Busy People*, 2nd Edition. She has also penned dozens of articles for newspapers, scientific and trade journals, and magazines and has edited more than 50 books. She currently operates her own freelance writing and editing business. Her clients have included World Almanac Books, Facts On File, Pearson Education, and pharmaceutical companies such as Roche, Genentech, Inc., and Watson Pharmaceuticals. She was a finalist in *Glimmertrain Stories* 2003 Very Short Fiction Award contest. She holds a master's degree in English from Fordham University and bachelor's degrees in English and journalism from Rutgers College.

Questions and comments on *The Encyclopedia of Business Letters, Faxes, and E-Mails* may be sent to:

Bob Bly
Center for Technical Communication
22 E. Quackenbush Avenue
Dumont, NJ 07628
phone 201-385-1220, fax 201-385-1138
E-mail: rwbly@bly.com Website: *www.bly.com*

Regina Anne Kelly
Editing, Writing, and Layout
23 Cindy Lane, Building 5
Ocean, NJ 07712
phone 732-693-7749, fax 732-450-1858
E-mail: reginaannekelly@verizon.net